I th...
passed our trial.
I love you even
more now than
ever before.

With all my Heart,
Erin

Valentine's 1989

THE
TRIAL
OF
SOCRATES

❧❧❧

Also by I. F. Stone

THE
TRIAL
OF
SOCRATES

I. F. STONE

LITTLE, BROWN AND COMPANY
BOSTON   TORONTO

FIRST EDITION

Library of Congress Cataloging-in-Publication Data

Stone, I. F. (Isidor F.), 1907–
    The trial of Socrates.

    Includes index.
    1. Socrates. I. Title.
B317.S76   1988   183'.2   87-22855
ISBN 0-316-81758-9

MV

Designed by Robert G. Lowe

*Published simultaneously in Canada
by Little, Brown & Company (Canada) Limited*

PRINTED IN THE UNITED STATES OF AMERICA

To my wife, Esther

without whom this,
and so much else of me,
would not have been possible

CONTENTS

❦❦❦

PREFACE
How This Book Came to Be Written

ᆼᄀᄀᄋᄀ

THIS IS REALLY A FRAGMENT of what was originally meant to be a larger, a much larger, work.

No book can be fully understood unless the writer discloses the motivation that led him to embark on his onerous task. How, after a lifetime of "muckraking" — that invidious term for critical and independent journalism — was I drawn into classical studies and the trial of Socrates? When angina pectoris forced me to give up *I. F. Stone's Weekly* at the end of 1971 after nineteen years of publication, I decided to embark in my retirement on a study of freedom of thought in human history — not freedom in general, which has too many ambiguities, and may even be identified with the freedom of the strong to exploit the weak, but freedom to think and to speak. This project had its roots in a belief that no society is good, whatever its intentions, whatever its utopian and liberationist claims, if the men and women who live in it are not free to speak their minds. I hoped that such a study would help a new generation, not only to preserve free speech where it exists — and is always threatened from motives good as well as bad — but to help embattled dissidents in the communist world find their way to a liberating synthesis of Marx and Jefferson.

In my youth I was drawn both by philosophy and journalism. I read the fragments of Heraclitus the summer after I graduated from high school. I majored in philosophy at college, but I was also working my way as a journalist full time when I dropped out in my junior year and made newspaper work my lifelong career.

But I never lost interest in philosophy and history, and turned to them in my retirement. I began my explorations into freedom of thought by spending a year studying the two English revolutions of the seventeenth century, which played so large a part in the development of the American constitutional system.

I soon felt that I could not fully understand the English seventeenth-century revolutions without a fuller knowledge of the Protestant Reformation, and the close connection between the struggle for religious liberty and the struggle for free expression.

To understand the Reformation, it was necessary to go farther back again and probe into those premonitory stirrings and adventurous thinkers in the Middle Ages who sowed the seeds of free thought. This in turn was closely associated, of course, with the impact on Western Europe when Aristotle was rediscovered through Arabic and Hebrew translations and commentaries in the twelfth century.

This led back to the sources of these liberating influences in ancient Athens, the earliest society where freedom of thought and its expression flourished on a scale never known before, and rarely equaled since. There, like so many before me, I fell in love with the ancient Greeks.

When I first got back to ancient Athens, I thought in my ignorance that I would be able to do a cursory survey, based on standard sources, of free thought in classical antiquity. But I soon found that there were no standard sources. Almost every point in classical studies was engulfed in fierce controversy. Our knowledge resembles a giant jigsaw puzzle, many parts of which are forever lost. Scholars of equal eminence are able to fashion from the surviving fragments contradictory reconstructions of a vanished reality. These tend to reflect the preconceptions with which they began.

So I turned to the sources for myself. There I found that one could not make valid political or philosophical inferences from translations, not because the translators were incompetent but because the Greek terms were not fully congruent — as one would say in geometry — with their English equivalents. The translator was forced to choose one of several English approximations. To understand a Greek conceptual term, one had to learn at least enough Greek to grapple with it in the original, for only in the original could one grasp the full potential implications and color of the term.

How can one understand the word *logos,* for example, from any one English translation, when the definition of this famous term — in all its rich complexity and creative evolution —requires more than five full columns of small type in the massive un-abridged Liddell-Scott-Jones *Greek-English Lexicon?* A thousand years of philosophic thought are embodied in a term that begins by meaning "talk" in Homer, develops into "Reason" — with a capital R, as the divine ruler of the universe — in the Stoics, and ends up in the Gospel of St. John — by a subtle borrowing from biblical sources — as the creative Word of God, His instrument in the Creation.

In my day, even in a country high school, one had four years of Latin to prepare for college, and Catullus and Lucretius were among my early enthusiasms. But I had only one semester of Greek in college before I dropped out in my junior year.

I decided in retirement to learn enough Greek to be able to grapple with conceptual terms for myself. I started on my own with a bilingual edition of the Gospel of St. John, then went to the first book of the *Iliad*. But the study of Greek soon led me far afield into the Greek poets and Greek literature generally. Their exploration continues to be a joy.

But the more I fell in love with the Greeks, the more agonizing grew the spectacle of Socrates before his judges. It horrified me as a civil libertarian. It shook my Jeffersonian faith in the common man. It was a black mark for Athens and the freedom it symbol-ized. How could the trial of Socrates have happened in so free a society? How could Athens have been so untrue to itself?

This book is the fruit of that torment. I set out to discover how it could have happened. I could not defend the verdict when I started and I cannot defend it now. But I wanted to find out what Plato does not tell us, to give the Athenian side of the story, to mitigate the city's crime and thereby remove some of the stigma the trial left on democracy and on Athens.

THE
TRIAL
OF
SOCRATES

PRELUDE

❧❧❧

NO OTHER TRIAL, except that of Jesus, has left so vivid an impression on the imagination of Western man as that of Socrates. The two trials have much in common. There is no independent contemporary account of either, not even a fragmentary allusion. We have no transcripts, no court records. We do not hear the prosecution. We know the story only as told later by loving disciples.

In the case of Socrates, we do have the indictment. But we do not have what lawyers call a bill of particulars — the specific charges rather than the general allegations. We do not know under what law or laws the charges were brought.

Both Jesus and Socrates achieved immortality through martyrdom. For Christian theology, the Crucifixion fulfilled the divine mission. But for Socrates even martyrdom would not have been enough. Socrates left no writings of his own. Of his many and diverse disciples there have survived only the writings of Plato and Xenophon. If only Xenophon's recollections of Socrates had survived, even the final cup of hemlock would not have been enough to immortalize him. (The Socrates of Xenophon is rather platitudinous and banal, sometimes a downright philistine, capable even in one passage of Xenophon's *Memorabilia* — his recollections of Socrates — of jokingly offering to act as a panderer to a well-known Athenian courtesan.) Had Socrates been acquitted, had he died comfortably of old age, he might now be remembered only as a minor Athenian eccentric, a favorite butt of the comic poets.

It was Plato who created the Socrates of our imagination, and to this day no one can be sure how much of his portrait is the real Socrates and how much is the embellishing genius of Plato.

The search for the historical Socrates, like the search for the historical Jesus, continues to generate an ever more enormous literature, a vast sea of speculation and learned controversy.

The debt of Socrates to Plato is, however, no greater than the debt of Plato to Socrates. It is to Plato's literary genius that Socrates owes his preeminent position as a secular saint of Western civilization. And it is Socrates who keeps Plato on the best-seller lists. Plato is the only philosopher who turned metaphysics into drama. Without the enigmatic and engaging Socrates as the principal character of his dialogues, Plato would not be the only philosopher who continues to charm a wide audience in every generation. No one reads Aristotle or Aquinas or Kant as literature.

One of Plato's ancient biographers, Olympiodorus, tells us that Plato originally wanted to be a playwright, a tragic or a comic poet. In his time the theater was the foremost achievement of Athenian literary genius. Olympiodorus says that when Plato met Socrates and fell under the older man's spell, he burnt his efforts at tragic poetry and turned instead to philosophy.[1]

This proved only a detour to Plato's original goal. The four dialogues that describe the trial and death of Socrates — the *Euthyphro, Apology, Crito,* and *Phaedo* — live as tragic drama. It is hard to read Socrates' serene farewell to his disciples in the *Phaedo* without a tear, nor can one fail to be moved in the *Apology* — no matter how many times one has read it — by Socrates' last words to his judges. The Platonic account is theater at its highest level. Socrates is as much a tragic hero as Oedipus or Hamlet.

The trial occurred in 399 B.C. How does a reporter cover a trial that was held almost twenty-four hundred years ago? The first obstacle is the frightening ratio of controversy to fact. The Socratic literature is mountainous; the evidence, meager; and much of the literature is controversy many times removed from the original sources: Scholar X attacks Scholar Y's criticism of Scholar Z's interpretation of an ancient text. The first step is to turn from these distant and often acrimonious debates and reexamine the basic documents themselves.[2]

Three contemporary portraits of Socrates have survived. In addition to the accounts by Plato and Xenophon, we also have the portrait that emerges from the comedies of his friend Aristophanes, a friendship attested by the *Symposium* of Plato. Aristophanes devoted a whole play, the *Clouds,* to Socrates and also refers to the philosopher in three other of his surviving comedies: the *Birds,* the *Frogs,* and the *Wasps.* Their testimony may be supplemented by the fragmentary scraps remaining from other lost comedies about Socrates that were produced in his lifetime.

In addition, we catch some useful glimpses of Socrates only two generations later in the works of Aristotle, Plato's greatest pupil, born fifteen years after Socrates died. Aristotle differed with Plato on many questions. Indeed, Aristotle and Plato may be read together as an ongoing philosophical and political debate; even in our own time, Platonists and Aristotelians are not always on speaking terms. The references to Socrates in Aristotle are brief and scattered, but they add some fresh insights. These are valuable because Aristotle distanced himself from the cult of Socrates and treats his contribution to philosophy with a precise astringency, in striking contrast to Plato's adoration.

So we have a Xenophontic, a Platonic, an Aristophanic, and an Aristotelian Socrates. How is one to determine, amid the differences in these primary sources, which was the real Socrates? There is no way to achieve an indisputable answer. But where we find common features in the various portraits, there is a substantial probability that we may have reached the historical Socrates.

The search for the "real" Socrates also finds helpful hints — and additional contradictions — in what little we know of his other disciples and in the scattered references to Socrates in Greek and Latin literature down to and including the Church Fathers.[3]

Getting a grip on the historical Socrates is only part of our task. Equally important is reconstructing the missing case for the prosecution and seeing how Socrates appeared to his fellow citizens. We have to dig out of the ancient records what our principal source, Plato, does not disclose, and what the defenders of Socrates tend to gloss over. In pursuit of this goal, we will find ourselves wandering over the whole of classical antiquity, Latin as well as Greek.

All knowledge may be reduced to comparison and contrast; if only one thing existed in an otherwise void universe, we could not describe or "know" it. Much can be learned in dealing with any Greek problem if we turn to the analogous aspect of Roman civilization. The comparison — and even more, the contrast — between these two kindred but widely divergent societies is illuminating. For example: To study the voting procedures and rules of debate in the popular assemblies of the Roman Republic side by side with the Athenian assembly is to see clearly the contrast between the two political systems, the former a thinly disguised oligarchy, the other a full and direct democracy. So our attempt at a new understanding of the trial of Socrates will also become a fresh look at classical antiquity. It is our yesterday, and we cannot understand ourselves without it.

PART I

SOCRATES AND ATHENS

Chapter 1

THEIR BASIC DIFFERENCES

ᘇᘐᕽᗋᕽᘊᘈ

T O JUDGE only by Plato, one might conclude that Socrates got into trouble with his fellow citizens by exhorting them to virtue, never an endearing occupation. But if we turn away from the *Apology* for a wider view, we will see that the conflict between Socrates and his native city began because he differed so profoundly from most of his fellow Athenians and, indeed, from the ancient Greeks generally, on three basic philosophical questions. These differences were not mere distant abstractions, of no concern to ordinary mortals, but challenged the very foundations of the self-government they enjoyed.

The first and most fundamental disagreement was on the nature of the human community. Was it, as Greeks would have said, a *polis* — a free city? Or was it, as Socrates so often said, a herd?

A good place to start is with one of the most famous observations of antiquity — Aristotle's remark, at the very beginning of his treatise on politics, that man is a political animal.

The English translation is unfortunate. The English words *political animal* are, it is true, an exact and literal rendering of the Greek term, *zoon politikon*. But in English this conjures up the picture of a ward heeler who spends his life in the seedy chores of a modern political machine.

The Greek word *polis*, or city, and its various derivatives carried very different connotations. To be a *polites*, a citizen of a *polis*, was a badge of honor. It implied that the citizen had a right to debate, and a right to vote on, the decisions that affected his life and that of his city.

A *polis* meant something more to the ancient Greeks than "city" does to us in a modern nation-state. It did not mean merely to live in an urban rather than a rural area. The *polis* was an independent and sovereign "state" in the full modern sense. The *polis* made law within its borders, and — outside them — it made war or peace as it saw fit.

But when Aristotle began his *Politics* with the proposition that man was a "political animal," he was not concerned with the *polis* in its outward manifestations as a sovereign body but in the inner relations that made the city possible. Aristotle's point was that man alone had the qualities that made a communal existence possible, and for him as for most Greeks the highest form of such *koinonia* — literally "community" — was the *polis*. It was made possible, Aristotle said, because of all the animals man alone had the *logos*.[1] The *logos* was more than the power of speech. It also denoted reason and morality.

There are, as Aristotle observed, other social or gregarious forms of life. Certain insects lead a communal existence in hives and certain wild animals live together in herds. But it is man's "special distinction from the other animals that he alone has perception of good and bad and of the just and the unjust." It is this intrinsic sense of justice that gives man his social instinct, his "impulse" as Aristotle calls it, to a social life, and makes man "a political animal in a greater measure than any bee or any gregarious animal."[2]

When Aristotle said that the *polis* exists "by nature," he meant that it springs from the nature of man, from an intrinsic sense of justice.

For the Greeks, *polis* had a special characteristic that distinguished it from other forms of human community. It was, as Aristotle says, "an association of free men," as distinguished from such other and earlier forms of association as the family, which was ruled by its patriarch, or monarchy, or the relation of master and slave. The *polis* governed itself. The ruled were the rulers. As Aristotle described it, the citizen "takes turns to govern and be governed."[3] Whether in oligarchies, where citizenship was restricted, or in democracies like Athens, where all freeborn males

were citizens, major offices were filled by election but many
others were filled by lot to give all citizens an equal chance to
participate in their government. Every citizen had the right to vote
and speak in the assembly where the laws were enacted, and to sit
in the jury courts where those laws were applied and interpreted.
These were the basic characteristics of Greek *politics* — the admin-
istration of its cities — long before Aristotle described them in the
fourth century B.C. They governed the life of Athens in the
lifetime of Socrates, and it was with these premises that Socrates
and his disciples disagreed.

The difference was fundamental. Politics in Athens and the
Greek city-states generally, as in Rome under the Republic, was a
kind of two-party class struggle. Both sides agreed that the city
should be governed by its citizens. They divided over how wide
that citizenship should be. Was citizenship to be restricted, as in
the oligarchies, or widespread, as in the democracies? Was the city
to be ruled by the few or the many, which also meant the rich or
the poor? But for both sides, politics — the very life of the city —
lay in self-government, and to oppose self-government was to be
not just antidemocratic but anti*political*. This is how Socrates
looked to most of his contemporaries.

Socrates was neither an oligarch nor a democrat. He stood apart
from either side. His ideal, as we see it variously expressed in both
Xenophon and Plato and reflected in what we know of the other
Socratics, was rule neither by the few nor the many but by — as
he put it in Xenophon's *Memorabilia* — "the one who knows."[4]
This must have looked to his contemporaries as a reversion to
kingship in its most absolute form. And to advocate kingship was
to set oneself wholly in opposition to the *polis*. In fifth- and
fourth-century Athens, advocacy of kingship must have looked as
quirky as a monarchist political party would in twentieth-century
America — too quaint and eccentric even to be alarming.

Neither the few nor the many wanted to revive kingship,
wanted to give up control over the government of their own lives.
They differed bitterly — and fought miniature civil wars — over

who should be counted in the citizenry. But they agreed that the citizens should rule their city.

The controversy is not so comfortably ancient as it may at first seem. The twentieth century has seen — and still sees — new forms of one-man rule in the totalitarianisms of right and left. Indeed, the germ of totalitarianism is already evident in the way Socrates formulated his theory of government in the *Memorabilia*, the earliest and fullest expression of his views.

Socrates would have argued that he was proposing not kingship in its ancient form but a new kind of one-man rule, the basis of an ideal society. In the *Memorabilia*, Socrates set himself up as an opponent of all forms of existing government. He itemized — and rejected — them one by one.

"Kings and rulers," he said, "are not those who hold the sceptre," the symbol of their high office, which they often claimed to have received from Zeus himself. That took care of monarchy in its conventional form. Nor are they, he continued, "those who are chosen by the multitude." That took care of democracy. "Nor those on whom the lot falls" — that rejected public officials chosen by lot. "[N]or those who owe their power to force or deception" — that took care of "tyrants." The true or ideal "kings and rulers" are "those who know how to rule."

An Athenian democrat would have said that it is just such men who are sought out by popular vote and — to guard against mistaken judgment and abuse of authority — are limited in their powers and terms of office. But Socrates did not envisage any such safeguarding limits on the rulers. His basic premise — according to Xenophon — was "that it is the business of the ruler to give orders and of the ruled to obey." This must have looked like the old kingship refurbished and made absolute. But Socrates would have said that he was advocating a new form of rule — rule, as we would say, by experts. In Xenophon, Socrates defended his advocacy of absolute rule with analogies also familiar in the Platonic dialogues. Socrates "went on to show," Xenophon recalls, "that on a ship the one who knows, rules, and the owner [of the ship] and all the others [on board] obey the one who knows." Similarly, Socrates argued, "in farming the landowners, in illness the patients" and "in training" the athletes send for experts, "those who know," that "they may obey them and do the right thing." He even added a little joke, in that era of male supremacy, saying that "in spinning wool . . . the women govern the men because they know how to do it and men do not."[5]

These are all imperfect analogies, from which fallacious conclusions are drawn. A Greek democrat could argue that the shipowner, the patient, the landowner, and the athlete were free to pick their "experts," and if these experts proved unsatisfactory they could be discharged and others hired in their place. This was what a free city did in picking — and replacing — its officials. Otherwise, behind the façade of "the one who knows" there lurked the face of tyranny. The problem was not only to find the right expert but to have the means to get rid of him if he turned out badly.

To understand the first grapplings with this problem in the Greek city-states — the first beginnings of what we call political science — we are largely dependent on the pages of Plato and Aristotle. To evaluate their contribution one must begin with an essential difference between them.

Plato was a theorist, Aristotle a scientific observer. Aristotle prized practical over theoretical knowledge in dealing with human affairs. Aristotle had a strong bias in favor of experience and common sense. In contrast, Plato in a famous passage of the *Republic* proposed to limit the study of "the dialectic" — and thus the future rulers of his utopia — to those who could "let go of the eyes and the other senses and rise to the contemplation of *to on*" — "pure being" or "being itself."[6] This would no doubt be a contemplative joy to the mystic, but it hardly offers guidance to the statesman, forced to deal with tangled affairs and obdurate human nature.

Aristotle takes issue with Plato at the very beginning of his own masterwork on philosophy, the *Metaphysics*. It starts off by saying, "All men naturally desire knowledge. An indication of this is our esteem for the senses." Without them, and especially sight, Aristotle asks, how can we know and act? In the same way, at the beginning of the *Politics* Aristotle makes it clear that he is taking issue with the political views of Plato and Socrates. There, as in the *Metaphysics,* he does not mention them by name. But the reference is unmistakable. "Those then who think," Aristotle writes, "that the nature of the statesman, the royal ruler, the head of an estate and the master of a family are the same, are mistaken."[7] The *polis* commanded the loyalty of free men because it embodied the consent of the governed. To the Greek, all this would have seemed indisputable.

The *politikos,* the political leader or statesman in a *polis,* was an elected official, subject to a limited term — usually a year — of office, answerable in a popular assembly and the popular jury-courts for the conduct of his office, and invested even in time of war with far less than absolute power. The citizens he led were not his inferiors in legal status or rank but (as Aristotle observed in his *Politics*) "equal and like."[8] They shared a common humanity.

Here lay the first and most fundamental of the conflicts between Socrates and Athens.

The various followers of Socrates disagreed, often as violently as modern scholars, as to just what Socrates *had* taught them, even — and especially — on the nature of virtue. But on one matter they agreed: They all rejected the *polis.* They all saw the human community not as a self-governing body of citizens with equal rights but as a herd that required a shepherd or king. They all treated democracy with condescension or contempt.

Xenophon's ideal, as set forth in his own utopia, the *Cyropaedia,* or *Education of Cyrus,* was monarchy under law. This was the Persian model as Xenophon imagined its establishment by Cyrus the Great, founder of the Persian empire.

Antisthenes, the oldest disciple of Socrates, considered monarchy the ideal form of government and agreed with Xenophon that Cyrus was the ideal monarch.[9] These views were presumably expressed in his lost dialogue, the *Statesman,* mentioned by Athenaeus.[10]

Antisthenes was the founder of Cynicism, and he was especially cynical about democracy. Two stories gibing at it are attributed to Antisthenes, one by Diogenes Laertius, the other by Aristotle.

In the first, Antisthenes is supposed to have asked the Athenians why they did not vote that asses were horses since (as he said) they sometimes elected generals who had as little resemblance to real commanders as an ass did to a horse![11] This satirical comparison may have originated with Socrates himself, since in Plato's *Phaedrus*, Socrates speaks of a popular orator palming off an ass as a horse on an ignorant city.[12]

Aristotle in his *Politics* attributed to Antisthenes a sardonic fable about the lions and the hares. "When the hares made speeches in the assembly and demanded that all should have equality," Antisthenes related, "the lions replied, 'Where are your claws and teeth?' "[13] This was the cynical reply to the democratic demand for egalitarianism.

Plato sketched several utopias. All but one of them, the *Laws*, was based on one form or another of monarchy. In the *Politicus*, or *Statesman*, as we have seen, the ideal rule was absolute monarchy. In the *Republic*, it was absolute rule by one or several "philosopher kings." In the *Timaeus* and its sequel, the *Critias*, Plato pictured the Golden Age of man as a time when the gods tended their human herds as men later tended their cattle.

Even in the "moderate" utopia of Plato's old age, the *Laws*, the narrowly restricted citizen body would have operated under the watchful eye of a Nocturnal Council, an inquisitorial body empowered to root out dissent, the archetype of our late but unlamented House Un-American Activities Committee. Travel abroad was severely restricted to keep the community from "spiritual pollution" — as the Chinese Communists now say — by foreign ideas. These Platonic innovations in thought-control went beyond any kingship the Greeks had ever known. They were in fact the first sketches of what we now call totalitarian societies.

In Plato's *Gorgias*, Socrates makes clear that no form of the *polis* met with his approval. There the two most famous conservative statesmen of Athens, Cimon and Miltiades, are treated with the same impartial scorn as the two most famous democratic leaders, Themistocles and Pericles. Socrates said of Pericles, who had recently died, that he must be judged a failure as a statesman because he had left the human herd in his care "wilder than when he took them in hand. . . . [W]e know of nobody," Socrates concludes, "who has shown himself a good statesman in this city of ours."[14] "I think," Plato has him say, "I am one of few, not to say the only one, in Athens who attempts the true art of statesmanship."[15] It was not his most modest moment.

Socrates laid it down as his basic principle of government in the *Memorabilia* "that it is the business of the ruler to give orders and of the ruled to obey." Not the consent of the governed but their submission was required. This was of course an authoritarian principle most Greeks, and particularly the Athenians, rejected.

Fundamental to all the Greek city-states was the equality of the citizenry, whether restricted to the few or the many. The Socratic premise was a basic inequality; nobody was a citizen, all were subjects. A gulf separated the ruler from the ruled.

In one respect the Socrates of Xenophon differs from the Socrates of Plato. In Xenophon's *Memorabilia* Socrates advocates kingship within the limits of law, but in Plato's *Republic* Socrates imposes no such restriction upon the philosopher kings. This may reflect the differences between the two disciples. Absolutism is the hallmark of the Platonic utopias, whereas Xenophon, in the *Education of Cyrus,* puts forward as his ideal a kingship exercised within the bounds of law. Xenophon and Plato may have "heard" Socrates differently on the subject in accordance with their own preconceptions, as disciples so often do.

At one point in Xenophon's *Memorabilia* Socrates even speaks not only of law but of popular consent as necessary ingredients of a true monarchy. Xenophon wrote that Socrates distinguished between "kingship and despotism" by saying that the "government of men with their consent and in accordance with the laws of the state was kingship; while government of unwilling subjects and not controlled by laws, but imposed by the will of the ruler, was despotism."[16] But what if a lawful king began to act lawlessly? Did his subjects then have a right to overthrow him, as a shipowner might discharge a pilot who had become alcoholic or a patient change a physician who had abused his trust? Socrates is forced to confront the problem of what to do about a bad ruler or one who turns bad. After he has just laid down the proposition that "it is the business of the ruler to give orders and of the ruled to obey," two questions are put to him. What if the ruler disregards good advice? What if he kills a loyal subject, who dared to give him such advice?

Socrates is evasive and answers with a question of his own: "How can he [the ruler] refuse when a penalty waits on disregard of good counsel? All disregard of good counsel is bound surely to result in error, and his error will not go unpunished."

To the second question, about killing a loyal subject, Socrates offers a similar reply. "Do you think," he asks, "that he who kills the best of his allies suffers no loss, or that his loss is trifling? Do you think that this conduct brings him safety, or rather swift destruction?"[17]

These simplistic replies would have satisfied few of his contemporaries. What Socrates did not say is more impressive than what he did say. Nowhere does he affirm the right of citizens to get rid of a ruler who rejects good advice and kills those who offer it. He asks them to rely, like a free-market theorist, on the supposedly inevitable consequences of bad judgment and misconduct. The "destruction" Socrates predicts for the bad ruler is no consolation to the ruled. The city and the citizens may be destroyed along with the stubborn and willful ruler. Or he may decamp, like a Marcos or a Duvalier, with the wealth he stole from his subjects. Tyrants all too often get away with their plunder.

Socrates thinks like a loyal monarchist. His basic view is expressed at another point in the *Memorabilia,* when he asks why in Homer King Agamemnon is called "shepherd of the people"? Answering his own question, he replies: "Because a shepherd must see that his sheep are safe and fed."[18]

The good shepherd does indeed see that his flock is safe and fed, and to that degree there is a common interest uniting them. But the ultimate purpose of the shepherd is to shear the sheep for their wool and eventually to sell them for mutton. The herd is destined for the meat market, and the sheep are not consulted by the shepherd when he decides their time has come. The lesson the

Greeks drew from the shepherd analogy is that the sheep cannot trust their shepherd, nor a community entrust itself to one man's absolute will, however benevolent he claims his purpose to be. They preferred to become a *polis* rather than be treated as a herd.

By the time of Socrates, kingship had disappeared from the Greek city-states, and lived on only among the barbarians or in semibarbarous areas like Macedonia. Aristotle, surveying the Greek city-states two generations after the death of Socrates, could say, "There are now no royalties. Monarchies, where they exist, are tyrannies."[19]

In Sparta, which the Socratics admired, the one Hellenic city-state in which there were still hereditary kings, their authority had dwindled to no more than that of military commanders in time of war. Even then they had to operate under the watchful eye of annually elected "ephors" or overseers, Sparta's highest executive officers. And there were two kings, from two different royal families; division of authority and rivalry kept them in check.

Elsewhere the name of *basileus,* or king, survived as an anachronistic relic. Certain religious rites were still administered by priests chosen from ancient royal families. In Athens there were nine annually elected *archons,* or magistrates. The *archon basileus,* or king magistrate, also exercised quasi-religious functions. He was chosen from certain priestly families who claimed royal ancestry. But his authority was in no way kingly. He was not the head of the state even for ceremonial purposes. Thus the last vestige of kingship in the Athens of Socrates figures in his trial. We meet Socrates in Plato's *Euthyphro* on the portico of the *archon basileus.* The old philosopher has come there for the preliminary examination before trial because one charge against him was impiety, and the king magistrate was the *archon* who presided over such cases.

Even when Athenian democracy was twice overthrown in the lifetime of Socrates, the antidemocrats tried to substitute not kingship but an oligarchy much like the patrician Senate in Republican Rome.

In Rome, as in the Greek city-states, kingship was overthrown by the aristocracy many generations before Socrates. The very word *rex,* or king, was in such disrepute in Rome that when the

Republic was finally overthrown, the new monarchs did not call themselves kings but caesars, from the name of the aristocrat who had toppled the oligarchic Republic. Socrates and his followers were totally out of step with their time in advocating kingship of any kind.

Chapter 2

SOCRATES AND HOMER

ᘓᘓᘓᘓ

WHILE XENOPHON chose Cyrus the Great as his utopian ruler, Socrates reached back many centuries to Homeric times for his ideal king, invoking the legendary memory of Agamemnon as the archetypal ruler.

Homer, as the Bible of the Greeks, could be quoted on either side of most controversies since he is as rich in ambiguities and contradictions as our own Holy Writ. This is true of the debate over whether the human community is a herd, dependent on a shepherd for its safety, or a *polis* best governed by its citizens themselves.

Homer does call Agamemnon "the shepherd of the host" or "people." But this was a polite and formulaic salutation, not to be taken at face value, as his actual conduct and his tumultuous relations with his troops attest. In one passage, as we shall see, Homer does affirm the divine right of kings. But the *Iliad* can also be read as an object lesson in the dangers of relying on a monarch's unfettered will. The *polis* itself, of course, was a product of later times. But the word appears in the *Iliad,* though not in the later sense of a self-governing community. Its basic meaning in Homer seems to be merely a fortified dwelling place. The term is applied to Troy, but its inhabitants curiously enough are called *politai* in the *Iliad,*[1] though it was ruled by King Priam and his queen, Hecuba. Presumably *politai* then denoted city-dwellers rather than citizens in the later sense.

In general, the Homeric story does not fit the Socratic ideal of rule by "the one who knows" in which the ruler commands and the ruled obey. Agamemnon was commander in chief of the assembled troops but far from being their absolute ruler. Agamemnon's leadership was hardly a success story. When the *Iliad* begins, it is the ninth year of the war against Troy, and the Greeks have yet to break into the city. All they have to show for their arduous efforts and their long struggle is the loot from the smaller surrounding towns. When the *Iliad* ends, Troy has yet to be conquered, though its hero, Hector, has been slain.

Agamemnon may have been "a doughty warrior" — another formulaic Homeric phrase Socrates loved to quote — but as a commanding general he was no genius. He seems to have been the prototype of the dogged generals who persist in the frontal assault long after it has proven useless, like so many generals in the stalemated and bloody trenches of the First World War. Troy did not fall until later, in the *Odyssey*, and then only to the wily stratagem of the Wooden Horse, which breached by deception walls that could not be taken by force. But that was the triumph of guileful Odysseus and not of the stubbornly unimaginative Agamemnon.

Agamemnon was not the absolute king the Socratics idealized. Instead, the Greek host before Troy already exhibited in embryo features common to the *polis* and modern parliamentary and presidential systems. Agamemnon was the presiding officer. He was advised by a council of elders made up of aristocratic landowners and warriors. Below this council, there was a general assembly of the warriors. So the *Iliad* shows us not absolute kingship but a government of three branches, an Executive, a Senate, and an assembly of the "Commons." The authority of the Homeric assembly was vague and undefined. Even the council of elders had to speak softly in its dealings with Agamemnon. But the "shepherd of the people" could not ignore the wishes of his flock. He was not a Louis XIV. The state was not he. He could not simply issue orders and be certain they would be obeyed. The phrase "shepherd of the people" and the Homeric word customarily translated as *king* are both deceptive. And the words translated as *king* in Homer — *basileus* or sometimes *anax* — were as yet far from having the connotations of the word *king* as we know it from the modern nation-state. Every large landowner seems to have been addressed as *basileus* or "king."

The unwary reader of the *Memorabilia* is apt to believe that "shepherd of the people" was a phrase Homer reserved as a special tribute to Agamemnon. Actually it is applied by Homer to any king or chieftain.

Indeed, when we first encounter the term in the *Iliad,* it is applied to an obscure figure named Druas, whom Cunliffe's Homeric lexicon lists among "various minor heroes" so addressed.[2] Agamemnon was only the foremost king, as he was only the foremost "shepherd" of the Greek host. Achilles, Odysseus, and Hector are among the many other notable warriors also called "shepherds of the people."

The metaphor has benevolent connotations, but the *Iliad* casts a sardonic light on how Agamemnon fulfilled his duties as a shepherd of the host. It opens with one betrayal of trust by Agamemnon and revolves around a second. When the curtain rises, the *Iliad* shows Agamemnon blindly willful and doubly imprudent, (1) in ignoring the will of the assembled warriors and (2) in insulting a priest of Apollo, who was a god both of healing and of plague.

The priest comes to save a daughter the Greeks have taken captive. He is no ordinary suppliant. He comes with a rich ransom. He carries the symbols of his holy office as a priest of Apollo, and he even offers his prayers for their success against Troy if only they will restore his child.

Homer tells us the warriors gathered in assembly to hear the suppliant father and "shouted assent" to his proposal. Only Agamemnon — to whom the girl captive had been allotted — dissented, and it was with his dissent that all the troubles recounted in the *Iliad* began. Agamemnon is infatuated with his captive and is even foolish enough to declare publicly that he prefers her to his own queen, Clytemnestra; it is not surprising that on his return home, she will murder him. He not only rejects the ransom offer but humiliates and threatens the old man. Apollo, angered by this affront to his priest, sends a plague upon the camp. Soon the camp is thick, Homer says, with the burning pyres of the dead.

Then we get our first glimpse of the limitations of royal power in the Homeric age. Achilles summons an assembly without the king's permission. The assembly, after a bitter debate, forces Agamemnon to give up the slave-girl and send her back to her father with appeasing sacrifices to Apollo. The plague is lifted and the king humiliated. The host has saved itself by overruling its shepherd. It has proved it is not a mere herd but already has the germs of the *polis*.

Still, Agamemnon has not learned his lesson. In revenge and as recompense, he unleashes a new disaster by seizing the favorite slave-girl of Achilles. Achilles thereupon cuts as poor a figure as the king. Achilles in anger not only deserts the battle but turns traitor out of wounded pride. The hero runs to his mother, the sea nymph Thetis, and begs her to persuade Zeus to revenge Achilles by intervening in the war on the side of Troy and against Agamemnon and the Greeks. Zeus obliges by sending Agamemnon a false dream, promising an early victory and thereby leading him into rash frontal assaults on Troy and a series of costly defeats.

So, as we see, the *Iliad* can easily be cited against the Socratic ideal of kingship. It is hard to believe that among the sharp-witted Athenians, steeped as they were from their school days in Homer, none ever confronted Socrates himself with these disillusioning sidelights on "shepherds of the people."

If an Athenian democrat turned from the *Iliad* to the *Odyssey*, he could find another Homeric argument against the Socratic ideal of kingship. This appears in the encounter between Odysseus and the Cyclops. There Homer drew the distinction between a civilized and an uncivilized man. In it we can see that while the Homeric community was not yet a *polis*, it was already more than a herd.

We meet the Cyclops in the ninth book of the *Odyssey*. Odysseus and his men are on their long and tortuous way home from the war in Troy. On their way they come to the land of the Cyclops. The circumspect Odysseus orders his men to wait on a nearby islet while he and a few trusty comrades spy out the land.

In the course of this exploration, Homer gives us a rudimentary lesson in sociology and political science. He shows us what in his own time were already considered the hallmarks of civilization.

Odysseus fears that he will meet a creature of great strength, "a savage man who knows nothing of justice or of law,"[3] the primary elements that characterize the civilized man. A glance at the Greek text gives us a fuller understanding of their meaning. The words translated as *justice* and *law* are *dikas* and *themistas*. These words are plural forms of *dike* and *themis*. In the singular these are abstract terms: the former denoted custom, law, or justice while the latter meant what is decent or proper as established by custom, tradition, or precedent. The plural forms describe the methods used to settle disputes in an orderly society. A closer translation might be "lawsuits and adjudications." The uncivilized man is not familiar with such procedures. What Odysseus finds in the land of the Cyclops confirms his apprehensions. The land of the Cyclops is not organized as a community. Each lives a solitary life in a dank and smelly cave of his own, with his wives, his children, and his flocks. Homer says the Cyclops knew neither farming nor seamanship, the primary occupations of the early Greeks. He is more monster than man. He has only one eye, glaring from the middle of his huge forehead, and he is given to cannibalism.

Odysseus and his men are taken captive and imprisoned by a Cyclops, Polyphemus, in his cave. He proceeds to eat two Greeks for breakfast and then two more for his supper. The wily Odysseus, however, soon finds his weak spot. Like other aborigines since, Polyphemus knew nothing of liquor, and fell an easy victim to firewater. The Greeks got him drunk, burned out his one eye, and escaped.

Homer adds a tantalizing touch to his portrait of the Cyclops. Each was "a lawgiver to his own children and wives" but he had no concern for others and, Homer says, he knew nothing of "deliberative assemblies." So this was another point that differentiated him from the civilized man of his time. No such phrase appears in the *Iliad*. There the king consults his council of elders before making a decision and then announces it to the warriors, who can indicate approval or disapproval by shout or murmur, but their assembly did not ordinarily "deliberate."

Perhaps this indicates that the *Odyssey* is somewhat later than the *Iliad* and reflects a somewhat later stage of political development, or perhaps the *Iliad* deals only with the more restricted assemblies of wartime. In any case we have here an indication in the *Odyssey* that centuries before Socrates "deliberative assemblies" were already a salient feature of the Greek community. This was more like a constitutional monarchy than the Socratic conception of a polity in which "the one who knows" gives the orders and the rest obey.

We cannot leave the story of Odysseus and the Cyclops without pausing for a moment to look at it from the "uncivilized" man's viewpoint. There is still a sardonic lesson in it for later times.

Odysseus looked down upon the uncivilized man because he had "no concern for others" outside his own family. But before encountering the Cyclops, our civilized friend Odysseus had another adventure that showed that the civilized man's concern for others was also quite limited.

Odysseus tells us that before reaching the land of the Cyclops, his ships were blown by the wind to the city of Ismarus in the country of the Cicones. "There," he relates matter-of-factly, "I sacked the city and slew the men; and from the city we took their wives" — for sale or use as slaves, of course — and then made off with "great store of treasure." This loot was carefully divided "among us," Odysseus reports with satisfaction, so that "no man might go defrauded of an equal share."[4]

There is no moral qualm in this confession of piracy. The hero's only ethical concern is that his fellow sailors should feel that they had been given their fair share of the plunder. This is no more than the proverbial honor among thieves.

Polyphemus, had he known about the slaughtered and enslaved in Ismarus, might well have asked: Where was that "concern for others" on which the civilized Odysseus had prided himself? If the Cyclops was concerned only for his immediate family, was not Odysseus concerned only for his fellow pirates?

When Odysseus set out to explore the land of the Cyclops, he wanted to know whether "they were friendly to strangers and god-fearing."[5] Polyphemus might have wondered what kind of stranger-loving and god-fearing men were these who could make a surprise attack without provocation or grievance against a city, destroying it, without the slightest remorse.

Of course if Polyphemus had known the outside world, he would have been aware that piracy was then a respectable occupation — as it was until fairly recently in modern times. What was Sir Walter Raleigh but Queen Elizabeth I's favorite pirate on the Spanish Main? "In early antiquity," Professor Ernest Badian of Harvard writes in the *Oxford Classical Dictionary*, piracy "was not clearly distinguished from trade on the one hand and war on the other."

The Cyclops was not wholly unsophisticated. When Polyphemus first caught sight of his visitors, he asked them, "Strangers, who are you? From where do you come over the watery ways? Do you come on business or do you wander at random over the sea as pirates, who wander about, risking their lives and bringing evil to men of other lands?"[6] The key phrase here was "men of other lands." The laws of the civilized community apply only within it. Outside its confines other lands were fair game. What was the Trojan war but a giant plundering expedition?

Indeed law and order within the community may intensify its repressed savagery. War may be a welcome way to let savage impulses loose outside it, as Freud speculated after the carnage of World War I in his essay "Civilization and Its Discontents." Freud believed that the lawless urges men subdue to make communal life possible find relief in the mass murder of war. There we see again the truth of Aristotle's observation that where man is perfected by communal life, he is the best of animals but when separated from law and justice man is the most savage of animals.[7] The planet will not be safe until it, too, becomes a *polis,* and man — fully civilized at last — becomes in that prescient ancient Greek term a *cosmopolites,* or citizen of the world.* Odysseus and the Cyclops, the civilized and the uncivilized, were not all that different. One —

* The Greek word makes its earliest appearance in the Greek Jewish philosopher Philo Judaeus of Alexandria, but is said to have originated some centuries earlier with the Cynics.

when opportunity offered — robbed and enslaved his fellows; the other put them on his menu for supper.

We end this digression on a lighter note. It comes from the great Irish classicist, the late W. B. Stanford. In his commentary on the *Odyssey,* Stanford pointed out that the questions put to Odysseus by the Cyclops in book nine of the *Odyssey* are identical with those put to Telemachus, son of Odysseus, in book three when he comes to Pylos in search of some clue to the fate of his long-missing father.[8] There in Pylos the wise Nestor also asks his visitor whether he is a pirate. The three lines in both passages are identical. But the circumstances are different. And here we come to another distinction between the civilized man and the uncivilized, as measured by the standards of Homer.

Nestor did not put the question to his visitors until, in accordance with the laws of hospitality, he had fed his guests and after the strangers had, as Homer says, taken their "joy of food." In a footnote to the passage in the ninth book, Stanford wrote, "Contrast Nestor's polite postponement of such questions till after his guests had been made comfortable with the Cyclops' boorish directness."[9] The Cyclops was not a gentleman.

Chapter 3

THE CLUE
IN THE THERSITES STORY

જાજાજી

THERE is one passage in Homer, however, that does support absolute kingship. But neither Socrates nor his defenders quote it though this would, one might think, have lent "scriptural" support to the Socratic ideal. Their curious silence may provide a hitherto overlooked clue to the prosecution's case.

We were led back to this Homeric passage when we set out to investigate a murky section of the *Memorabilia* where Xenophon in discussing the trial refers to the charges brought against Socrates by an "accuser," whom he does not identify. But modern scholars long ago decided that this reference is not to a prosecutor at the actual trial but to a lost pamphlet by a prodemocratic writer named Polycrates, which was published soon after the trial was over. In any case the few tantalizing bits that Xenophon gives us from this vanished work provide our only glimpse of the case as seen by the prosecution. These throw fresh light on that portion of the indictment which alleged that Socrates "corrupted" the youth.

The word *corrupted* may create a false impression. It sounds to modern ears like the allegation of a homosexual offense. But pederasty — an erotic attachment between a man and a beardless youth — was socially respectable in classical Greece, as the Platonic dialogues make clear. The verb used in the indictment — *diaphtheirein* — can mean destroy, corrupt, seduce, or lead astray. The same Greek word turns up in Plato's *Statesman,*[1] where Plato uses it to mean leading the youth astray *politically*. The fragments of Polycrates in Xenophon show us that the word had the same meaning in the indictment of Socrates. "Subverting" or "alienating" the youth might therefore be a better modern rendering than "corrupting."

According to Xenophon "his accuser" said Socrates "taught his companions" to look down upon the laws of Athens, led them "to despise the established constitution and made them violent," that is, ready to use force to overthrow it. The accuser cited Critias and Alcibiades as the foremost examples of this corrupted youth and said that "none wrought so many evils to the state." Critias as the leading figure in the dictatorship of the Thirty "bore the palm for greed and violence," while Alcibiades under the democracy "exceeded all in licentiousness and insolence."[2]

In addition the accuser said Socrates "selected from the most famous poets the most immoral passages" and used them in teaching his youthful followers "to be tyrants and malefactors."[3]

It is a pity we do not have the text of the accusation by Polycrates so we could see for ourselves just which poets Socrates is supposed to have quoted in alienating youth from the democracy. There were famous aristocratic poets who could have been so used. Two who spring to mind are Pindar and Theognis. Indeed in the only other but little known surviving *Apology* of Socrates, that of Libanius in the fourth century A.D., Pindar and Theognis are named among the poets Socrates was accused of quoting against democracy. Pindar sang odes in honor of many famous tyrants. Theognis in his elegies expressed the furious hatred of the old landed nobility for middle-class upstarts, the craftsmen and merchants who were demanding the right to vote and to public office.

In one ferocious outburst, Theognis compared them to a herd of oxen and advised,

> *Stamp on the empty-headed people! Jab*
> *With your pointed goad, and lay the heavy yoke*
> *Around their necks! You won't find, under the sun*
> *A people who love slavery so much.*[4]

This view of the common people as a herd is not unlike that of Socrates. It would be surprising if such well-known and antidem-

ocratic verses were not cited by the "accuser." But Xenophon
limits his examples from those supposedly quoted by Polycrates to
one passage each from Homer and Hesiod. The quotation from
Hesiod is so irrelevant we can only conclude that it is dragged in
as a diversionary tactic. As his first example of poetry used to
teach young men to be "tyrants and malefactors," Xenophon
quotes a line from Hesiod: "No work is a disgrace, but idleness is
a disgrace." This verse is from Hesiod's *Works and Days*.[5] It is
simply an expression of the work ethic and has no relevance
whatsoever to the issue raised by Polycrates.

Hesiod wrote before the rise of democracy but unlike Homer,
who reflected the aristocratic point of view, Hesiod was a
struggling peasant farmer, and voiced the feelings of his class
against the great landowners. His *Works and Days* is the first poem
of social protest and "kings" — the aristocratic landowners — are
his favorite targets. Like the British gentry centuries later, they sat
as justices of the peace in settling disputes among the tenant
farmers and laborers within their rural domains.

Hesiod had a low opinion of their integrity as judges. He calls
them those "who devour bribes" and "oppress their fellows with
crooked judgments." He warns them that "watchers" sent by
Zeus roam the earth "clothed in mist" to record their misdeeds for
divine retribution.[6] Hesiod could hardly be used to inculcate
antidemocratic ideas.

Only the Homeric passage which Xenophon cites is relevant to
the charge against Socrates, but this is so carefully truncated by
Xenophon that its significance is hidden from the reader. To
understand this, however, we must step back for a moment and
see what preceded and provoked it. The quotation is from the
second book of the *Iliad*, where the Greeks make a rush for their
ships in a burst of eagerness to give up the war and go home.

As we have seen, Zeus, on the urging of Achilles' mother, had
sent a false dream to lure Agamemnon into a disastrous frontal
assault on the walls of Troy, to punish the king for humiliating
Achilles in the affair of the slave-girl. Agamemnon in turn decides
on a wily stratagem of his own. He tells his council that he will
issue an order to lift the siege of Troy and launch the ships

homeward in order to test the morale of his troops. He hopes that the troops will protest the order lifting the siege before they have had a chance to take and loot the city.

Should the troops instead rush joyfully for the ships, the councilors were instructed by Agamemnon to warn them not to take the king's order seriously but to come back for new instructions in a fresh assembly. The result of the order to lift the siege is just what Agamemnon had feared. His words are hardly out of his mouth when there begins a mad rush for the ships. Not only the common soldiers but their officers — the "notables" — join in. All alike show themselves sick of the long and fruitless war.

Odysseus leads the councilors in stemming the rout and bringing the army back to the assembly. But in doing so Odysseus treats the army's officers one way and the common soldiers another. "Whenever he found one that was a 'king' and a notable," Xenophon quotes from Homer, Odysseus "stood by his side and restrained him with gentle words." But whenever he encountered "a man of the people," he treated the common soldier with blows and insults. "He drove him with his sceptre," Homer said, "and chid[ed] him with loud words." Odysseus ordered him "to sit still and hearken . . . to thy betters: but thou art no warrior and a weakling never reckoned whether in battle or in council."[7]

The accuser said Socrates interpreted these lines from Homer "to mean that the poet approved of chastising common and poor folk." Xenophon's answer is that Socrates "never said that" and would have thought himself "worthy of chastisement" if he had. On the contrary, Socrates "showed himself to be one of the people and a friend of mankind" for despite his "many eager disciples" he "never exacted a fee" but gave "of his abundance . . . to all."

But Xenophon was discussing the accusations of Polycrates like a skillful defense lawyer. If we turn back to the *Iliad* for ourselves we see that Xenophon made two significant omissions from the Homeric account that a democrat like Polycrates would never have overlooked. The first omission is the rest of Odysseus's rebuke to the common soldiers. The lines Xenophon quoted are lines 198 to 202 inclusive of the second book. The conclusion of his speech, the four lines which follow, would have provided a major point in the accusation of Polycrates. Here democracy is directly attacked and — for the first time in Western literature — the divine right of kings asserted. These omitted four lines are the climax and the point of the lesson Odysseus was administering. Odysseus says:

> *"There is no way all we Achaeans can be king here,*
> *"It is not good for a multitude to rule, let there be one lord only,*
> *"One king, on whom the son [i.e., Zeus] of crooked-counselling Cronos has conferred*
> *"The sceptre and the power of setting forth the law, that he may deliberate for his people."*[8]

An antidemocrat could find no better text in Homer: "It is not good for a multitude to rule." The people are to listen, the king to command. This exactly fits the ideal formula Socrates himself puts forward elsewhere in the *Memorabilia,* that "the one who knows should rule, and the others obey." No wonder Xenophon omitted these four lines.

There is a second, equally important, omission in the Xenophontic version: the scene that follows the speech of Odysseus on the divine right of kings. When the rush to the ships has been ended and the assembly called to order, a common soldier dares to challenge Odysseus and the doctrine he has just been expounding.

There are many assemblies of the warriors in the *Iliad,* but this one turns out to be unique. It is the first and only time in Homer that a common soldier speaks up, expresses the views of the army's rank-and-file, and reviles the king, Agamemnon, to his face. It is the debut of the common man in written history, the first exercise of free speech by a commoner against a king, and it is suppressed by force: Odysseus answers the speech not by argument but with a beating.

No accuser of Socrates who cited the mutiny in the second book of the *Iliad,* as Polycrates did, would have omitted this climactic scene. It certainly offered a bad example to disaffected young aristocrats and encouraged their "chastising common and poor folk." Xenophon may have suppressed it because it was too damaging. Xenophon nowhere mentions even the name of Thersites. But there may be an unconscious echo of the name in his text. Xenophon could simply have denied that Socrates ever used these passages from Homer if in fact that was the truth. Instead, the rebuttal he offers on behalf of Socrates is more admission than denial.

"What he [Socrates] did say," Xenophon argues, "was that those who render no service either by word or deed, who cannot help army or city or the people in time of need, ought to be stopped, even if they have riches in abundance, above all if they are insolent as well as inefficient."[9] Except for that attempt at populistic demagogy in the phrase "even if they have riches in abundance," this is no more than a paraphrase of what we already heard from Odysseus. Socrates too is saying that insolent upstarts should be "stopped," i.e., from speaking. That is what Odysseus did to Thersites. Curiously, the word Socrates here uses for insolent is derived not from the more familiar Greek term *hybris* but from the adjective *thrasos* (bold or brash) whence this number one upstart got his name.* A Freudian might say that the name Xenophon was suppressing slipped out in the choice of the adjective.

Homer shows a distinct class bias in his very description of Thersites. Homer can be touching and affectionate in describing common folk, even swineherders and slaves — provided that these common people "know their place." Toward Thersites, who didn't, the aristocratic bard shows no mercy. No other character in Homer — not even the cannibal Cyclops — is pictured more repulsively than Thersites.

The Greeks liked their heroes handsome. Homer makes Thersites so misshapen as to be virtually a cripple. Homer describes him as the ugliest of all the men who marched on Troy.[10] He is "bandy-legged" and lame in one foot; his round shoulders were

---

* There is an alternative form of *thrasos* that in the Aeolic dialect — one of the main linguistic strains in the Homeric epic idiom — would be *thersos*, whence the name Thersites.

stooped forward over his chest; he was pointy-headed and almost bald, only a scant stubble grew on his head. In short, this was one man Helen would never have run away with.

The modern reader wonders how Thersites ever got past the recruiting officer. One Homeric commentator, the Byzantine scholar Eustathius, suggested that the only reason Thersites was allowed to join the expedition was the fear that if left behind he might incite a revolution![11] The ancient fabulist Lucian, waxing satiric about Homer's description of Thersites, says that when the rebel got to Hades he sued Homer for libel.[12]

The Greeks also loved eloquence and Homer made sure to let them know Thersites was as unpleasant to listen to as he was to look at. Homer says he was an endless talker, his mind full of "disorderly words, with which to revile kings." He did not speak with grace (*kata kosmon*), and he was ready to say anything that would get a laugh from the troops. Homer adds that Thersites was especially hateful to Achilles and Odysseus, for they had frequently been the objects of his coarse humor. Apparently he had been an agitator and activist for some time.

When Odysseus has finally prevailed on everyone else to sit down at the assembly, only Thersites refuses to be silent. Despite Homer's invidious description of Thersites as a man of disorderly speech, he speaks here not only boldly, but succinctly and to the point.

Thersites scolds the monarch to his face. "Son of Atreus," he says, "what are you dissatisfied with now? Your huts are full of bronze and plenty of women, the choice spoils we Achaeans give you whenever we take a town. Are you greedy for the gold that the horse-taming Trojans may yet bring you as ransom for a son, whom I or some other Achaean may have taken captive? Or some young girl to sleep with, that you will keep apart for yourself? It is not seemly," this commoner lectures Agamemnon, "that you, our leader, should bring evil on the sons of the Achaeans," i.e., by dragging out the war any longer in his greed for more spoils.

Then Thersites turns to his fellow soldiers and calls them "soft fools, base things of shame, ye women of Achaia, and men no more." Thersites urges them to make for their ships and home "and leave this fellow here to digest his prizes in his old age and learn whether he can get along without us." It seems as if Thersites had been stung by Odysseus's reference to the common soldiers as men of no account in battle.

It is Thersites in this speech who first calls Agamemnon "shepherd of the people" — the line Socrates loved to quote in the *Memorabilia* — but Thersites does so in derision. He concludes with the most serious grievance of all against the king: he has "dishonored" Achilles, "a man better far than he," by taking away the hero's favorite girl captive. Achilles sulks in his tent and Agamemnon has endangered the whole expedition by alienating the army's foremost warrior. The "shepherd of the people" has betrayed his sheep. His lust has proven stronger than his royal duty.

Odysseus replies with violence. In front of the whole assembly, he beats Thersites until he bleeds, humiliating him and threatening that if Thersites ever again dares "take the name of kings in your mouth," Odysseus will strip him naked before the assembly and send him "wailing to the swift ships." So ended the mutiny Agamemnon himself had stirred up by the false announcement he made to test the morale of the troops. And the siege went on, still unsuccessful through twenty-two more books of the *Iliad*. And that's the last we hear of Thersites and the first attempt of the common man to exercise freedom of speech.[13]

Actually if we now go back to the *Iliad* again, we will see that it's not so much what Thersites said about Agamemnon that riled Homer and much classical scholarship ever since, but that a common man dared to say it.

Indeed, what Thersites says of Agamemnon in book two of the *Iliad* is no more than an echo of what Achilles said of Agamemnon in book one. There, in the quarrel between the two "kings" over their favorite slave-girls, Achilles calls Agamemnon "greediest of all men," "clothed in shamelessness," a drunkard "heavy with wine," and a coward who has "the [fierce] eyes of a dog but the [timid] heart of a deer." "Never," Achilles tells him, "hast thou had courage to arm thee for battle with thy folk, or go forth to an ambush with the chiefs."[14]

Like Thersites, Achilles also complained that Agamemnon took the pick of the spoils while others bore the brunt of the battle.[15] Achilles even adds what Thersites dared not say — that he himself had no quarrel with the Trojans: "they never stole my cattle or my horses." Achilles says he came to the war only as a favor to Agamemnon and threatens to quit; indeed, he proceeds to sit out most of the *Iliad,* until book eighteen.

The foremost hero of the *Iliad* had a swollen ego; wounded pride meant more to him than loyalty to his fellow warriors. But Homer has no word of criticism for the petulant and willful Achilles even when the crybaby — there is no other word for him — runs to his sea goddess mama, Thetis, and persuades her to enlist the aid of Zeus against the Greeks: an act of treason. The double standard applied by Homer to the two rebels against Agamemnon is blatant. He idealized the aristocrat and caricatured the commoner.

But Achilles is not the only aristocratic critic of Agamemnon in the *Iliad.* Though Odysseus beats Thersites for speaking against the monarch, he is as bitter against Agamemnon in book fourteen. There the king suggests taking to the ships in flight. "I count it no shame," he says, "to flee from ruin." Then Odysseus "with an angry glance from beneath his brows," says to Agamemnon, "Doomed man that thou art, would that thou wert in command of some other, inglorious army, and not king over us."[16] The scene was hardly a testimonial for absolute kingship.

Since there is no reference to Thersites in Xenophon, we never learn from the *Memorabilia* how Socrates felt about him. But there are two references to Thersites by the Platonic Socrates, and both are scornful. In the *Gorgias,* where Socrates describes the punishment awaiting evildoers after death, he dismisses Thersites as a common criminal unworthy of the eternal torments reserved for malefactors of high rank and notable misdeeds.[17] In the *Republic,* when Socrates tells the story of Er's trip to the underworld of the dead, Thersites appears as a buffoon clothing himself in the body of an ape for his next reincarnation.[18] Agamemnon in the same tale chooses rebirth as an eagle.

The reverence for Agamemnon expressed in the *Memorabilia*

obviously is not confined to the Xenophontic Socrates. The king is as venerable a figure to the Platonic Socrates. At the end of Plato's *Apology*, where Socrates is bidding farewell to his judges, he says that, if there is a hereafter, he looks forward to the joy of conversing with the great men of the past. Among them he longs to see Agamemnon. "What would not one give, gentlemen," he asks, "to be able to question the leader of that great host against Troy?"[19] In the *Symposium* Socrates quotes the same phrase from Homer he uses in the *Memorabilia*, calling Agamemnon "sturdy and warlike."[20] In the *Cratylus*, a minor dialogue that deals with the etymology of names, Socrates argues that a man's name determines his nature — a quirky notion that later inspired Sterne's *Tristram Shandy*. Socrates finds roots in the name Agamemnon that indicate he was admirable for "patience and perseverance."[21]

In the *Republic* the Platonic Socrates goes a step further than the Xenophontic in devotion to the king. Where Homer shows Agamemnon as less than virtuous, Socrates proposes to censor such offensive passages out of the *Iliad*, lest they create disrespect for authority. Socrates singles out for censorship the speech in which Achilles criticized Agamemnon.[22] In the Platonic utopia, literature is to inculcate "self-control" (*sophrosyne*) in the subject population on two levels: (1) "to be obedient to their rulers" and (2) to be rulers over their own "bodily appetites." Achilles presumably set a bad example by criticizing his king. But Socrates says nothing of the bad example set by the ruler in failing to control his own "bodily appetites" for a slave-girl.

Socrates was particularly anxious to censor the lines in which Achilles described Agamemnon as "heavy with wine, with the face of a dog and the [timid] heart of a deer,"[23] along with "other impertinences in prose or verse" on the part of "private citizens to their rulers." Plato's Socrates says they "certainly are not suitable for youth to hear."

In the second book of the *Republic* Socrates also advocates censorship of the false dream sent Agamemnon by Zeus. Socrates says "though there are many other things that we praise in Homer, this we will not applaud."[24] He cites this passage — along with a similar false dream sent by Apollo to Thetis in a lost play of Aeschylus — as examples of representations of the gods which will not be allowed on the stage or in the schoolbooks of the Republic.

Similarly in the *Republic* there is an obscure reference that even shows (according to James Adam's commentary) annoyance with lost plays that made fun of Agamemnon for his ignorance of arithmetic![25] Agamemnon, as the archetypal king, is to be safeguarded from all criticism.

Imagine what such censorship would have done to the *Oresteia* of Aeschylus. When Agamemnon dares bring his concubine, the prophetess Cassandra, home from Troy, Clytemnestra kills them both and exults in full-bodied fury unfit for prudish ears:

"Here lies the man who did me wrong; darling of the slave-girls at Ilium; and here she lies his captive, and prophetess, and concubine, his oracular faithful bedfellow, yet equally familiar with the seamen's benches. The pair has met no undeserved fate."[26] The phrase "equally familiar," implying that on the voyage back Cassandra also slept with the common sailors, is a decorous translation of the Rabelaisian *isotribes* in the original. The literal meaning is that Cassandra "rubbed [it] up equally" with the sailors. Aeschylus would never have been allowed that speech in the Platonic theater.

So we conclude our first point in demonstrating the fundamental philosophical divergences between Socrates and Athens. He and his disciples saw the human community as a herd that had to be ruled by a king or kings, as sheep by a shepherd. The Athenians, on the other hand, believed — as Aristotle later said — that man was "a political animal," endowed unlike the other animals with *logos,* or reason, and thus capable of distinguishing good from evil and of governing himself in a *polis.* This was no trivial difference.

Chapter 4

THE NATURE OF VIRTUE
AND OF KNOWLEDGE

ကြသသော

WE NOW come to a second basic divergence between Socrates and his city. This concerned two questions that for Socrates — though not for the city — were inextricably interrelated. One was: What is virtue? The only definition of virtue Socrates ever ventured in his many fruitless attempts to define it was to equate virtue with knowledge. This raised the second question: What is knowledge?

These are of course fundamental problems of philosophy, and they are still being debated, unresolved. They may seem distantly abtruse and obscurely metaphysical — and best left to be wrestled with by candidates for Ph.D.s. But they had inescapable political implications. If virtue was knowledge, then presumably — like other forms of knowledge — it was teachable. And if it was teachable, then it could not be limited to a few, the old landed aristocracy, but could be learned by the many, the rising middle class of traders and craftsmen, and even to the common people. If they shared in virtue, then the many qualified for, and could not be denied, a share in governing the city.

But Socrates, in dealing with the question "what is knowledge?" went off in an opposite direction. Real knowledge, Socrates taught, could be obtained only through absolute definition. If one could not define a thing absolutely, then one didn't really *know* what it was. Then Socrates demonstrated that such knowledge was unobtainable, even by him. Modestly, he claimed that, in this sense, all he knew was that he didn't know. Virtue was knowledge, but real knowledge was inaccessible. Even this much of the truth could be grasped only, if at all, by a very few. So behind his immeasurable modesty there lurked an equally immeasurable conceit.

It followed — at least for Socrates and his disciples — that since virtue was knowledge and knowledge was unattainable, ordinary men, the many, had neither the virtue nor the knowledge required for self-government. By this labyrinthine metaphysical route Socrates was back to his fundamental proposition that the human community was a herd, and could not be trusted to govern itself.

To understand the contrasting Athenian view, which was the general Greek view in the time of Socrates, we turn again to Aristotle. The basic premise of his ethics as of his politics is that virtue is *arete politike.* The first word means virtue and the second word means political but the better English equivalent, as we have seen, is civic or social. For Aristotle as for most Greeks every citizen possessed — *by his very nature as a social animal* — those elementary virtues required for communal life. He didn't have to be a master of metaphysics. But he had to have that necessary modicum of reason, the *logos,* and with it the ability to distinguish right from wrong.[1] This "political virtue" gave men a sense of justice, and sufficient consideration for the rights of others, to make the *polis* — the civilized community — viable.

Of course, then as now, not everybody measured up to this requirement, but most did. Otherwise even the primitive community could not have come into being and grown into a city-state. This was the basic ethical premise of the Greek *polis,* whether its citizenship was restricted to a relative few or extended to all freeborn males. By refusing to recognize this modicum of basic virtue and of basic knowledge, the Socratic teaching struck at the very core — the necessary premises — of the *polis.* The dominant Greek view gave dignity to the common man. The Socratic view demeaned him. This was an irreconcilable divergence.

This divergence is reflected in the antagonism between Socrates and the so-called Sophists. The Sophists claimed to be teachers of knowledge and virtue. If Socrates was right, they were impostors, for neither knowledge nor virtue was teachable. The many could hope to attain neither. Their definition even eluded the grasp of the select few, including — by his own cheerful admission — Socrates himself.

The antagonism between Socrates and the Sophists, as portrayed in Xenophon and Plato, has blackened their name. Until then the term *sophistes* had a complimentary, not a pejorative, connotation. In Homer a *sophie* denoted a skill of any kind. The word *sophistes* came to mean a skilled workman or artist and was soon also applied to diviners, poets, and musicians. The legendary Seven Wise Men of Greece were called *sophistai,* as were the pre-Socratic philosophers. It became an honorable appellation again in the Roman empire for teachers of Greek rhetoric and philosophy.

There is a strong element of class prejudice in the Socratic animosity toward the Sophists. They were teachers who found their market in democratic cities like Athens among a rising middle class of well-to-do craftsmen and traders whose wealth had enabled them to acquire arms. Their participation as *hoplites* — or heavy-armed infantry — in the defense of the city had also won them a share in political power. They wanted to be able to challenge the old landed aristocracy for leadership by learning the arts of rhetoric and logic so they could speak effectively in the assembly. They wanted to share in the arts and culture of the city. The Sophists served as their teachers.

The landed aristocracy had long had its teachers too. Aristocrats like Plato — who had distinguished lineage on both his paternal and maternal sides — did not leap fully educated from the womb. They had private tutors. The archetype of such a relationship appears in Homer. There an exiled aristocrat named Phoenix found a home with Peleus as tutor to his son Achilles. In the *Iliad,* Phoenix recalls that when he became the tutor of Achilles the latter was still a child, knowing nothing as yet "of dreaded war, or of the assemblies in which men strive for pre-eminence."[2] Rhetoric even then was as important as arms in the aristocratic curriculum.

The service Phoenix performed for Peleus in the case of his son was no different from that which Sophists offered well-to-do middle-class parents in the time of Socrates. Phoenix reminds

Achilles that his father assigned him "to instruct thee in all these things, to be both a speaker of words and a doer of deeds."

Phoenix did not charge a fee for his services. The landed estates were not run on a money economy, and he was paid in protection and, as we would say, in room and board. The Sophists are treated with snobbish disdain in the pages of Plato for accepting fees. Generations of classical teachers have echoed this uncritically, though few of them could afford to teach without pay either.

Elementary education for all citizens was achieved early in Athens, at least a century before Socrates, and literacy seems to have been widespread. This reflected the rise of democracy. But the higher education remained the monopoly of the aristocracy until the Sophists came along. They provoked upper-class antagonism by teaching the arts of rhetoric — for an ability to speak well in public was the open door to middle-class political participation in the debates of the assembly and the higher offices of the city. Rhetorical skills were also, and perhaps even more important, to enable citizens to defend themselves in the law courts. The Athenians were very litigious and, since there were no lawyers in our sense of the term, citizens needed some skill in speaking and in logic to defend their rights in civil and criminal cases. Even those who could afford the services of professional speechwriters like Lysias and, later, Demosthenes needed training in the art of recitation and in the give-and-take of argument.

All this is better understood if compared with education in ancient Rome. There the Republic was an aristocratic oligarchy and the teaching of Latin rhetoric was discouraged lest it widen participation in government and break the hold of the senatorial patricians on the levers of power. When Greek teachers began to appear in Rome, they were regarded with suspicion.

The famous Cato, a dour and hard-fisted old farmer, who treated his own slaves as they aged with notorious callousness, was then the censor, an office with wide powers over Roman morals and manners. Though himself an able speaker, he was hostile to those who taught the art. In 161 B.C. teachers of rhetoric were expelled from Rome.

When, after Cato's time, Latin rhetorical textbooks began to appear, they provoked senatorial anger, and the *OCD* (under "Rhetoric, Latin") tells us that "in 92 B.C. *rhetores Latini* [i.e., teachers of Latin rhetoric] came under the castigation of the censors." Greek teachers of Greek rhetoric, however, were not affected. Facility in Greek was an upper-class accomplishment beyond the ken of the Roman *hoi polloi*. Greek rhetoric added to the graces of the Roman aristocracy.

The close relationship between rhetoric and politics was demonstrated when the caesars overturned the Republic and ended free debate both in the oligarchic Senate and the carefully restricted popular assemblies. Oratory degenerated into showy and empty declamation, a wordy exhibitionism deprived of the vigor it had when it was the voice of free men, whether aristocratic or democratic, determining their own destiny. Without free speech, oratory became mere wind.

A basic reason for the antagonism to the Sophists in Socratic and Platonic circles is that among these teachers were thinkers who for the first time affirmed the equality of man. One Sophist, Antiphon,* appears in Xenophon's *Memorabilia* as a rival and critic of Socrates, whom he twits for not taking part in political life.[3] A fragment of a work, *On Truth,* by Antiphon the Sophist, which turned up on a papyrus in Egypt during the past century, seems to be the earliest explicit affirmation in Greek philosophy of the equality of man.[4] Antiphon was a kindred spirit of Jefferson and the Jacobins. He disparaged nobility of birth and recognized no distinction between Greeks and barbarians. "We revere and honor those born of noble fathers," Antiphon wrote, "but those who are not born of noble fathers we neither revere nor honor. In this we are, in our relations with one another, like barbarians, since we are all by nature born the same in every way, both barbarians and Hellenes." For Antiphon, too, virtue was associated — though

---

* Antiphon the Sophist is not to be confused with Antiphon the speechwriter, a man of oligarchic views who led the conspiracy that overthrew Athenian democracy in 411 B.C., established the short-lived dictatorship of the Four Hundred, and was tried and executed when it was overthrown and democracy restored.

not wholly identified — with knowledge. But the knowledge was teachable and all men could acquire it. "It is open to all men," he wrote, "to observe the laws of nature, which are compulsory. Similarly all of these things can be acquired by all, and in none of these things is any of us distinguished as barbarian or Hellene. We all breathe into the air through mouth and nostrils, and we all eat with hands . . ." Here the fragment breaks off.

In another fragment, Antiphon introduces the concept of "the consent of the governed." He distinguishes the law of nature from the man-made law of the city.[5] The laws of nature, he wrote, are compulsory on all men, but the laws of the city — which vary from place to place — "are arrived at by consent." In this emphasis on the consent of the governed, as in his affirmation that all men are created equal, Antiphon anticipated the American Declaration of Independence. Another of the lost works of Antiphon was a treatise *On Concord,* or social stability. In this he may have been the first theoretician of the welfare state. He expressed the view that "the chief cause of dissension is inequality of wealth" and concluded that "the rich should be encouraged to help their neighbors."[6] Neither the Xenophontic nor the Platonic Socrates makes any mention of the poor. They never seem to enter his field of vision.

Another Sophist, Alcidamas, a pupil of Gorgias, seems to be the first philosopher to challenge the institution of slavery. We owe our knowledge of this to an ancient and anonymous commentator's marginal note on a curious break in the manuscript of Aristotle's *Rhetoric.* Aristotle, in discussing the idea of a universal natural law, says, "Alcidamas also speaks of this precept in his *Messeniacus. . . .*"[7] The rest of this tantalizing sentence was blanked out of the ancient manuscript, almost as if the scribe were afraid of a dangerous and inflammatory thought that might provoke a slave revolt. Such indeed it may have been. We cannot know for certain what Aristotle quoted, but an anonymous ancient marginal note at this point (translated in a footnote to the Loeb edition by J. H. Freese) quotes Alcidamas as saying, "God has left all men free; Nature has made none a slave." I wonder whether that quotation ever got into the literature of American abolitionism. (Judging by its name, the *Messeniacus,* that lost work by Alcidamas, may have dealt with the revolt of the Messenians against the Spartans who had enslaved them.)

Before our hearts thrill unduly to this noble sentiment, I must add a final and melancholy little footnote of my own. One of the saddest observations in the study of antiquity is to see how the Stoics, St. Paul, and the Roman jurists all affirmed the equality of man — whether free or slave — and all settled down quite comfortably with the institution of slavery. So did most but not all of our Founding Fathers.

But Alcidamas, one of the Sophists, at least transcended the prejudices of his time (as, we shall see, did Euripides) and opened men's eyes to a higher morality. Philosophers like Socrates, Plato, and Aristotle shared the conventional view of slavery in their time and were in this respect at least inferior in sympathy and insight to a Sophist like Alcidamas.

Socrates and Plato never questioned slavery and Aristotle thought it "natural." Yet all three lived in a society among slaves who had lost their freedom through the misfortunes of war or piracy. It was an ill fate, not any inferiority of nature, that had brought them to the slave markets of antiquity. Even those born into slavery, as in Rome, often rose above their origins. Homer was wiser than the philosophers. He said that when a man is captured in battle and made a slave, he becomes "half a man." Having lost his freedom, he no longer cares; what he henceforth produces belongs to another. It was not his nature that had made him a slave but enslavement which had changed his "nature." The moral is even the greatest philosophers may share the blinkers of their time, where clearer vision would threaten a property right.

Never in Xenophon and only once in the many dialogues of Plato is the case for democracy stated and Socrates confronted with it. But instead of picking up the challenge and giving us his reply, Socrates evades the issue, and takes us off instead into a semantic fog. This occurs in the Platonic dialogue that bears the name of Protagoras. Protagoras was the most famous of the rival teachers and philosophers whom Socrates and Plato stigmatized as "Sophists."

Athens in the fifth century B.C. was an open market for ideas. Teachers flocked to it from all over Greece attracted by a prosperous middle class eager for culture and philosophy. Protagoras is the only one of them who is treated respectfully in the Platonic dialogues. He was a close friend of Pericles and when the latter established a model colony at Thurii in 443, he chose Protagoras to write its code of laws. Protagoras, as Plato himself so often did, sometimes put forward his ideas in the form of a myth. The myth of Protagoras in the Platonic dialogue of that name embodied the basic premises of a democratic society.

The exposition of this myth was provoked in the dialogue by a speech in which Socrates speaks contemptuously of the Athenian assembly. Socrates says to Protagoras that when the assembly, the governing body of the city, has to deal with a construction project, it sends for builders to advise it. If its naval fleet or merchant marine is to be expanded, the assembly sends for shipwrights. The assembly depends on trained and professional experts. If a nonexpert tries to speak up, "no matter how handsome and wealthy and well-born he may be," the assembled citizens "merely laugh him to scorn."[8] But when it meets to debate basic issues of government, Socrates says, "the man who rises to advise them on this may equally well be a smith, a shoemaker, a merchant, a sea-captain, a rich man, a poor man, of good family or of none, and nobody thinks of casting in his teeth" his lack of instruction or training in the matters under discussion.[9]

This struck at the very basis of Athenian democracy, as initiated almost two centuries before when the great Athenian lawgiver and social reformer, Solon, gave all male citizens, including the poorest, the right to vote in the assembly and in the jury-courts.

To appreciate just how revolutionary an event this was, we need only recall that men without property did not win the right to vote in Western Europe until the late nineteenth and early twentieth centuries. Even in the United States men without property did not win the right to vote — even in the North, much less the oligarchic slave-holding South, where they remained "poor white trash" — until the 1820s and 1830s, the so-called Jacksonian Revolution.

Protagoras replied to Socrates' criticism of every man's right to speak in the assembly with a fable or myth about the origins of civilized life. Protagoras said that when man was first created he lived a solitary existence and was unable to protect himself and his family from wild animals stronger than he was. Consequently men banded themselves together to "secure their lives by founding cities." But the cities were torn with strife because their inhabitants "did wrong to one another," for they did not yet have "the art of politics" (*politike techne*) that would have enabled them to live peacefully together. So men "began to be scattered again and to perish."

Protagoras said Zeus feared that "our race was in danger of utter destruction." So he sent his messenger, Hermes, down to earth with two gifts which would enable men at last to practice "the art of politics" successfully and establish cities where they could live together in safety and in amity. The two gifts Zeus sent down to man were *aidos* and *dike*. *Aidos* is a sense of shame, a concern for the good opinion of others. It is the shame a soldier feels in betraying his fellows on the battlefield, or a citizen if he is caught doing something dishonorable. *Dike* here means respect for the rights of others. It implies a sense of justice, and it makes civic peace possible by settling disputes through adjudication. In acquiring *aidos* and *dike,* men would at last be able to ensure their survival.

But before Hermes set out to earth, he asked Zeus a crucial question, and the answer Zeus gave is the point of the myth of Protagoras. "Am I," Hermes asked Zeus of *aidos* and *dike,* "to deal them out as the other arts have been dealt?" To understand the question, one must keep in mind that "arts" in this quotation is an inadequate translation of the Greek word *techne,* from which our words *technique* and *technical* are derived. For the ancient Greeks, *techne* included much more than what we call "arts." It included all the crafts and professions, high and low, from the shoemaker and smith to the physician and sculptor.

Hermes reminds Zeus that the other "arts" were given out in

such a way that "one man possessing the medical art is able to treat many ordinary men, and so with the other craftsmen." Hermes asked Zeus whether he was to give out the "political art" to a select few, or to all. The answer of Zeus was the democratic answer. "To all," is his reply, "let all have their share" of the civic art. "For cities cannot be formed," Zeus explains, "if only a few" possess *aidos* and *dike*. All must share them to make communal life possible. To drive the point home, Zeus further instructed his messenger, "And make thereto a law of my ordaining, that he who cannot partake of respect [*aidos*] and right [*dike*] shall die the death of a public pest."

Then Protagoras draws the moral of his myth. "Hence it comes about, Socrates," Protagoras says, "that people in cities, and especially in Athens," listen only to experts on matters of special expertise, "but when they meet for a consultation on political art," i.e., on a general question of government, "where they should be guided throughout by justice and good sense they naturally allow advice from everybody, since it is held that everyone should partake of this excellence or else that states [i.e., cities, the *polis*] cannot be."[10]

This was — to use a portentous modern term for it — the ideology of the Periclean Athens in which Socrates grew up but to which he was never reconciled. It assumed that all men shared in what Protagoras called the "political art," and therefore could be trusted — and had a right — to govern themselves. The myth of Protagoras may be read as the founding fable of democracy.

Socrates does not pick up the challenge of the myth and reply directly to it. He might have replied that the myth was a pretty fable but only a way of asserting, and investing with divine sanction, a proposition that had to be proven. But it would have been embarrassing for Plato to put that into the mouth of Socrates because Plato himself so often uses myths in the same way to get a point across.

The frankest reply for Socrates would have been to argue that the government of cities is an art or *techne* like any other; that only a few possess it, as only a few have a gift for medicine or sculpture; and that those who do not have it — the many — should submit for their own good to their rule, and not waste time foolishly airing their uninformed views.

But to have confronted Protagoras then and there with this thesis would have made Socrates look too clearly and simply an enemy of Athenian democracy. So instead Socrates dismisses the myth with a compliment. He calls the speech of Protagoras a "great and fine performance"[11] and then drops the subject, like an astute lawyer who dismisses a witness rather than elicit further testimony on a ticklish topic. A real debate on democracy, and its basic premises, is dodged. We never get another opportunity elsewhere in the Platonic dialogues, where democracy is constantly slurred and satirized but never seriously and fully debated. Though the *Protagoras* has only run a third of its length when the myth is dropped, the rest of the discussion is taken up with a tortuous and inconclusive effort to define virtue.

The first question Socrates asks Protagoras is whether the various virtues are one or several. Soon we are off on a tiresome interrogation over whether virtue is teachable, a familiar topic in Plato. The dialogue ends, of course, in a victory for Socrates. But it is victory of a strange sort. Socrates and Protagoras end up by changing sides. Socrates begins by denying that virtue is teachable and ends up by arguing that it is. Protagoras, perhaps out of sheer fatigue, also does a dialectical somersault. He ends up arguing that virtue is not teachable — an embarrassing position for a professional teacher. Along the way they have lost sight of the crucial question — just what was this "virtue" whose teachability they have been debating?

The dialogue culminates in a mutual collapse. At the end the exhausted Protagoras calls attention to "the extraordinary tangle into which we have managed to get the whole matter." He expresses the hope that on some other occasion he and Socrates may work their way through it again "until at last we reach what virtue is."[12] That never happens.

Protagoras was only the most prominent victim of Socrates' genius for confusing his interlocutors and the issues. He (and Plato) often do this by gross oversimplification and the search for absolute abstractions where there are only complex realities. Of course statesmanship is a craft few possess in the highest degree, and those who have it do not always exercise it for the public good. Of course very few Athenians in their assembly could claim to be statesmen. But the case for giving them a voice and a vote does not rest on the assumption that they are experts in statecraft; instead, it involves several propositions. The first, as voiced by Protagoras and later by Aristotle, is that you cannot have a community or city unless everyone — generally speaking — has that modicum of civic virtue, that respect for public opinion and that sense of justice, which makes living together possible. The second is that it makes for social stability if the citizens feel that they have some voice in determining the issues that affect their own lives and welfare. The myth of Protagoras provided the philosophical underpinnings for the right to self-government. Such parables seem to have been familiar in fifth-century Athens, for Plato has Socrates remark at one point in the *Protagoras* that "one could probably hear similar discourses from Pericles or some other able speaker."[13]

The coming of democracy provided another benefit to Athens. It increased its military power because free men fought with a new devotion and bravery when it indeed became "their" city that they were defending and aggrandizing. This was the lesson Herodotus drew in his history when he came to explain the victories of Athens against the far more numerous armies and wealth of the Persian empire in the first half of the fifth century B.C. Herodotus writes that the Persians were driven into battle with whips while the Greeks, and especially the Athenians, who bore the brunt of the long struggle, fought as free men. "Thus grew the power of Athens," Herodotus says, "and it is proved not by one but by many instances that equality is a good thing; seeing that while they were under despotic rulers the Athenians were no better in war than any of their neighbors, yet once they got quit of despots they were far and away the first of all." Under despotism, Herodotus adds, they were cowardly, "as men working for a master, but when they were freed each man was zealous to achieve for himself."[14]

The Athenian point of view appears in an eloquent passage of Aeschylus, the first and in some ways the greatest of the city's tragic poets — himself a veteran of the victory over the Persian host at Marathon. It is in his play *The Persians,* first produced in 472 B.C., three years before the birth of Socrates. The play's ancient preface explains that Xerxes, "the youthful and impetuous King of Persia," has gathered a mighty host from all over his vast and populous domains "to conquer all Greece and especially to take vengeance on Athens, at whose hands his father Darius had suffered cruel defeat at Marathon."[15]

The curtain rises on Susa, the Persian capital, where the regents and the Queen Mother are worried by the lack of news from the battlefield. A messenger arrives and the Queen Mother asks him a key question about the Greek forces: "Who is the shepherd set over them, as lord and master of their army?" The messenger replies, "Of no man are they the slaves or subjects."

"How, then," the Queen Mother asks, "can such men withstand the attack of an invading army?"

The messenger did not argue political theory with the Queen Mother. He simply appealed to the facts. "These are the men," he tells her, "who destroyed the army of Darius, though it was both numerous and splendid." One can easily imagine what heady language this was to an Athenian audience, so soon after the Persian wars.

"Then," the Queen Mother says sadly, "the fathers and mothers of the army we have sent there have good grounds for apprehension."[16]

Soon a courier comes with the news that the Persian fleet has been destroyed at Salamis, and that the Persian army, retreating homeward, is suffering heavy losses.

For Aeschylus, and for the Athenians, it was not just a victory of Greeks over Persians but of free men over "slaves." The victors at Salamis were men elevated and inspired by the freedom to speak their minds and govern themselves. This is something that Socrates, though he himself had fought bravely as a soldier, never acknowledged.

Chapter 5

COURAGE AS VIRTUE

ও৯৯৩

THE GREEK WORD *arete,* which we translate as *virtue,* seems originally to have been associated with valor in battle, and may be connected with the name of the Greek god of war, *Ares,* whom we know better under his Roman name, Mars. Both the Greek word *arete* and its English equivalent, *virtue,* have connotations of machismo, manliness. (This is in fact the basic meaning of the Latin word, *virtus,* from which our word *virtue* is derived.) So when Socrates came to define virtue, he thought of courage as one of its prime components, and he came up with the proposition that courage, therefore, as virtue is also knowledge.

Certainly knowledge, in the sense of training in weaponry and experience in battle, plays an important role in war, which men have regarded from time immemorial as the test of manliness and courage. But other factors than knowledge play their part in courage, and it is strange that Socrates, who had himself made a record of bravery in war and was to show preeminent courage of another kind at his trial, should have overlooked them.

Courage has many manifestations. Though combat is its primitive test, there are times when a refusal to fight and kill takes the greatest courage of all. Under any circumstances, courage is certainly a virtue. If we take courage as a test of the Socratic view that virtue is knowledge, we will soon see how inadequate that conception is and how it impoverishes our view of man's nature. Aristotle in his *Nichomachean Ethics* disputes "Socrates' notion that Courage is Knowledge" by considering the case of the professional soldier. His is the courage that at first glance does seem to spring from knowledge. Warfare, Aristotle says, "is full of false alarms," and the professional soldier is better prepared by training and experience to size up the real danger. "Experience," Aristotle says of professional troops, "renders them the most efficient in inflicting loss on the enemy" with minimum damage to themselves because "they are skilled in the use of arms" and equipped with the best "both for attack and defense." They are "like . . . trained athletes against amateurs."

But, Aristotle observes, there are circumstances where knowledge may undermine courage. "Professional soldiers prove cowards when the danger" becomes too great and they find themselves "at a disadvantage in numbers and equipment." They "are the first to run away," Aristotle observes, "while citizen troops stand their ground and die fighting." This, he concludes, is because citizens "think it disgraceful to run away, and prefer death to safety."[1] The mercenary professional soldier is too quick to decide that a cause is lost, where the citizen soldier — prepared to die — may win over odds that the cowardly see as insuperable.

Courage in such cases transcends knowledge. It springs from motivation, from duty, devotion to one's fellows, patriotism, belief in a cause. These overcome fear of death itself, and make men ready to die for what they believe in.

Just as Aristotle defined virtue in general as political or civic, so he also defined courage as a social virtue. "First, as most closely resembling true Courage," he says, "comes the citizen's courage." True courage is defined by Aristotle, in accordance with his Doctrine of the Mean — or what we might call the sensible moderate course — as the middle point of prudence between the two extremes of cowardice and rashness. Aristotle traces this civic courage to a twofold source. One source is in a system of rewards and punishments by which the community molds the individual and habituates him to virtue. Thus citizen soldiers, the always realistic Aristotle observes, "endure dangers" not only because of civic devotion but also "because of the legal penalties and the reproach attached to cowardice."

This fear of "reproach" brings us to the other source of civic courage cited by Aristotle. This is *aidos* — that innate sense of shame — concern for how one appears in the eyes of one's fellow citizens. Citizen troops are "prompted," Aristotle says, by "the sense of shame, and by the desire for something noble." Aristotle sees motivation and habituation molding men's character to virtue. This contrasts with the simplistic view of Socrates that courage as part of virtue was the product of knowledge. Just what he meant by knowledge is unclear, but in the case of courage it seems to have been an ability to determine what is really dangerous and what only appears to be so. Civic courage — and full and true courage of any kind — transcends such ignoble and utilitarian calculations.

Aristotle might have cited Socrates' own conduct at his trial against the Socratic definition of courage. He knew the danger was real, but preferred death to submission. Aristotle also contrasts the valor of citizen troops with the conduct of troops like the Persians who fought because they were afraid of their officers. Aristotle says the officers "beat them if they give ground" and notes that the Persian commanders had trenches dug *behind* their own troops to make it harder for them to run away![2]

The Athenians, and the Greeks generally, marched to a different music. Its proud tunes reverberate in the great funeral oration with which Pericles in the pages of Thucydides honors those Athenians who fell in the Peloponnesian war. This Athenian patriotism finds no echo in the Socrates of Plato. The music of free men did not register on his ears. To hear it would mean to admit a link between the martial courage he admired and the democracy he rejected. The one apparent exception, Plato's *Menexenus,* on closer inspection appears to be a spoof on patriotic Athenian oratory, perhaps a parody of the Periclean funeral speech itself

In one dialogue, the *Laches,* Plato actually has Socrates discuss the nature of courage — and other military matters — with two eminent Athenian generals, Nicias and Laches. The encounter is amusing, perhaps more amusing than Plato intended it to be. The dialogue bears the ancient subtitle "On Courage" and was described as *"maieutikos,"* an adjective that refers to "midwifery."

Socrates frequently compares his art with that of a midwife — by his interrogations bringing to birth his interlocutor's own thoughts. But in the *Laches,* as so often elsewhere, he stifles them one by one as they emerge from the dialectical womb. The midwife seems to be an expert abortionist.

The *Laches* begins with a demonstration in the art of fighting in heavy armor. Two anxious fathers must decide whether their sons should learn the art, and whether the man demonstrating it would be a capable teacher. The two generals and Socrates are present as consultants, the former as experts in the arts of war, the latter because of his fame as a wise man. The dialogue, of course, soon becomes a one-man show. We never hear from the teacher whose skills were to be tested. The generals turn out only to be foils for Socrates. They prove — not surprisingly — that they are no match for him in logic. The supposed subject *hoplomachia* — fighting in heavy armor — is brushed aside almost at once for an attempt to define courage, which then turns into a discussion of virtue in general. That is defined as knowledge, and it appears that what the boys really need to defend themselves is "a knowledge of good and evil." The discussion is tortuous, often charming, but always frustrating. Socrates confesses at the end that he, too, does not know the answers to his own questions. He suggests that all of them, the generals and the boys, and Socrates himself, ought to go back to school and start all over again. So the dialogue ends with an engaging chuckle, and an impasse.

Nowhere in the dialogue does any brash voice raise the question, "My dear Socrates, when you acquitted yourself so bravely at the battles of Delium and Potidea did you do so because you then had a satisfactory definition of courage? If you had no more knowledge of courage then than you do now, but still behaved courageously, this would seem to show that courage is not a form of knowledge at all." A brash heckler might even have cited the generals to prove his point. Neither of them were capable of defining courage. In that sense, by Socratic standards, they had no knowledge of it. But they themselves had never been accused of lacking courage in battle, nor of being unable to distinguish a coward from a brave soldier among the men under their command. The logic of Socrates led down a blind alley. The dialogue is good clean fun for professional logicians but frustrating when translated into practical terms, where all kinds of useful work is performed by men from generals to shoemakers who could not define — at least to the satisfaction of Socrates — either the courage they displayed or the shoes they made.

Socrates was the master of a negative dialectic that could destroy any and every definition or proposition put to him. But he rarely offered a definite proposition of his own. This complaint about Socrates' negative dialectic was a familiar one in his time and in later antiquity. It was characteristic not only of the Platonic but of the Xenophontic Socrates. It is leveled at Socrates in the *Memorabilia* by the Sophist Hippias, himself a versatile philosopher and teacher, who is credited with a major discovery in mathematics. On one of his many visits to Athens, Hippias encounters Socrates holding forth on a favorite theme and asks him derisively, "Are you still saying the very same things I once heard long ago from you?"[3] Socrates is piqued and challenges Hippias to a debate. But Hippias declines on the ground that Socrates engages in a purely negative dialectic. "You mock at others," Hippias says, "questioning and examining everybody, and never willing to render an account yourself or to state an opinion about anything."

Oddly enough, the best testimony to the exasperation provoked by this negative dialectic is in Plato. We have already seen the clash between Socrates and Hippias in Xenophon's *Memorabilia*. Their encounters must have made a strong impression on the disciples of Socrates because there are two dialogues devoted to them in the Platonic canon, the *Hippias Major* and the *Hippias Minor*. These sometimes seem to be satires not only on the Sophist but on Socrates himself. Both, like most of the Socratic dialogues, are concerned with problems of definition. The theme of the *Hippias Major* — "major" because the longer of the two — is the search for a definition of "the beautiful." The Greek word is *kalos,* which has many more meanings and ambiguities than its English equivalent. Socrates takes full advantage of these ambiguities.[4] He invites Hippias to advance the definitions and then knocks each one down in turn, but never advances one of his own. "The final result," as

H. N. Fowler, the Loeb translator, observes in his preface, "is negative."[5] The Sophist is pictured as completely helpless in the relentless coils of Socrates' negative dialectic. But the victory is so overwhelmingly complete in this most "fixed" of all the fixed boxing matches of Plato as to strain our credulity. It is so one-sided as to verge on caricature and its net effect is fully to confirm the complaint made by Hippias in the *Memorabilia* about the ineradicable negativism of Socrates. The dialogue makes one wish we had an account of the debate as seen from the other side, by a disciple of Hippias.

The other dialogue, the *Hippias Minor,* or *Lesser* (but only because shorter) *Hippias,* though more generally accepted as Plato's own handiwork than the *Hippias Major,* goes further in exposing Socrates himself to criticism. It could easily have been turned into an Aristophanic comedy. Again Hippias is made to appear absurd. But in the process Socrates emerges as even more so. "The whole," as Fowler admits in his preface to the *Lesser Hippias,* "seems almost a *reductio ad absurdum* of the Socratic method."[6]

The discussion is opened by Socrates. He asks Hippias to address the relative merits of the honorable Achilles and the crafty Odysseus. This in turn leads to a comparison of the truthful and the false man. The conclusion, as Fowler summarizes it, "is that he who best knows the truth is most able to tell falsehood, and that therefore" — buckle your dialectical seatbelts! — "the true man is most false." This was paradox turned into slapstick.

Socrates here outdoes the Sophists in sophistry. For how could a true man become false without ceasing to be true? Hippias is not allowed this obvious retort. He only says wearily at the end, "I cannot agree with you, Socrates." The big surprise of the dialogue is the answer of Socrates. He says, "Nor I with myself, Hippias." And Socrates adds a sad confession. "As I was saying all along," he concludes, "in respect to these matters" — his constant efforts to define the virtues — "I go astray, up and down, and never hold the same opinion."[7] So Socrates, too, at least in the *Lesser Hippias,* confesses himself a victim of his own skill in the negative dialectic.

The authenticity of the *Hippias Major* is questioned mostly because it lacks the grace and wit of the best Platonic dialogues. The doubts about the *Lesser Hippias,* which purports to be its sequel, are similar. But the satiric light thrown by both on the negative dialectic can be matched in other Platonic dialogues whose authenticity is not questioned. The *Meno* is an outstanding example. It was subtitled by the ancients, "On Virtue"; a sequel to the *Protagoras,* it picks up where the latter left off. The reader will recall that the *Protagoras* ended in a dialectical somersault. Protagoras and Socrates reversed the positions from which they started and Socrates — for once — took a positive stance. He concluded that since virtue was knowledge, it must be teachable.

If it is teachable, then common men can by education be made fit to rule themselves. This admission was a victory for Protagoras as a teacher and a pro-democrat. But he never gets a chance to draw this inference in the dialogue that bears his name.

The sequel takes its name from a charming young disciple who is an aristocrat from Thessaly, a backward rural hinterland where the landowners were still the ruling class and their estates were worked by serfs. In the *Meno,* Socrates begins by reversing himself again and denying that virtue is teachable. He returns to the negative dialectic and leaves Meno in complete confusion. But he does make one positive but fragile admission. Socrates admits at the very end of the discussion that virtue is "neither natural nor taught," but comes to us "by a divine dispensation."[8]

But if virtue is a divine dispensation, then it is not solely to be found among the learned and superior few. This implication is not developed in the dialogue but it is there. This seems to be the only place in the Platonic canon where one comes upon a fleeting admission that one may find virtue among the many, including even the unlettered and the humble. But this proposition leads in a democratic direction, and Plato's Socrates quickly undermines it by a curious qualification. He says that this divine dispensation is imparted "without understanding in those who receive it." So a common man, if virtuous, cannot thereby claim "knowledge." And the man "who knows," as Socrates has often told us, alone has the right to rule.

But the interrelations of virtue, knowledge, and teachability are left in a denser fog than ever by the time Socrates bids farewell to his young friend Meno. Meno expresses the frustration many readers of this dialogue feel to this day, despite its charm. Meno complains that "on countless occasions I have made abundant speeches on virtue to various people — and very good speeches they were, so I thought — but now," he feels, he can no longer venture "one word as to what it is." Meno says that before he met Socrates he was warned about his negativism. "I used to be told," Meno says, "that yours was just a case of being in doubt yourself and making others doubt also; and so now I find you are merely bewitching me with your spells and incantations, which have reduced me to utter perplexity."

Meno even makes a little joke at his teacher's expense. "And if I am indeed to have my jest," Meno says, "I consider that both in your appearance and in other respects you are extremely like the flat torpedo sea-fish; for it benumbs anyone who approaches and touches it. . . . and something of the sort is what I find you have done to me now. For in truth I feel my soul and my tongue quite benumbed."9

One wonders, in reading this charming passage, whether it may be in some sense autobiographical, whether the youthful Plato himself had sometimes felt this same frustration in his early encounters with Socrates. In any case, here Plato's genius as a writer of philosophic drama transcended devotion to the memory of his master. The scene confirms the satiric verisimilitude of the *Major* and the *Minor Hippias*.

There is one more melancholy observation to be made about the *Meno*. The dialogue is supposed to have taken place at Athens in 402 B.C., three years before the trial of Socrates.10 And Meno, in a foreboding and dramatic touch, warns Socrates that his negative dialectic might get him into trouble. "You are well advised, I consider," Meno tells Socrates fondly, "in not voyaging or taking a trip away from home; for if you went on like this as a stranger in any other city you would very likely be arrested as a wizard."11 The Greek word Meno uses — *goes* — does not carry the complimentary connotations with which we use the word *wizard* in English. In Greek it meant literally a male witch and was used figuratively for a juggler or cheat. So the bell tolls for Socrates in the *Meno*.

This complaint about Socrates' negative dialectic is familiar in later antiquity. We find it in Cicero, who studied philosophy in Athens three centuries after the trial. Socrates was one of his heroes. But Cicero in his own dialogue, the *Academica,* which deals with the theory of knowledge (i.e., what knowledge *is,* or "epistemology"), records the opinion of his friend Varro, one of the most learned Romans of his time. "The method of discussion pursued by Socrates," Varro said, "in almost all the dialogues so diversely and so fully recorded by his hearers is to affirm nothing himself but to refute others."[12] Cicero agreed. In his treatise *On the Nature of the Gods,* he says that Socrates originated "a purely negative dialectic which refrains from pronouncing any positive judgement."[13]

St. Augustine offers a similar observation. Like Cicero, he was not a hostile critic of Socrates or Plato. On the contrary, in his *Confessions* he says that he was first led to Christ by certain Platonic works and — "having once gotten the hint from them, to search for incorporeal truth."[14] Yet in his *Against the Academics* (i.e., the Platonists), St. Augustine complains that they believed "they could defend themselves from error by being chary of committing themselves to positive statements."[15] In his *City of God,* Augustine traces this negative dialectic back to Socrates himself, and says it created an extraordinary confusion among his followers — even on so fundamental a question as what he meant by the supreme good, the ultimate goal of a virtuous life. Augustine says Socrates "was in the habit of starting every possible argument and maintaining or demolishing all possible positions." Then, "each one of his followers took one of his positions dogmatically and set up his own standard of the good wherever he thought best."

As a result, "so contradictory were the opinions maintained among the Socratics about this goal that, incredible as it seems for adherents of a single master, some, such as Aristippus asserted that pleasure is the supreme good, while others such as Antisthenes said that it is virtue."[16] Augustine even blames this negative dialectic for the enmity that led to the trial of Socrates, claiming that the old philosopher "used to mock and assail the folly of the uninstructed." To Socrates, Augustine observes, this seemed to include not only the common people but their leaders and any rival teachers.

St. Augustine credits Socrates with "employing a marvellous grace of discourse and a most refined wit." But "his practice," St. Augustine continues, "was either to confess his own ignorance or to conceal his own knowledge." The effect was to frustrate and sometimes infuriate his listeners. "In fact," St. Augustine concludes, "this is how it came about that he stirred up enmities, was condemned on a false charge and incurred the death penalty."[17]

One of the strangest traits in the character of Socrates was his attitude toward teaching, though teaching was his lifelong occupation. He never did any other work. Apparently he lived on a small income from an inheritance left him by his father, who is variously described as a sculptor or stone-cutter — the distinction between the artist and the craftsman was blurred in antiquity. Socrates was as much an itinerant teacher as the Sophists he (and Plato) are constantly denigrating. While they traveled about the cities of Greece, he spent his days in the gymnasiums and colonnades of Athens talking philosophy with anyone who would listen.

He was a town character, a home-grown philosopher. The comic poets cracked jokes about him in the theater, and even devoted whole comedies to his eccentricities as a teacher. The most famous and the one surviving example, of course, is the *Clouds* of Aristophanes, where Socrates is depicted as the head-master of a school. Aristophanes even invented a comic word for the school. He called it a "thinkery," a *phrontisterion* — adapted from the Greek verb *phrontizein,* to think — or as we now say of our research centers, a "think-tank." Socrates soon attracted disciples from all over Greece, and many diverse schools of philosophy began to claim derivation from his teachings.

Yet over and over again Socrates denies that he is a teacher. He

takes pleasure in discombobulating everyone he encounters who
claims to be a teacher. The more famous they are, the more he
enjoys their discomfiture.

He exhorts his fellow Athenians to virtue, but claims that it is
not teachable. He identifies virtue with knowledge, yet he insists
that this knowledge is unattainable, and cannot be taught. To cap
it all, after making his interlocutors feel inadequate and ignorant,
Socrates confesses that he himself knows nothing. This ultimate
humility begins to seem a form of boastfulness. To be told that
one knows even less than a man who cheerfully insists that he
knows nothing at all is to add insult to injury. Of all the paradoxes
of Socrates, this claim that he was not a teacher seems the most
paradoxical. We cannot, of course, ascertain what was in the mind
of Socrates. But we can infer from the circumstances why he
might prefer to deny that he was a teacher and to insist that neither
virtue nor knowledge could be taught. We can spell out three
possible reasons. One is political. Another is philosophical. The
third is personal. The three converge and support each other.

The political reason was linked to his antidemocratic point of
view. The Socratic doctrine that "the one who knows" should
rule and the rest obey would be undermined if knowledge and
virtue were teachable. The philosophical reason is that Socrates
was seeking for absolute certainties — absolute definitions of
virtue and knowledge — and found over and over again that these
were unattainable.

The personal reason may be that the two most famous of
Socrates' pupils — the future dictator Critias and the brilliant but
unreliable Alcibiades — turned out very badly and did Athens
much harm. Their careers could be cited as proof that, as a teacher
of virtue, Socrates was a failure. To deny that he was a teacher was
to clear himself of responsibility for their deplorable careers. If
virtue was knowledge and real knowledge was unreachable and
unteachable, then Socrates could not be blamed if two of his most
glamorous pupils turned out so badly.

This is more than surmise. It finds confirmation in the
Memorabilia. There Xenophon says "the accuser" charged that
"among the disciples of Socrates were Critias and Alcibiades and

none did more harm to the city." The accuser said that "during the oligarchy" of the Thirty, Critias was "the most thievish, the most violent and the most murderous" of the Thirty who then ruled Athens, while in the days of the democracy Alcibiades was "the most licentious, the most arrogant and the most violent."[18]

Xenophon agreed with the condemnation of Critias and Alcibiades. "I have no intention," he writes, "of excusing the wrong these two men wrought the state." Ambition, he says, "was the very life-blood of both: no Athenian was ever like them. They were eager to get control of everything and to outstrip every rival [for fame]."[19] But Xenophon argues that Socrates was not to be blamed for their misconduct. "They knew," Xenophon says, "that Socrates was living on very little, and yet was wholly independent" and that "he was strictly moderate in all his pleasures." But the example he set had no effect. His simple way of life held no appeal for them. "Had heaven granted them the choice between the life they saw Socrates leading and death," Xenophon says, "they would have chosen rather to die."

If virtue is knowledge, as Socrates taught, then Critias and Alcibiades should have been preeminently virtuous. For they were among the most brilliant and versatile Athenians of his time. Their lack of virtue sprang not from ignorance but from character. This was the dominant Greek view before and after Socrates. Its earliest surviving expression is in a famous fragment of the pre-Socratic philosopher Heraclitus: "A man's character is his fate" (*ethos anthropou daimon*). This lightning flash of insight is the basis of Greek tragedy. Both Critias and Alcibiades were tragic figures, doomed by the flaws in their characters. The very term, and the idea, of "ethics" originated in the Greek word *ethos,* which meant character. Aristotle's two great treatises on morality were called *ethica,* whence the term ethics derives. It had a hidden corollary. If virtue came from character and not knowledge, it was something the humble could have and the great could lack.

Xenophon says that what attracted Critias and Alcibiades to Socrates was his skill in argument: "He could do what he liked with any disputant." Their later careers "betrayed their purpose" in becoming pupils of Socrates "for as soon as they thought themselves superior to their fellow-disciples they sprang away from Socrates and took to politics: it was for political ends that they wanted Socrates."[20]

But the Xenophontic defense fails to meet a vital part of the accusation. Earlier in the *Memorabilia,* as the reader will recall, "the accuser" charged that the antidemocratic teachings of Socrates had "led the young to despise the established constitution and made them violent."

There is no evidence that Socrates preached the overthrow of the democracy by force. There is no reason to doubt Xenophon's argument that Socrates preferred persuasion to violence. But Xenophon does not answer the complaint that Socrates' disdain for Athenian democracy — and the derision with which he treated such egalitarian measures as the election to offices by lot — led his disciples "to despise the established constitution and made them violent."[21]

The denigration of democracy and of common men is a recurrent theme of both the Xenophontic and the Platonic Socrates. It might be seen as justifying or encouraging power-hungry men to overthrow the democracy as Critias had done or to manipulate it cynically as Alcibiades often did in the quest for power.

The dictatorship of the Thirty, as the narrow oligarchy that replaced the assembly in 404 was called, was set up with the connivance of the Spartans in the wake of their victory over Athens in the Peloponnesian war. Among the disaffected aristocrats who served as tools of the Spartan victors in the dictatorship were Critias and Charmides. Xenophon does not mention that both were relatives of Plato's, the former a first cousin, the latter his uncle. Both appear as glamorous figures, on friendly terms with Socrates, in the Platonic dialogues. Charmides in the dialogue which bears his name is seen as a lovely youth of intellectual promise being interrogated on virtue by Socrates. Critias appears as a respected participant in no less than four of the dialogues and his name and family are honored in the surviving fragment of another, the *Critias.* But except for one brief and disapproving passage in the *Seventh Letter* (which may or may not be authentic),

Plato never makes any reference to this bloody and painful chapter in Athenian history, and nowhere in the Platonic canon — not even in the *Seventh Letter* — is the name of Critias linked to its horrors. But it was still a fresh and bitter memory when Socrates was put on trial four years after the democracy was restored.

In his beloved Alcibiades, Socrates had living disproof of his favorite proposition. For Alcibiades had knowledge aplenty, in every common sense meaning of the term. But no one, not even Socrates, ever claimed that Alcibiades was a model of virtue.

Alcibiades flashes across the skies of Athenian history like a meteor. He was not only brilliant and handsome, a man of many talents, a military general of genius, dazzlingly proficient in political and philosophical discourse, an aristocrat who was idolized by the *demos,* erotically irresistible — in the bisexual world of antiquity — to women and men alike. (Socrates seems to have been the one exception to the sexual irresistibility of Alcibiades, as we know from the latter's rueful account in Plato's *Symposium,* of the austere and uneventful night he spent under the same blanket with Socrates.) The Athenian *demos* were fascinated by Alcibiades, and turned to him again and again in extremity as their last hope. But they never trusted him.

In the most daring initiative of the Peloponnesian war, the naval attack on Syracuse, the democracy picked Alcibiades as a commander but did not trust him with full authority. They ensured a disaster by dividing the command with the stodgy and superstitious Nicias. An eclipse of the moon frightened him from attacking when Syracuse might still have been taken unprepared. His hesitation ended in a disastrous defeat for Athens.

In the meantime, before the naval expedition reached Syracuse, Alcibiades was recalled to Athens in another manifestation of popular distrust. He was accused, perhaps as the result of an intrigue by aristocratic rivals, of having desecrated the sacred mysteries of Athens in a drunken party. He chose to flee instead of returning for trial, and took refuge not in a neutral area but with the enemies of his city, placing his military expertise and talents at the service of the Spartans.

Alcibiades had every gift but one that the gods could bestow, including the doting friendship of his teacher Socrates. The one and only thing he lacked was character. His death was made to order for Shakespeare, and one wonders why he — who drew so much from Plutarch — did not turn the latter's vivid *Life of Alcibiades* into one of his tragedies. The flawed hero died in exile fighting — naked, outnumbered, but brave with sword in hand — after he had been ambushed by a band of assassins in a woman's bed. According to Plutarch, the assassination was arranged by his old rival Critias. Critias, then still the leader of the Thirty, feared that the Athenian *demos,* whom Critias had driven out of the city, might turn to Alcibiades again to lead them in overthrowing his hated dictatorship. Critias himself was soon afterwards slain, along with Charmides, fighting the coalition of democrats and moderates who recaptured the city.

This dreadful murder, by one pupil of another, the one Socrates loved most, in a shadowy struggle over power is never allowed to obtrude upon the apologetic and adoring passages of Xenophon or Plato. But it is hard to believe it did not darken their old teacher's few remaining years before his trial.

The Socratic equation of virtue with knowledge has a famous corollary — that no one does wrong voluntarily. Or, as we might say, people do wrong "because they don't know any better." No doubt this is sometimes true. But one has to be very far down in the scale of humanity not to know right from wrong, or far down indeed in despair to forget the difference.

The crimes of Critias against the city could not be attributed either to lack of knowledge or despair. This aristocrat was as gifted as Alcibiades. Life and property in Athens were never as endangered as under his rule. His record has obscured his qualities. He was a poet, a dramatist, a master of the purest Attic prose. One story may illustrate what his reputation might now be if it were not for his bloody excursion into politics. Many centuries later a famous Athenian rhetorician, Herodes Atticus, became the tutor in Greek of Marcus Aurelius, the one philosopher among the Roman emperors, and the only true philosopher king ever to appear on the stage of history. Herodes admired the pure Attic style of Critias and may well have used his writings in teaching the Roman emperor to write Greek in the classic Athenian mode. So the noble *Meditations* (written in Greek, not Latin) of Marcus Aurelius — which can still elevate and console us in adversity — could owe their beauty of style in part to the model set by the hated Athenian dictator.

There is one vital difference between the careers of Alcibiades and Critias. Alcibiades was at times in his turbulent career a leader of the democracy. Critias was an unrelenting opponent. Critias was the first Robespierre. His crimes were the fruit of a cruel and inhumane but consistent logic. He was determined to remake the city to his own antidemocratic mold whatever the human cost. In a sense — however much Socrates might have disapproved it — Critias could well have claimed that he was only trying to act out the Socratic doctrine that "the one who knows" should rule and the rest obey. The formula itself was an invitation to the seizure of power by resolute ideologues like Critias, certain that the end they sought justified the means necessary to attain it.

Chapter 6

A WILD GOOSE CHASE
The Socratic Search
for Absolute Definitions

৩১৯৫৩৩

F OR SOCRATES, if you couldn't define something with unvarying comprehensiveness, then you didn't really know what it was. Anything short of an absolute definition he called *doxa*, or mere opinion as distinct from true knowledge, which he called *episteme*. The latter is often translated as "science" or "scientific knowledge." But that translation is misleading. The Socratic *episteme* is not science as we know it or as Aristotle established it — the patient observation and collection of particular facts, and their organization into general systems of knowledge. It was purely and simply definition, absolute definition.

Aristotle gave Socrates credit for opening up the question of definition. He regarded this as Socrates' major contribution to philosophy. In the *Metaphysics*, Aristotle says that "Socrates, disregarding the physical universe and confining his study to moral questions, sought in this sphere for the universal *and was the first to concentrate upon definition.*"[1]

But this concentration on definition could lead Socrates in nonsensical directions, and often into absurd statements. Definition is important to rid arguments of ambiguities, to focus clearly on the actual subject under discussion, so that opposing sides could avoid the trap of actually talking about two different things, as so often happens. The emphasis on definition was also important in the development of logic, for much of logic is inference from general definitions.

In the perspective of Greek philosophical development, the Socratic search for the absolute and unchangeable definition can also be understood as a reaction against the world view of the great

pre-Socratic philosopher Heraclitus. Change, perpetual and inescapable, was his central theme. He observed that all things change,
and that one could never — as he said — step into the same river
twice.

This was a profound insight and a major contribution to
philosophy. But, like other great truths, it could be carried too far
and the conclusions to be drawn from it could easily be overstated.
Heraclitus was a mystic and fond of affirming the identity of
opposites. The way up and the way down, he once said, is the
same. But he failed to allow for this doctrine when he affirmed
perpetual change. In accord with his own doctrine of the identity
of opposites, it is both true and untrue. Everything does change in
one sense but in another sense it often also remains the same.

We live among mysteries. One is the mystery of change. The
other is the mystery of identity. Both are realities, but inseparable
realities. Rivers constantly change and are never quite the same.
The water in them is ever flowing and changing. The riverbanks
and their courses are constantly shifting under the impact of floods
and droughts. These are observable and undeniable facts. But in
another sense — despite these changes — rivers have an enduring
and unmistakable identity. The Amazon, the Mississippi, the
Danube, and the Ganges have existed for millennia, in much the
same course and place, distinctly recognizable despite constant
changes.

In the same way, the child and the man are different, but
individual traits persist and are recognizable. Every human being
is constantly changing, throwing off old cells and creating new
ones, constantly growing and aging. Sometimes it is hard to
recognize an old friend, but familiar features persist and appear on
closer inspection. Change is a constant, but so is identity. The
whole truth can only be achieved by taking both into consideration. This is the ultimate inspiration of the Hegelian dialectic,
which sought the reconciliation of opposites in a higher synthesis.
It is also reflected in what the philosopher Morris R. Cohen of
New York's City College used to call "the principle of polarity."
To ignore either pole of a problem is to miss the full reality.

For Socrates and for Plato the search for definition became a search for an unchangeable, invariable, eternal, and absolute "reality" beneath, above, and beyond this Heraclitean universe of constant flux and inextricable contradictions. The history of this search is, in miniature, the history of philosophy. We simply find ourselves — as if trapped in a metaphysical maze — coming back century after century, though in a spiral of increasing sophistication and complexity, to the same half dozen basic answers worked out by the ancient Greek philosophers.

Socrates and his search for definition play a pivotal role in that never-ending debate. But it set his own disciples off in two wholly opposite directions. One was taken by Plato, the other by Antisthenes. Both started with the same observation, that their master had never been able to achieve the definitions he sought, as he himself admitted. They diverged in finding radically different ways out of this dilemma. These contradictory directions have marked philosophical thought ever since.

One led to complete skepticism, a denial that knowledge was possible. The other route, that of Plato, was to create another world somewhere far above this one, a world of eternal and unchangeable "ideas," and call that the real world. This real world of Plato's was filled with unreal, and therefore reassuringly changeless and comfortingly eternal, objects. He took refuge in this metaphysical heaven.

Plato was the archetypal conservative: Above all else, he feared change, and his philosophy sought for a way to escape it. In this search he erected a marvelous edifice of thought which is a joy to explore. But it is also rich in verbal quibbles, contradictions, flights from philosophy into theology, mystical raptures, and engaging absurdities, like gargoyles grimacing at us from the dark corners of a vast medieval cathedral.

Perhaps the earliest attacks on Plato's central theory of Ideas or Forms came from the Sophist, Antiphon. The Platonic Forms are, of course, the personification of universal concepts, as distinct from the particular objects that embody them. Plato, by the theory of Forms, was the first to draw attention to the "universals" as they were later called. But Plato took his insight so far as to enter the realm of the absurd. For he claimed, in Aristotle's words, that particular objects only exist by "participation" in the Forms or Ideas.[2] The Ideas alone were — in Plato's view — "real." The particular objects were but their changeable and evanescent reflection.

To put this in concrete terms, one's bed is "unreal." The Idea of the bed, existing eternally in some distant empyrean, is the true reality. To this Antiphon once made an effective reply. Antiphon observed — in a fragment of a lost work, *On Truth* — that if one buried a wooden bed in the earth and left it there to rot, it would eventually sprout a tree but not a bed. In other words, the material of the bed was anterior to the form or idea. The wood would regenerate itself. But it would require a new human craftsman in a new generation to take the wood and make a new bed from it. In this perspective, the universal concept, the Idea of the bed lives only as a metaphysical shadow of the particular. So Antiphon, by this materialistic and commonsense observation, turned the Platonic universe upside down, or rather right side up. This is the fascinating metaphysical morass into which Socrates led his disciples in the search for absolute definitions.

Socrates carried the search for definition to the point of absurdity. There are passages in the Platonic dialogues that read as if they were lifted from some lost Aristophanic comedy. One is in the *Theaetetus,* where — grappling with the problem of knowledge — Socrates discusses shoemaking. The other is from the *Phaedrus,* where, in a similar search, he discusses horse-trading.

Socrates begins his argument in both dialogues with the truism that you cannot make a shoe without knowing what a shoe is, nor can you be a trader in horses without knowing what a horse is. But to know what a shoe or a horse *is,* for the purpose of shoemaking or horse-trading, is it also necessary to meet the impossible standards of Socratic logic by coming up with an absolute and perfect definition of either shoes or horses? Must the shoemaker or horse-trader qualify for a Ph.D. in metaphysics? Socrates demands not only perfect definitions of the shoe and the horse but — more difficult — a perfect definition of knowledge itself. Here is how Socrates puts it to Theaetetus, who is perhaps the least wide-awake of all the submissive yes-men given Socrates in the Platonic canon:

> SOCRATES: Then he [the shoemaker] does not understand knowledge of shoes if he does not know knowledge.
> THEAETETUS: No.
> SOCRATES: Then he who is ignorant of knowledge does not understand cobblery or any other art.
> THEAETETUS: That is true.[3]

Any bright Athenian could have made the obvious objection to this stratospheric nonsense: A shoemaker need not be a philosopher, and a philosopher is not necessarily a good shoemaker. Indeed, the customer who brought a piece of leather to the cobbler was interested not — as a philosopher would say — in universals but in particulars. He wanted a pair made to fit his particular feet, not some metaphysically perfect definition of a shoe. Then as now, the right foot was not the same as the left. So no shoes even in the same pair were identical, however perfect the definition of "shoe." And the customer wanted his particular pair made in such a way as best to utilize the particular piece of leather he had chosen. At every point the "particular" was more important than the "universal." In one vital respect the shoemaker is ahead of the philosopher. The shoemaker *can* make a shoe. But the philosophers still can't turn out an absolutely perfect definition — either of shoes or of knowledge. Insofar as their respective crafts are considered, the shoemaker is clearly the better craftsman than the metaphysician. So with horse-trading. In the *Phaedrus* Socrates says how silly it would be "if I should urge you to buy a horse and fight against the invaders, and neither of us knew what a horse was. . . ."[4] An irreverent bystander might well have interrupted at this point to say that if neither Socrates nor Phaedrus knew what a horse was, they were obviously too low on the I.Q. scale to be of any use in the army anyway.

As with shoemaking, the art of horse-trading lies in the particulars not in the universal. The first thing the horse-trader would ask is what *kind* of a horse you wanted. For war? For

racing? For heavy work around the farm? Or a showy carriage
horse for a holiday outing? Then, too, the canny buyer would take
a good look at the horse's teeth, his legs, his hooves before closing
the deal. It was taken for granted that the buyer of the horse was
not an idiot who could be palmed off with a zebra or an ass. From
the commonsense point of view, the profundities of metaphysics
look straight out of cloud cuckoo-land. Everybody knows what a
horse *is;* everybody, that is, except the philosopher.

Yet this type of deceptive analogy and of semantic confusion
was used by Socrates and his disciples to cover democracy with
derision. Such analogies had antipolitical implications. If occupations as humble as shoemaking or horse-trading could not be
carried on successfully without unattainable definitions, how
could ordinary men be trusted to practice the far more complex art
of governing their cities?

Every disciple of Socrates may have drawn varying conclusions — and differing systems of philosophy — from their master's ambiguities. But all, without exception, drew such antidemocratic conclusions from them. Taken seriously, they would
have brought the life of the city to a halt.

Socrates' oldest disciple, Antisthenes, was the first of the
Cynics. He rejected human society and its conventions. The
Socratic search for the perfect definition drove Antisthenes to
skepticism. He may have been the first expounder of what the
Middle Ages called Nominalism — the view that universal concepts as general categories or definitions were merely names,
figments of the mind and not realities at all. But politically
Antisthenes wholly agreed with Socrates. He had nothing but
contempt for democracy. Diogenes Laertius in his *Lives of the
Philosophers* says that Antisthenes "used to recommend the Athenians to vote that asses are horses."[5] This gibe at governing a city
by majority vote seems to have been a commonplace in the
Socratic circle. A variant of it turns up in Plato's *Phaedrus.* There
Socrates cracks his own little joke on this theme. At the point
where we broke off our quotation about trying to buy a horse
without knowing what a horse is, Socrates goes on to say
jokingly, "But I merely knew this about you, that Phaedrus thinks

a horse is the one of the tame animals which has the longest ears."*
Phaedrus — who is not *that* foolish — interrupts Socrates to say,
"It would be ridiculous, Socrates." But Socrates hasn't finished his
little joke. He drags in the same cynical slur as Antisthenes:

SOCRATES: . . . but if I tried to persuade you in all seriousness,
    composing a speech in praise of the ass, which I called a horse,
    and saying that the beast was a most valuable possession at
    home and in war, that you could use him as a mount in battle,
    and that he was able to carry baggage and was useful for many
    other purposes —
PHAEDRUS: Then it would be supremely ridiculous.

Quite so. An ass is not a horse. But it is hard to imagine a
peasant stupid enough to buy an ass for a horse, no matter how
eloquent the sales oration and not even if Socrates himself were the
salesman. Yet Socrates uses this simplistic analogy for a broadside
attack on the Athenian assembly and its orators:

SOCRATES: Then when the orator who does not know what good
    and evil are, undertakes to persuade a state which is equally
    ignorant, not by praising "the shadow of an ass" under the
    name of a horse, but by praising evil under the name of good,
    and having studied the opinions of the multitude persuading
    them to do evil instead of good, what harvest do you suppose
    his oratory will reap thereafter from the seed he has sown?
PHAEDRUS: No very good harvest.[6]

Right again. But the assembly, and "the multitude" — a derog-
atory term in Plato's dialogues — have to consider many matters
that have little to do with simple problems of good and evil:
prosaic questions of administering the city or sometimes crucial
questions where even philosophers — or perhaps especially
philosophers — might find it difficult to distinguish the unmistakably good from the unmistakably evil. Indeed, it is not unknown
even for theologians to differ over God's will. The few, like the

---

* I suppose that in this automotive age I must explain here that it is the ass, not the horse,
which has the longer ears.

many, often stumble in the murk of life's complexities. Human affairs cannot find perfect masters nor wait for perfect solutions.

These Socratic homilies, which sound so profound to the unwary and uncritical, easily descend into the ridiculous. They are intended to cover democracy with derision but they often reflect instead on Socrates and Plato. They call to mind a sarcastic reflection by the English philosopher Hobbes in his *Leviathan*. In his stately seventeenth-century diction, Hobbes says that "the privilege of absurdity" is one "to which no living creature is subject, but man only," and he adds mischievously, "And of men, those are of all most subject to it that profess philosophy."* Hobbes goes on to say that "there can be nothing so absurd, but may be found in the books of Philosophy."[7] And on the very next page Hobbes takes aim at those who say "the nature of a thing is its definition." This applies squarely to Socrates. Among his examples of philosophic absurdity Hobbes includes those who affirm "there be things universal." This clearly targets the Platonists, who not only made "things" of univeral concepts, the Ideas or Forms, but claimed that these were not just useful figments for the purposes of analysis and classification but the only things truly "real." Thus the Platonists, in their celestial and enchanting meditations, turned topsy-turvy the plain meaning of the words they juggled, and used this in their vendetta against democracy.

Plato's theory of Forms developed out of the Socratic search for absolute definitions. But Socrates himself — according to Aristotle — "did not separate universals from particulars" and "he was right in not separating them."[8]

Nevertheless it was Socrates who started the metaphysical wild goose chase that Plato carried one step farther. The Forms were his substitute for the definitions Socrates never attained.

The longevity, complexity, and essential insolubility of the task Socrates pioneered may best be understood if one turns for a

---

* I owe this quotation to a charming essay on "Nonsense" by A. C. Baier in the *Encyclopaedia of Philosophy*, edited by Paul Edwards (New York: Macmillan, 1967).

moment to the article on "Definition" in the *Encyclopaedia of Philosophy*.

The article demonstrates that after more than two thousand years of intense dispute and recondite analysis, the philosophers have not yet been able to decide what a definition *is*, much less to determine whether any perfect definition is achievable.* This masterly summation provides an antidote to that "numbing effect" of which we heard poor Meno complain after his bout with the negative dialectic of Socrates — the ease with which he destroyed everybody else's definitions while offering none of his own. The article observes that "problems of definition are constantly recurring in philosophical discussion," but that "no problems of knowledge are less settled than those of definition." So after two thousand years our modern "sophists" still find these questions of definition as discombobulating as they do in the dialogues of Plato.

The problem is not only that things constantly change, thus eluding absolute definition. The problem is also, as every judge in a law court knows, that circumstances may not only alter cases — as the lawyers say — but can challenge the applicability of principles that usually appear unshakable.

This is true in dealing with Socrates' favorite theme — the definition of virtue. Socrates would surely agree that telling the truth is certainly basic to virtue: A liar is not a virtuous man. But is this always so? Can circumstances never alter even this basic proposition? Suppose you have a friend dying in a hospital who wonders why his beloved wife has not come to visit him in his final hours. Which is virtuous: to tell the poor fellow the full truth — that she has run off with their handsome chauffeur? Or soothe his mournful last hours with a sedative fiction? This is an extreme example, but extreme examples — as Socrates well knew — destroy perfect definitions. Our example shows how even the most fundamental notions of virtue and justice may

---

* This article by Raziel Abelson, one of the longest in the *Encyclopaedia*, fills twenty columns. It is recommended to anyone about to plunge into Plato's dialogues.

depend in "the instant case," as judges say, not on the universals Socrates sought but on the particular circumstances.

The fact that all laws and general propositions have their exceptions does not destroy the value of laws and generalizations as guides to human conduct — any more than the doctrine of justifiable homicide destroys the law against murder. But it does mean that in the agonizing choices with which real life so often confronts men and judges alike, true virtue, humanity, and kindness may call for bending the rules, sometimes considerably. The abstractions alone, no matter how ancient and venerable, sometimes prove insufficient. To decide when this is so may be painful and perilous. The law must be preserved but justice must be done. And they are not always the same. The ancient conundrum of Greek tragedy and Socratic/Platonic philosophy is still with us, and always will be.

Only once in the Platonic dialogues does Plato abandon "idealism" — the primacy of the abstraction and the tyranny of the absolute — and recognize this basic dilemma. But, characteristically, he abandons absolutism in one form, only to advance it in another. This occurs in the dialogue called the *Politicus,* or *Statesman*. There Plato is arguing that the ideal state is one ruled by an absolute monarch — absolute in the sense that the monarch should not be bound even by law.

In the *Politicus,* Plato introduces an argument which runs completely contrary to the idealism he generally espouses. But in doing so he shows an acute and sophisticated understanding of jurisprudence. Significantly his mouthpiece on this occasion is not Socrates but "A Stranger." His argument would be too incongruous in the mouth of Socrates. The Stranger argues that just decisions cannot be reached from abstract definitions of what is *ariston* (best) or *dikaiotaton* (most just). The Stranger asserts that in the ideal state absolute power must rest not with the laws but with the king. The reason for this, the Stranger goes on to explain, is that "law could never" determine "what is noblest and most just for one and all," because of "the differences of men and of actions" and the fact that nothing "in human life is ever at rest."

Consequently there is no way "to promulgate any simple rule for everything and for all time."

The Stranger says that "which is persistently simple," i.e., the law, "is inapplicable to things which are never simple," i.e., human life and conflict. Neither written nor unwritten law and custom are wholly adequate. As Mr. Justice Holmes once put it with Olympian conciseness, "General considerations do not decide concrete cases." This is the classic argument for supplementing the law with what in various legal codes is called "equity."

The cure for the law's inevitable shortcomings is not to place all power arbitrarily, as Plato would have us do, in the hands of one man. Indeed, Plato's own dialogue culminates in a vivid metaphor that can be turned against his own thesis. Here his argument is undone by his own genius as a writer.

The Stranger ends up his argument for absolute kingship by comparing the law to "a stubborn and ignorant man who allows no one to do anything contrary to his command, or even to ask a question, not even if something new occurs to some one, which is better than the rule he has himself ordained."[9] Too often in ancient times as in modern that is exactly how kings — and their modern equivalents, the dictators of various varieties — have operated. The law, for all its limitations, has proven a wiser and more adaptable master.

We are now in a position to understand the divine mission Socrates claimed to have received from the oracle at Delphi, and how that divine mission got him into trouble. There are two versions of the Delphic affair, one in Xenophon, the other in Plato. The former is simple and straightforward, but boastful to the point of embarrassment. The latter is subtle and engaging. But they have one essential point in common — Socrates' claim to be the wisest man around.

The earlier, and unadorned, version is in Xenophon's *Apology*. Plato's *Apology* bears all the marks of an account recollected and embellished in tranquillity many years after. Xenophon's, much less known, is no such masterpiece. It is sketchy and bald, a memorandum quickly written down, a plea to contemporary opinion. It may thus be closer to the historical facts. Xenophon says Socrates told the court that when his disciple Chaerephon "made inquiry at the Delphic oracle concerning me, in the presence of many people Apollo answered that no man was more free than I, or more just, or more prudent."

Socrates began by telling the jurors that when the legendary Spartan lawgiver Lycurgus once entered the sacred precincts of the oracle, the prophetic voice cried out that it did not know whether to call Lycurgus "god or man." Socrates acknowledged demurely that "Apollo did not compare me to a god" but added that "he did, however, judge that I far excelled the rest of mankind."[10]

Plato's version of the visit is less brash. The first difference between the two accounts is in the question put to the oracle. In Xenophon, Socrates says only that Chaerephon "made inquiry" at Delphi "concerning me." The response, as we have seen, was that Socrates "far excelled the rest of mankind."

But in Plato's *Apology,* Socrates says the oracle was asked an enigmatic question and gave an enigmatic answer, or at least Socrates chose to treat it as such. The question was whether "there were anyone wiser than I." The answer was "that there was no one wiser."[11] Plato's version differs in grace and whimsicality, or irony, but not really in substance from Xenophon's. In Plato, Socrates puts the story diffidently, as if to disarm the court. He asks the jurors not to "make a tumult" — using the same Greek verb, *thorubeo,* as does the Xenophontic account — "if I seem to you to be boasting" (which, of course, he was). Socrates is apologetic that such a question was even asked the oracle and blames this on Chaerephon, the disciple who dared broach it. He tells the jurors, "You knew the kind of man Chaerephon was, how impetuous in whatever he undertook." So blame for the boastfulness is shifted to Chaerephon.

This contrasts strongly with Xenophon's account. There after the "tumult" of protest from the jury, Socrates defends the oracle's high estimate of him. Socrates tells the jury not to believe the oracle "even in this without due grounds" but invites them to "examine the god's utterance in detail." "First," Socrates asks the jurors, "who is there in your knowledge that is less a slave to his bodily appetites than I am? Who in the world more free — for I accept neither gifts nor pay from anyone? Whom would you with reason regard as more just . . . and would not a person with reason call me a wise man? . . . And that my labor has not been in vain do you not think is attested by this fact, that many of my fellow-citizens who strive for virtue and many from abroad choose to associate with me above all other men?"[12]

But in Plato's account Socrates treats the god's praise of him as a divine jest. "For when I heard this," Socrates there tells the jurors, "I thought to myself, 'What in the world does the god mean, and what riddle is he propounding? For I am conscious that I am not wise either much or little. What then does he mean by declaring that I am the wisest?' "[13] Here Plato adds the final touch, and the major difference with Xenophon: the divine mission theme, which does not appear in Xenophon at all. Plato's Socrates says the god could not be lying, since he is a god. So it became Socrates' mission in life to go about and question his fellow townsmen to see if there *was* anyone among them wiser than he. And that, Plato's Socrates tells the jurors, is how he got into trouble and made himself unpopular. For he found that while he himself knew nothing, all the others he questioned knew even less — they were not even aware of their ignorance! So, despite the elaborate disclaimers, Plato's Socrates, like Xenophon's, did indeed consider that he excelled the rest of mankind.

There is not only a palpable conceit just under the surface of Plato's more graceful account but even a touch of cruelty at the expense of his interlocutors. The most humiliating — and infuriating — part of the Socratic mode of interrogation was that their ignorance was shown to be real while they felt that his self-proclaimed ignorance was ostentatious and pretended. This was the famous Socratic "irony." The Greek word *eironeia* from which our word irony derives meant dissembling or dissimulation, saying what one did not really mean. His interlocutors felt that, behind his "irony," his veil of mock-modesty, Socrates was laughing at them.[14] This was the cruelty that lurked behind the

Platonic account in its exquisite and aristocratic jesting, all the more deadly for its *politesse*.

Why, in Plato's *Apology,* does Socrates tell the story of the Delphic oracle? And why does Socrates claim that the oracle imposed a divine mission on him — the mission being to question his fellow citizens, and especially the leading Athenians, in order to determine what Delphi meant by saying that no one was wiser than Socrates?

Socrates says to the jury that he had become an object of suspicion in the city. His fellow townsmen were asking, "Socrates, what is the trouble about you? Whence have these prejudices against you arisen? . . . Tell us what it is, that we may not act unadvisedly in your case."[15] Socrates explains that he has acquired this unfavorable reputation on account of nothing else than a kind of wisdom, though he himself does not wholly understand what that wisdom is. It is at this point that, in explanation, he tells the story of the Delphic oracle.

Here a crucial question arises which is neither raised nor answered in Plato's *Apology.* Why should a reputation for wisdom get a man into trouble in a city like Athens, a city to which philosophers flocked from all over Greece and were not only welcomed but richly rewarded as teachers and popular lecturers? This was the most open city of antiquity, and perhaps of all time, the city that Pericles praised as "the school of Hellas," a city whose public places — as they live for us in the pages of Plato — were the happy scene of endless philosophical debate.

The answer seems to be that Socrates used his special kind of "wisdom" — his *sophia* or skill as a logician and philosopher — for a special political purpose: to make all the leading men of the city appear to be ignorant fools. The divine mission he claimed from Delphi turned out to be what we would call an ego-trip — an exercise in self-glorification for Socrates and of belittlement for the city's most respected leaders. He thus undermined the *polis,* defamed the men on whom it depended, and alienated the youth.

That is indeed what Plato's account tells us. His Socrates explains — as he may very well have done at the actual trial — that his investigation of the oracle led him to interrogate the three leading classes of citizens in Athens. First and foremost he started with the *politikoi,* the statesmen, the men who filled the highest offices of the city and as orators played a leading role in the assembly. Then he went to the poets, including — as he tells us — the tragic poets, whose surviving plays still stand amidst the highest peaks of world literature. Lastly he went to the Athenian craftsmen. The beauty and quality of their wares commanded a market all around the Mediterranean world and enabled crowded Attica to earn the bread for a population far beyond what its meager soil could feed. These craftsmen were also the men who built the Parthenon. Socrates found them all ignorant and deficient.

Socrates admits in Plato's *Apology* that "in addition" to the animosity aroused by his own interrogations, "the young men who have the most leisure, the sons of the richest men accompanying me of their own accord, find pleasure in hearing people being examined, and often imitate me themselves, and then they undertake to examine others; and then, I fancy, they find a great plenty of people who think they know something, but know little or nothing."

"Little or nothing" about what? What kind of questions did these fledgling imitators of Socrates put to the leading men of Athens to make them look as if they knew "little or nothing"? Socrates did not tell the jury. Instead he went on to say, "As a result, therefore, those who are examined by them are angry with me, instead of being angry with themselves, and say that 'Socrates is a most abominable person and is corrupting the youth.' "[16]

So, in a real sense, Socrates was. He had taught these youthful tyros, mere beginners in beardless wisdom, an easy way to make laughingstocks of the leading citizens, the officials of the city, along with its poets and its craftsmen, and of course the *hoi polloi,* the ignorant many, who presumed to vote on public questions in the assembly.

How did they do it? By that negative dialectic which we have seen was Socrates' stock-in-trade. He asked for definitions he himself was never able to attain and then easily refuted whatever definitions his interlocutors offered. Not infrequently this was accomplished by much the same verbal trickeries he attributed to the Sophists — by the quibbling about words we still call "sophistries." His "wisdom" — and the divine mission he claimed from Delphi — got him into trouble because this was an easy way to turn the city's gilded youth against the democracy. The most brilliant of them all was Plato and this is the testimony of his dialogues.

Even at its best, the Socratic negative dialectic provided an irrelevant standard by which to judge the competence of statesmen, tragic poets, or shoemakers in their respective crafts. Above all, it was no way to question the right of common men to participate in the government of their own lives and city.

Socrates was asking them to pass tests in metaphysics, to prove themselves as logicians. He called them ignorant because they could not cope with the most enduring problems of philosophy — the *epistemological* and the *ontological,* to use the modern vocabulary for the nature of knowledge and the nature of being. Socrates was himself baffled by them, and so are philosophers to this day. The very terms are metaphysical monstrosities, spooky conundrums. If even Kant, with the most systematic answers any metaphysician ever devised, has not wholly satisfied his fellow philosophers, how could Socrates deride his Athenian contemporaries as ignoramuses for failing the same test?

In one dialogue, the *Gorgias,* the Platonic Socrates drops the mask of mock-modesty — his claim to know only that he did not know. In that dialogue, he treats with scorn the four greatest leaders of Athens in his own and the previous generation. He asserts that he himself is one of the few, "if not the only," true statesmen Athens ever produced. That boast in the *Gorgias,* if Socrates indeed really talked that way on occasion, was enough to earn him the disapproval of practically everybody in Athenian politics except a few bitter-enders never reconciled to self-government in any form, whether democratic or oligarchic. All but one of the four statesmen Socrates treated with disdain in the *Gorgias* were themselves of aristocratic family; the rich and well-born continued to fill the highest offices of Athens long after universal male suffrage was achieved, and all propertied qualifications to office had been abolished. The one exception among the four was Themistocles, who was of poor and humble origin. Two of the four attacked by Socrates in the *Gorgias* — Themistocles and Pericles — were idols of the *hoi polloi.* But the other two — Miltiades and his son, Cimon — were the idols of *hoi oligoi,* "the few," the "better classes," the wealthy, and especially those of inherited wealth, the "nobility." These two were leaders of what we would call the conservative party, which would have liked some propertied restriction on the right to vote and hold public office. But both of these great conservative leaders were loyal to the city, and served Athens well in peace and war.

Each of the four meant much to Athenian pride. Miltiades and Themistocles were associated in the minds of the Athenians with the two most famous battles of the Persian wars — Marathon and Salamis. Miltiades commanded the outnumbered men who turned back the armies of Darius at Marathon in 490 B.C. when the invaders were at the very doorstep of Athens. Ten years later when the Persians tried again and came fearfully close to victory, ravaging Attica, forcing the evacuation of Athens, capturing the Acropolis and burning its sacred edifices, it was Themistocles who saved Athens by routing the mighty Persian fleet of Xerxes in the battle of Salamis in 480 B.C. A decade later it was Miltiades' son, Cimon, who ended Persian hopes forever when he crushed another Persian fleet and laid the foundations of the Athenian empire. Pericles, the latest of the four, assumed leadership of the city a decade later and led Athens to its heights. These four great leaders — and the quality of the Athenian common people — made possible all that symbolizes for us the glories of Athens: the Parthenon, whose serene ruins still stir our awe, Athens' great experiment in democracy and free thought, its theater, its wide-ranging philosophical debates, all that made Athens not only "the school of Hellas" but of all humanity since. These are the achievements Plato's Socrates brushes aside with querulous and crotchety conceit in the *Gorgias,* comparing the four to pastry-cooks and stigmatizing them as mere "flatterers" of the ignorant multitude.

The attack on the four reaches a ridiculous climax when Socrates accuses Pericles, the greatest of the four, of having made the Athenians "idle, cowardly, talkative, and avaricious."[17] Socrates, the most talkative Athenian of his time, a man who neglected the affairs of his family and his city to engage in constant conversation, the man who made talk his life and his monument, accuses Pericles of having made his fellow Athenians "talkative"! Socrates drank the final hemlock with heroic and exemplary equanimity. But can one imagine him serene if the Athenians had suddenly lost their love of talk and glumly evaded his engaging inquiries?

Of course we do not know whether the historical Socrates ever delivered such an attack on the four statesmen. The *Gorgias* was written long after his death when Plato had returned from self-imposed exile and founded his academy. But the attack on the four is not inconsistent with what we learn elsewhere of Socrates, particularly the description by Xenophon of Socrates' demeanor before his judges. In Plato's dialogues, Socrates' high estimate of himself is usually veiled by "irony." But his low estimate of Athenian statesmen is unmistakable in Plato's *Apology,* and it recalls the warning to Socrates in Plato's *Meno.*

In that dialogue Socrates meets Anytus, a well-to-do master tanner and a middle-class political leader. The topic of discussion — what else? — is virtue: how and if it can be taught. Anytus argues that young men are taught virtue in a city by example, by the role model set for them by their elders, and by the great men of the city's past. This was as much a truism then as it is now. Socrates dismisses this argument scornfully. Obviously he does not like to admit that the community, the *polis,* is itself a teacher, inculcating by example and tradition. Socrates is here as always anti*political,* in the Greek as well as in the modern sense. To rebut the notion that the city's great men set a salutary example, Socrates takes aim at four Athenian statesmen, much as he did in the *Gorgias,* though a little more gently. Once again he equally attacks oligarchs and democrats. He picks the same democrats, Themistocles and Pericles. But this time from the conservative and oligarchic side he chooses two other outstanding statesmen. One is Pericles' great rival, the general (not the historian) Thucydides. The other is that paragon of ancient rectitude, Aristides, who was known and remembered as "Aristides the Just." All are treated as disparagingly in the *Meno* as the four in the *Gorgias*.

Plato, ever the dramatist, has Anytus say as a premonitory parting shot, "Socrates, I consider that you are too apt to speak ill of people. I, for one, if you will take my advice, would warn you to be careful."[18] Anytus was to turn up several years later at the trial as the most prominent of his three accusers. The four were to have their day in court.

I do not wish to imply that Socrates was finally brought to trial for casting aspersions on Athenian statesmen. Insulting them was not a crime in Athens. It was a popular sport. The comic poets — who played something of the same role in Athens as independent journalists in our world — did it all the time, to the intense enjoyment of the Athenians.

Socrates' real offense lay in his gross oversimplifications — in the simplistic philosophical premises from which he leveled his attacks on the city, its leaders, and the democracy.

Of course the ruler of a city, or any other polity, should be "one who knows." But what should he know? A commonsense answer then as now would be: enough about foreign affairs, trade, defense, public works, economic and social problems to lead the city wisely. But for Socrates, the man "who knows" had to be a professional philosopher. His "knowledge" had to be a specialized metaphysical figment.

The Socratic formula giving rule to the man "who knows" had in it the germ of Plato's philosopher kings. But Socrates went further than Plato. Socrates could find no one — even among the philosophers — who possessed *episteme* or real knowledge in his narrow sense of the term.

No one could provide the perfect and absolute qualifications he required. Neither could he, as Socrates cheerfully confessed. No one "knew" and no one was fit to rule. Where did that leave the city? Up a creek. His dialectic led to a dead end.

What was legitimate if sometimes ponderous philosophical playfulness — whales of the intellect flailing about in deep seas — became disruptive when applied to the affairs of the *polis*. An example is the famous Socratic corollary of the virtue = knowledge equation: the "paradox" that no one does evil voluntarily. This would wreck any system of criminal justice. It is true that men sometimes commit crimes because, as we say, "they didn't know any better." But how can they ever "know better" in the peculiar world of the Socratic logic? If virtue is knowledge but "knowledge" is unattainable, then no one can ever "know any better." No one is guilty and every criminal can go free.

In normal jurisprudence, a man who commits arson or murder can avoid conviction if his lawyers can prove insanity. In the jurisprudence of Socrates, any criminal could escape punishment by pleading that the crime was involuntary due to "ignorance." How could anyone be convicted of bank robbery when a philosophically sophisticated burglar could so easily show by Socratic standards that he did not even know what a bank *was?*

In a realm created by idealist philosophers, their constant search for the perfect in an imperfect world hobbles reasonable solutions to the complexities with which men must wrestle in the search for order and justice. To say that no man does wrong voluntarily is to assume in advance that he does not know right from wrong. In what sense is it true that men do not know right from wrong? Only in the sense that they cannot come up with definitions of right and wrong so perfect as to cover any conceivable contingency. But a man who does not really know it is wrong to burn a neighbor's house or to rob and kill him would be very hard to find outside an insane asylum or a home for the hopelessly retarded. Most criminals know very well what they're doing, and there are few who do not in their hearts feel their guilt, and some even confess and seek punishment to rid themselves of that feeling. The criminal, as often as not, may be superior rather than inferior in his knowledge of the real world. He may be more daring and enterprising than his peers, and contemptuous rather than ignorant of right and wrong.

Besides basic problems of morality there are simpler aspects of law the Socratic logic would destroy. In Athens as elsewhere it was "wrong" to disobey the law of the city even if no ethical standard was involved, just as a matter of civic peace and order. So in our time it is "wrong" to drive on the left in New York and "wrong" to drive on the right in London. These are what legal scholars call "normative" rather than ethical rules. Then as now ignorance of the law was not accepted as an excuse, else the standard of proof would be almost impossible. How can anyone prove a man "did know" who claims he didn't?

The law imposes an elementary duty on the citizen to know the law. He cannot escape by pleading ignorance. One of the earliest victories of the common people in their struggle for justice was forcing the ruling class of great landowners to write the law down so everyone could see it and know just what they were accused of violating. That victory was won in Athens more than a century before Socrates was born.

Proposed laws were debated and voted on in the assembly. Literacy was widespread in Socrates' time and laws were posted on the equivalent of civic billboards. In Athens you didn't need a lawyer to know the law. In this sense no Athenian could claim ignorance of what was legally "right" or "wrong." Indeed, he would certainly have resented the imputation of such ignorance.

As for broader ethical norms, in no city were right and wrong in this sense more fully debated than in Athens, as the Platonic dialogues themselves attest. So does the tragic theater; agonizing moral conflicts were its central theme, as they were in the greatest of the public debates recorded by Thucydides. So do the eager audiences which the Sophists and Socrates himself attracted to ethical discussions.

When the Athenians "did wrong" they did so knowingly and voluntarily, either because as individuals they thought they could get away with it, or as a city when confronted with a choice of evils, and they chose what they considered — though often only after bitter and divisive debate — the lesser evil than military defeat and the loss of empire. So it was in the decision to massacre the people of Melos for revolting against Athens during the Peloponnesian war, the gravest "war crime" Athens ever committed but one which, in all their discussion of virtue, neither Socrates nor Plato ever mentions. Perhaps this is because it illustrates that life's complexities cannot be squeezed into their oversimplified universe.

Neither in Xenophon nor Plato is Socrates ever confronted by the basic social questions raised by his paradoxical doctrine. How could men be trained in virtue if they were assured in advance of escaping punishment by the doctrine that they never did wrong voluntarily?

Chapter 7

SOCRATES AND RHETORIC

ভ৶৲৹

L IKE EVERYTHING ELSE in Greek literature, oratory or
rhetoric had its beginnings in Homer. But it took on new
and critical importance when the Greek city-states, whether
oligarchic or democratic, achieved self-government. The principal
organs of self-government were the assembly, where the laws
were made, and the jury-courts, where they were interpreted and
applied. The citizenry, whether the few or the many, had to learn
how to speak clearly and argue persuasively in order to protect
their interests in the assembly and in the law courts. Some skill in
speaking and argument became a political and practical necessity
as participation widened with the evolution toward democracy.

The practicality of some training in rhetoric is demonstrated by
the circumstances under which the first manuals on the art of
rhetoric made their appearance. These are recorded by a fragment
from a lost work by Aristotle, preserved by Cicero in his essay on
oratory, the *Brutus,* named for the Republican aristocrat who
assassinated Caesar.

Aristotle said that the first two Greek writers on oratory, Corax
and Tisias, wrote their manuals after the tyrants were driven out
of Sicily in the middle of the fifth century B.C. Exiles whose
property had been expropriated by the dictators returned home
and sued in the law courts for restitution. They needed training in
rhetoric to argue their cases successfully against those who had
acquired these "stolen goods" from the tyrants. Cicero argued
that the art of oratory was thus "the offspring" of a well-
established constitutional order.[1] But the Platonic Socrates is

scornful of rhetoric and launches two destructive attacks upon it, one in the *Phaedrus* and the other in the *Gorgias*. The former is one of the most enchanting of the Platonic dialogues but it soars into a mystical realm midway between poetry and theology. It sets the standard of knowledge required for a "true" rhetoric so high that few could approach it. Socrates says the orator must begin to apprehend the nature of the soul and its relation to the divine and must have caught some glimpse of the ideal Forms that exist, invisible to ordinary mortals, far above the celestial spheres. "The acquisition of this knowledge," says the introduction to this dialogue in the Loeb edition, "is a great task, which no one would undertake merely for the purpose of persuading his fellows; a higher purpose, the perfection of his soul and the desire to serve the gods, must animate the spirit of the student of the real art of rhetoric."[2] In the *Apology,* too, Socrates similarly rejects participation in politics for the perfection of the soul.

On the other hand, in the *Gorgias,* the most intemperate of all Plato's dialogues, Socrates takes so low a view of rhetoric as actually practiced that no student of his would care to be caught engaging in it. He compares the art of the orator to that of the pastry-cook and equates rhetoric with flattery. Socrates says to Gorgias, one of the most famous teachers of oratory in his time, that rhetoric is "a pursuit that is not a matter of art, but showing a shrewd, gallant* spirit which has a natural bent for clever dealing with mankind." Socrates adds, "I sum up its substance in the name *flattery*. This practice, as I view it, has many branches, and one of them is cookery, which appears indeed to be an art" but is only "a habitude or knack . . . rhetoric [is] another branch of it, as also personal adornment and sophistry."[3]

This is so sweeping that one blushes for Socrates. It seems to be name-calling rather than serious analysis. Socrates here, as so often, treats his subject from an either-or rather than a more-or-less point of view. Not all the oratory in the assembly and the law courts was base flattery. The austere and aristocratic Pericles was

---

* The word used in the original is *andreias,* which means manly and would perhaps better be rendered here as bold.

no back-slapper. The so-called demagogue Cleon who succeeded him was quite capable of scolding his followers, and often did, as we know from Thucydides.

Socrates was contemptuous of the vulgar tradesmen in the assembly. He would never admit that they might sometimes act wisely and rationally as they did in their own affairs; nor that these canny traders were shrewd enough to size up mere flattery. Persuasion is not always flattery nor flattery always persuasive. The unspoken premise of the Socratic assault on oratory was disdain for the common people of Athens. This comes out in the *Gorgias* when Socrates includes the tragic poets with the orators as practitioners of flattery. This low opinion of Athenian tragedy seems to stem from Socrates' low opinion of the audience. He describes tragic poetry as "a kind of rhetoric addressed to such a public as is compounded of children and women and men, and slaves as well as free; an art that we do not quite approve of, since we call it a flattering one." So Aeschylus, Sophocles, and Euripides were flatterers of an ignorant mob audience!

The orators, Socrates concludes, "like the poets" are "set on gratifying the citizens . . . sacrificing the common weal to their own personal interests" and behaving "to these assemblies as to children."[4] Coming from any less venerable figure than Socrates, this outburst would be dismissed as antidemocratic demagogy. The best antidote to the poisonous nonsense in the *Gorgias* is Aristotle's *Rhetoric*. It reflects the dominant Greek and Athenian view with which the teachings of Socrates and Plato came into sharp conflict. Aristotle, as we have seen, began his *Politics* and his *Ethics* by affirming that the *polis* and civilized life were made possible because mankind generally possessed that modicum of "civic virtue" and the *logos* to distinguish right from wrong and the just from the unjust. So he began the *Rhetoric* with a similar affirmation that mankind generally had sufficient intelligence to be reached by reasoned argument. Such a faith lies at the very foundation of democracy; free government has no future where men can be treated as a mindless herd. Thus from the very opening lines of the *Rhetoric,* we are in a different universe from that of the Socratic and the Platonic, and breathe a different air.

Aristotle treats rhetoric, the mode of argument in the law courts and the assembly, on an equal level with dialectic, the mode cultivated in the philosophic schools. "Rhetoric," he begins his treatise, "is a counterpart* of Dialectic; for both have to do with matters that are in a manner within the cognizance of all men and not confined to any special science. Hence all men in a manner have a share of both [i.e., rhetoric and dialectic]; for all, up to a certain point, endeavor to criticize or uphold an argument."[5] Men argue, and love to argue, among themselves. So Aristotle sets out to study the modes of argument as practiced in the assembly and the law courts.

Aristotle, of course, recognizes that popular oratory is subject to abuse. As if in direct answer to Socrates, he says, "If it is argued that one who makes an unfair use of such faculty of speech may do a great deal of harm, this objection applies equally to all good things." Aristotle finds hope in the belief (1) that "rhetoric is useful, because the true and the just are naturally superior to their opposites," (2) that "generally speaking, that which is true and better is naturally always easier to prove and more likely to persuade," and (3) that "men have a sufficient natural capacity for the truth and indeed in most cases attain to it."[6] History's darker pages, some quite recent, often make all this seem optimistic but without some such faith good men must succumb to despair.

Where Socrates was constantly searching for absolute certainty in the shape of perfect definitions — and never finding them — and where Plato abandoned the real world for a celestial stratosphere of unchangeable Ideas or Forms, Aristotle approached the problem of knowledge from a point of view close to what we call common sense. In systematizing logic for the first time, and inventing the syllogism as its principal instrument, Aristotle distinguished two forms of the syllogism, the dialectical and the

---

* The reader indoctrinated by the Platonic dialogues tends to read "counterpart" as implying that rhetoric is a lower species of argument than dialectic. But the word used by Aristotle has no such demeaning or belittling connotation. It is *antistrophos* — a term borrowed from the theater when the chorus sings a "strophe" on one side of the stage and then moves to the opposite side and sings an "antistrophe" in the exact same meter.

rhetorical. Both begin with propositions believed to be true; the dialectical, with those believed to be necessarily and always true; the rhetorical, with propositions believed to be probably, though not always, true. Aristotle called the rhetorical syllogism an *enthymeme,* and the Liddell-Scott-Jones *Greek-English Lexicon* defines the term as a "syllogism drawn from probable premises."[7]

The distinction arises not from the difference between the capacities of learned dialecticians and those of ordinary men, but from the nature of the material with which the latter must deal in their assemblies and law courts. The nature of the decisions to be made in them compel the citizenry as legislators and judges to argue from probabilities rather than unattainable absolute certainties. The assembly has to make decisions of policy to deal with the future, and the future is unpredictable. The law courts have to determine what actually happened in a past event, where honest witnesses often differ remarkably. In such elusive matters even Plato's philosopher kings could no more be certain than the most ordinary Athenian citizen. Here Socrates' ideal ruler, "the one who knows," would find it impossible to live up to his billing.

Men do not have to deliberate upon what is certain but upon what is uncertain, and on which their judgments are no more than probabilities. That is the best guide they can find, Aristotle explains in discussing the *enthymeme,* because "no human action, so to speak, is inevitable."[8]

The Aristotelian view is illuminating and encouraging where the Socratic and the Platonic viewpoints are frustrating and calculated to undermine men's faith in their ability to govern themselves.

The Aristotelian respect for observation and distrust of absolutes may reflect the fact that he was a physician's son. In his philosophical work, he often thinks like a physician and reflects medical experience. Thus in the *Nichomachean Ethics,* rebutting the idealist conception of knowledge, Aristotle says that the doctor does not treat a disease, he treats a patient, a particular patient, each with his own complications. No two patients, though suffering from the same disease, are quite alike.

Of course the physician had to learn the definitions and general rules of treatment for various diseases. But this was only the beginning of the healing art. It was in combining the general theory with the particular observation that medicine became both science and art in ancient Greece — indeed, it was the first branch of Greek inquiry to become truly scientific in the full modern sense. Its greatest figure, Hippocrates, who became a legend in his lifetime, was — to borrow modern terminology — empirical and pragmatic. His extensive works, says the article on him in the *Oxford Companion to Classical Literature,* "reveal a true scientific spirit, in the insistence on the permanence of the relation of effect to cause, *and the necessity of careful observation of medical facts"* (italics added).

As with medicine, so also with law. Aristotle's wariness about absolutes comes out again in his great contribution to law. He was the first to formulate the concept of equity as a necessary component of any just legal system. This was centuries before what we now know in Anglo-American law as "equity" grew up in the Chancery courts of the English kings as a corrective of the common law.*

Legislators, Aristotle said in the *Rhetoric,* "are obliged," in framing a law, "to make a universal statement which is not applicable to all, but only to most, cases" since "it is difficult to give a definition" (i.e., an absolute definition) "owing to the infinite number of cases," each with its own peculiarity.[9] Hence equity "bends" the law to do justice in the specific case. The Greek word Aristotle used for equity is *epieikeia.* It meant fairness. Aristotle further defined it as "the spirit as opposed to the letter of the law."[10] Aristotle in the *Nichomachean Ethics* called equity "a rectification of law where law is defective because of its generality."[11] Generality was the Socratic goal, as indeed it is of all knowledge. Generality is a fundamental necessity of law, but Aristotle in the same passage goes on to observe that "there are some cases for which it is impossible to lay down a law." This was not, of course, an Aristotelian discovery. Aristotle's remark about

---

* When the Napoleonic Code came to be formulated in France, its framers went back to Aristotle for inspiration in providing it with a system of equity.

cases for which there was no law reflected more than two centuries of experience with the Athenian popular jury-courts — the *dikasteries,* as they were called — where citizens of all classes sat as both jurors and judges.

The notion of equity was implicit in the oath taken by the Athenian *dikasts,* or juror-judges. They swore "to vote according to the laws where there are laws, and where there is not, to vote as justly as in us lies."[12]

What Aristotle says about the inherent inadequacy of any general rule of law was stated earlier — as we have seen — by Plato in the *Politicus,* the one place in the Platonic canon where Plato wholly abandons absolute idealism. It is startling to hear "The Stranger" — Plato's mouthpiece in the *Politicus* — argue almost in the same words as Aristotle that law cannot determine what is "most just" because "the differences of men and of actions" make impossible "any simple rule for everything and for all time." This was for Plato a complete departure on the metaphysical side. It cut loose from the tyranny of absolute Forms and absolute definitions.

As the Stranger put it, while lawmaking belongs to "the science of kingship" (i.e., the king makes laws for the community), ideally he himself should not be bound by them. "The best thing," the Stranger asserts, "is not that the laws be in power, but that the man who is wise and of kingly nature be ruler,"[13] a new version of the Socratic doctrine that "the one who knows" should rule and the rest obey. So this anti-absolutistic view of law — unexpected in Plato — became an argument for absolutism as the ideal government! But human experience, ancient and modern, demonstrates that absolutism breeds injustice and dictators set repressive policies, as the recent careers of Stalin and Mao Tse-tung demonstrate.

In Aristotle's hands, the observation from which the idea of equity developed became a way to escape metaphysical and political blind alleys by combining elements of idealism with elements of what we have come to call empiricism or pragmatism. Aristotle's solution was not to choose "either-or" but "both" — to escape the tyranny of either extreme by combining elements of both. This was an application of what he called the Doctrine of the Mean, or the middle way.

Equity moves from the general definitions of law to the particulars of the case. Then it adapts the law to achieve "justice." In this, it turns back to the transcendental universal standard of which Socrates and Plato made us aware. "Justice," though we cannot absolutely define it, and men often differ about it, remains "the ideal" — the concept we owe to Plato.

Much like the notion of the unattainable limit in calculus, it provides an indispensable component in the fruitful analysis of social and political problems. It is Plato's great contribution and Socrates prepared the way for it. But Aristotle added a component they were unwilling to recognize because it moved in a democratic direction, and gave dignity to the common man. Aristotle recognized that the very concept of "justice," instead of being something only the rare few could achieve, sprang from deep roots in common human experience and in man's very nature as a "political animal."

So the oath taken by the Athenian jurors — to act "justly" — implied that they had an innate sense of justice. To add "as in us lies" was to recognize that while they were imperfect — were kings or philosophers perfect? — they would strive to do their best. This common stock of "civic virtue" was the basis on which Athens practiced democracy and Aristotle formulated equity.

The negative dialectic of Socrates — if the city had taken it seriously — would have made equity and democracy impossible. His identification of virtue with an unattainable knowledge stripped common men of hope and denied their capacity to govern themselves.

Chapter 8

THE GOOD LIFE
The Third Socratic Divergence

❧❀❧

ARISTOTLE SAYS that a cityless man is like "a solitary piece in checkers."[1] A solitary checker piece standing alone has no function. It has meaning only when associated with other pieces in a game. The vivid metaphor implies that men fulfill themselves only in a *polis*. The individual can find the good life only when associated with others in a community. This conception did not originate with Aristotle. It was the general Greek view. To become "cityless" — *apolis* — already denoted a tragic fate in Herodotus and Sophocles a century before Aristotle. And this brings us to a third fundamental philosophical point on which Socrates differed from his fellow Athenians.

Socrates preached and practiced withdrawal from the political life of the city. In Plato's *Apology* he defended this abstention as necessary for "the perfection" of the soul.[2] The Athenians and the Greeks generally believed that the citizen was educated and perfected by participating fully in the life and affairs of the city.

"Man," Aristotle wrote, "when perfected, is the best of animals; but if he be isolated from law and justice he is the worst of all . . . if he be without virtue, he is a most unholy and savage being."[3] The sense of justice that alone can lift him above his own savage impulses, Aristotle said, "belongs to the *polis;* for justice, which is the determination of what is just, is an ordering of the political association."

A solitary man lives in a world where the very word *justice* has no meaning. Where there are no "others," no conflicts arise that call for a "just" solution. The problem of justice appears only in a community. The *polis* was a continuous school molding its people by its laws, its festivals, its culture, its religious rites, its traditions, the example of its leading citizens, its theater and by participation in the government of the city, particularly the debates of the assembly and the jury-courts, where questions of justice were argued and decided.

The Athenians lived in a city so beautiful we are still awed by its ruins. Its tragic and comic poets still enchant us. We are still inspired by the best of its political orators. We still learn from them lessons for our time, as other men have done for centuries. If ever a city deserved the full energy and devotion of its citizens, that city was Athens. Participation in "politics" — managing the city — was a right, a duty, and an education. But all the Socratics, from Antisthenes to Plato, preached withdrawal from it.

Early in the sixth century B.C. the Athenian social reformer and lawgiver Solon, who first opened membership in the assembly and the jury-courts to the poorer classes, enacted a law that any citizen who remained neutral and took no position on either side in a time of *stasis* or severe political contention and class struggle should be punished by loss of citizenship.[4] Plutarch in his *Life of Solon* explains that the great lawgiver believed "a man should not be insensible or indifferent to the common weal, arranging his private affairs securely and glorying in the fact that he has no share in the distempers and distresses of his country."[5] The same attitude is reflected in the funeral speech of Pericles, perhaps the most eloquent exposition ever of the democratic ideal. After asserting that the councils of Athens were open to all, rich and poor alike, Pericles added that the Athenians "regard the man who takes no part in public affairs, not as one who minds his own business, but as good for nothing."[6] The city's business — as Athenians saw it — was every citizen's business.

By these standards, Socrates was not a good citizen. He did his duty as a soldier, and acquitted himself bravely. But it is extraordinary that so prominent an Athenian managed in his seventy years to take almost no part at all in civic affairs. Had Solon's law against nonparticipation in times of civil strife been in effect in the fifth century B.C., Socrates might have been disfranchised under it. The two greatest political convulsions of Socrates' lifetime —

indeed the worst in the city's history — were the overthrow of the democracy in 411 and again in 404 B.C. Socrates took no part on either occasion in the overthrow or in the restoration of democracy. He sided neither with the disaffected aristocrats who seized power, nor with the democrats they killed or expelled from the city, nor even with the moderates whom the dictators soon drove into opposition. Except for one act of courageous but silent civil disobedience during the second dictatorship — that of the Thirty — he stood aside from the conflict.

In a famous and delightful passage of Plato's *Apology*, Socrates tells his judges, "If you put me to death, you will not easily find another, who, to use a rather absurd expression, attaches himself to the city as a gadfly to a horse" — a "sluggish" horse, he added, which needs a bit of "stinging" for its own good.[7] This is the origin of the cliché somewhat disparagingly attached to critical and radical journalists in our own time. But the Socratic gadfly never seemed to be around when its sting was most needed. Socrates never raised his voice in the assembly when the fateful decisions of his lifetime were made. He must have looked to most of his fellow citizens less like a gadfly than as what Pericles in his funeral speech called an *idiotes* — a disparaging term for a citizen who took no part in public affairs. That is why *idiotes* was translated as "good for nothing" in the quotation we just cited from the funeral speech. (The word is the ultimate etymological ancestor of our word *idiot,* but it did not then connote mental incapacity.)

A similar contrast is drawn in Plato's *Apology* between the verb *idioteuo* and the verb *demosieuo*.[8] The latter means to take part in public business, the affairs of the *demos*. Socrates was aware of the criticism he had provoked by abstention from politics. These verbs are used by Socrates in the second of the several excuses he gives for not taking part in the affairs of the city. "Perhaps it may seem strange," he tells his judges, "that I go about and interfere in other people's affairs* to give this advice in private, but do not venture to come before your assembly and advise the state." The

* The Greek word thus translated is *polypragmono,* which also means to be a busy-body.

use of the adjective "your" rather than "our" is indicative. In his very language, as in his life, he stood apart.

His first excuse in the *Apology* is that his famous *daimonion* — the private warning inner voice, or guiding spirit he claimed to possess — had warned him against engaging in politics. The *daimonion* never explained its premonitions. But Socrates does. "Do not be angry with me for speaking the truth," Socrates tells the court; "the fact is that no man will save his life who nobly opposes you or any other populace [the Greek word he uses is *plethos* — the multitude] and prevents many unjust and illegal things from happening in the state."

This excuse was insulting to the city and a confession of cowardice, as Socrates makes clearer in what he says next. "A man who really fights for the right, if he is to preserve his life for even a little while, must be a private citizen, not a public man."⁹ The Loeb translation here fuzzes the real force of the Greek original. What Socrates says is *idioteuein alla me demosieuein* — one had to be an *idiotes* and abstain from the affairs of the *demos,* if one wanted to be safe.

But only a few minutes earlier Socrates had called himself a gadfly and boasted that he stung the sluggish horse of Athens for its own good! How could a man really fight for the right, as Socrates has just phrased it, without taking the risks of the battle? And how prevent "unjust and illegal" things from happening without speaking and voting against them in the assembly? The city allowed free speech and the right to vote in the assembly as a means of preventing unjust policies. How could these safeguards be effective if citizens lacked the courage to exercise those rights? Socrates was providing a lesson in expediency, not in virtue.

No one asked Socrates to give up philosophy for public office. But there were moments in the life of the city when it confronted urgent issues of a profoundly moral character. On such occasions, the voice of a philosopher in the assembly could make a difference. And, for a philosopher, what better forum than the assembly to dramatize the struggle for virtue? There were two memorable and contrasting debates of this kind in the lifetime of Socrates during the Peloponnesian war. Both involved the fate of a rebellious Athenian ally. One debate was over Melos, the other over Mytilene. The outcome of the former left a dark stain forever on the name of Athens. The latter, on the other hand, did the city honor. Each was a test of the city's virtue. Both were worthy of a philosopher's participation.

How one wishes — for the sake of the city's reputation and his own — that Socrates had put in an appearance. Though Socrates denied that he was a teacher, he could hardly deny that he was a preacher. He was constantly exhorting his fellow citizens to be virtuous. These were occasions when virtue was at stake. To understand the debates over Melos and Mytilene, one must recall what happened to the Greek city-states in the wake of their victory over the Persians in the first half of the fifth century B.C. That victory was won under the leadership of Athens in unity with Sparta. But after the war, what had been a protective alliance of equal states soon became a kind of Athenian empire.

Empire is perhaps too strong a word if it conjures up images of the Persian empire or the Roman. But more and more the decisions of a protective alliance not only on defense but on other matters fell into the hands of its most powerful member, Athens. So did what was supposed to be a common treasury. Contributions for the maintenance of the Athenian navy in mutual defense soon became tribute money. With it Athens enriched and beautified itself. It financed the building of the Parthenon, a majestic symbol of that shift from protectorate to empire.

This bred rebellion. Athens and Sparta split from each other. Each organized a rival bloc. Smaller states turned to Sparta for protection against Athens, and to Athens for protection against Sparta. The Hellenic world was split into two, and the next great armed struggle in the fifth century was between these two rival combinations. This culminated in the long and ruinous Peloponnesian war. This internecine, fraternal, and mutually destructive struggle among kindred peoples sharing a common civilization was a miniature of the two World Wars of our own time, and of the third and final planetary conflagration that may now be shaping up.

In that "World War" of the Hellenic people, there was war

within war. Within each alliance there were constant revolts by the smaller members against protectors who became increasingly unpopular with those they were supposed to protect, like NATO and the Warsaw Pact in our time. Class war was enlisted in the struggle for empire. Within each city-state there was recurrent strife between rich and poor. Long before the Spanish Civil War invented the term, Athens and Sparta both had their "Fifth Columns" within the other's domain. Democratic Athens connived with disaffected democrats in the cities under the Spartan yoke. Oligarchic Sparta conspired with disaffected aristocrats in the cities Athens dominated, and Sparta had its Fifth Column of wealthy antidemocrats within Athens itself. Cities changed — or tried to change — sides as one faction or other seized power. And inhumanity gained the upper hand everywhere.

Melos has gone down in history as a classic example of the brute injustice bred by war and power politics — what the Germans called *Realpolitik,* and all the world's powers, whatever their ideology, still practice. Melos illustrated the cruel logic imposed on the strong as well as the weak by the relations between supposedly sovereign states in a world without law between them. That logic is still at work today. Each Greek superpower, to forestall or stifle rebellion among its satellites, often acted brutally, in fear of appearing weak — like a bully in a schoolyard, afraid of looking "chicken." Injustice to smaller allies looked to the big powers like a necessity of self-preservation. This is the story as spelled out in the incomparable pages of Thucydides, a political parable for all time.

Melos was an island city-state, a Spartan colony that had long been an exasperating holdout in the Aegean waters Athens otherwise dominated. Though Spartan in sympathy and governed by an oligarchy, Melos did not dare to take the Spartan side in the Peloponnesian war. It stayed neutral, and that was its offense in Athenian eyes. During the Persian war, ships from Melos took part in the decisive Greek naval victory at Salamis. The Melian fleet and Melian resources would have been a help to Athens in the struggle with Sparta. And there was the danger that Melos might open its harbors to the Spartan fleet and give it a base in the Aegean.

In 426 B.C. Athens made an unsuccessful attack on Melos, and a decade later threatened another, demanding that Melos join forces with Athens. When the Melians resisted an alliance with Athens, offering only to remain neutral, the Athenians besieged the city. After a winter of starvation, Melos surrendered, throwing herself on Athens' mercy. Athens responded by killing all the men, enslaving the women and children, and handing over the island to Athenian settlers. It was the cruelest episode of a cruel war.

That was in 416 B.C. Socrates was then about fifty-three, a leading character of the city, surrounded by admiring disciples from all over Greece. Did Socrates think this was justice? Did he think it virtuous to destroy a city that had already surrendered? Did he think it wise policy? Surely on so traumatic an occasion the city had a right to ask Socrates to join in the debate. Where was the self-appointed gadfly? There is no mention of the Melian massacre either in Xenophon or in Plato. The silence is all the stranger because it was so obviously a black mark against the democracy the Socratics despised. Or perhaps they, too, thought the massacre justified for reasons of *Realpolitik.* Philosophers have often been no more immune than the common man to the nationalistic passions aroused by war.

It may be that the silence of Socrates about Melos in the pages of Xenophon and Plato is linked to his painful knowledge of the discreditable role played in the Melian massacre by his beloved Alcibiades. We know from Plutarch and from an Athenian orator that Alcibiades was a prime mover in the assembly's decision to show no mercy to the Melians.[10] We also know from the same sources that Alcibiades created a scandal in Athens itself by fathering a son on one of the newly widowed women taken captive at Melos.

Socrates' voice at that time in the assembly might have saved the Melians from a massacre. A decade earlier, in a similar debate over Mytilene, one voice did make a difference, turning the assembly from massacre to mercy. Mytilene was the most important city on the rich and populous island of Lesbos, a city famous for the lyric poets Sappho and Alcaeus. It led an uprising of all but one of the island's cities against Athens in 428 B.C. The moment Mytilene chose for abandoning the Athenians in the Peloponnesian war was a dark one for Athens. All the lands of Attica outside the city walls had been laid waste by the Spartan invaders. Their siege of Athens itself had brought on a plague in a city overcrowded with refugees from the surrounding countryside. Under primitive sanitary conditions, these were days of horror. The worst blow was the death of Pericles in that plague.

Athens had barely begun its recovery from these terrible misfortunes when the news came of the revolt on Lesbos. The Spartans, who had encouraged it, thereupon began their fourth invasion of Attica. Athens feared, and Sparta hoped, that the example of Mytilene and the distress of Athens would spread the infection of rebellion. By the following year, when Mytilene finally capitulated to the hunger and class conflict brought on by the Athenian siege, Athens was in an ugly mood.

On the first day of the debate in the assembly on the fate of Mytilene, the hard-liners won an easy victory. Mytilene was to be crushed to strike terror in the hearts of other cities where rebellion was smoldering. The assembly, on the motion of Cleon, who had succeeded Pericles in the leadership of the city, voted to destroy Mytilene, to kill its entire male population, and to sell the women and children into slavery. This was the logic of terror as a deterrent.

A trireme was at once dispatched to impose these orders on the prostrate city. But a reaction set in overnight. It was strong enough to force the assembly to be reconvened the very next day to reconsider its cruel and hasty action. Cleon was furious. He denounced any wavering as a sign of weakness and a lack of resolve, threatening the solidity of the alliance and Athenian security. The argument is not unfamiliar to modern experience, nor indeed lacking in weight. Cleon was exasperated. The "demagogue" scolded the *demos*. He upbraided the assembly, saying he had often recognized, but never more than in the case of Mytilene, that a democracy was incapable of governing other peoples.[11] He warned against pity. He urged the Athenians to remember that their alliance was really a despotism. Humanity was a luxury an empire could not afford.

His speech provided a vivid, if hostile, picture of the Athenians. "You are adepts," Cleon complained, "not only at being deceived by novel proposals but also at refusing to follow approved advice." Cleon called the Athenians "slaves . . . of each new paradox and scorners of what is familiar," ready "to applaud a smart saying before it is out of the speaker's mouth."[12] This is not the portrait of an assembly unwilling to listen to contrary opinion. The leader of the unexpected opposition was a man named Diodotus, otherwise unknown to history. He had argued in vain for clemency the first day of the debate, and took advantage of the changing mood to challenge Cleon's leadership. Remorse had set in and compassion had made itself felt. Diodotus now sought by a cool and objective logic to win over those still wavering. He argued that even from an imperial point of view clemency was wiser policy than ruthless terror. Diodotus made three main points. The first was the unwisdom of destroying a city ready to surrender. It was not easy to take a walled city intent on resisting. The walls of Mytilene had not been breached. It was hunger that brought the city to its knees. It had not yet fallen when its leaders decided to surrender. It could have fought on, and waited for the help Sparta had promised. The destruction of the city now would teach other rebellious allies they could expect no mercy from Athens, and could find no safety in surrender. This would make it harder to suppress future rebellions.

The second argument was based on the logic of class struggle. The strategy of Athens was to appeal to the democrats against the ruling oligarchs in the cities friendly to Sparta. If Athens now subjected Mytilene to indiscriminate massacre and enslavement, it would be treating oligarchs and democrats, rich and poor, alike.

The internal situation in Mytilene was complex. It had been firmly ruled by a pro-Spartan oligarchy. The turn toward peace came after its rulers in desperation had armed the masses. They were starving, sick of the war, and ready to shift the city's allegiance to Athens. Once they had arms, they defied the oligarchs and tried to sue for peace. The oligarchs thereupon surrendered to circumvent them, fearing the result would be their own loss of power to a democratic government in Mytilene. Why,

Diodotus argued to the Athenian assembly, kill potential allies as well as natural enemies?

The third reason given by Diodotus for clemency was equally dispassionate and practical. Why destroy a city whose fleet, manpower, and financial resources could contribute so much to Athens' own survival and victory? The quarrel between Athens and Mytilene had arisen when the latter tried to leave the alliance. Why destroy her now when her surrender signaled a readiness to join forces with Athens? "He who is wise in counsel," Diodotus concluded, "is stronger against the foe than he who recklessly rushes on with brute force."[13]

Like so many crucial decisions of real politics, the choice was not an easy one. Either course — reprisal or clemency, toughness or conciliation — had its risks. Neither guaranteed success. Conciliation might make revolt seem less hazardous to other discontented allies. But a massacre would sow more hatred of Athens and fiercer rebellion. The arguments of Diodotus prevailed. The assembly reversed itself, though by a narrow margin, and this time voted for clemency.

Unfortunately the trireme with the earlier decision had already set out for Mytilene. By the time the assembly voted the next day, the trireme with the order for a general massacre had a head start, Thucydides tells us, of "about a day and a night." In one of the most dramatic episodes in his history, the second trireme with the reprieve set out in haste hoping it would not find Mytilene already destroyed. The rowers ate as they rowed, "and took turns sleeping and rowing." Nevertheless the first trireme had already arrived. The decree of death had been read aloud. The first Athenian emissaries were about to execute the orders when the second ship landed. "By just so much," Thucydides tells us, "did Mytilene escape its peril," and Athens save its honor.[14] The decision proved wise: Mytilene became a faithful ally of Athens. Was this not virtue put into action, albeit by men who could not define it to the satisfaction of Socrates?

In Plato's *Apology*, Socrates offered an unworthy excuse for never participating in the affairs of the city. "Do you believe," he asked his judges, "that I could have lived so many years if I had been in public life and had acted as a good man should act, lending my aid to what is just and considering that of the highest importance?"[15] The debate over Mytilene showed that Socrates was wrong. The *demos* he despised had a conscience that could be appealed to. An obscure citizen who did indeed "act as a good man should" turned the tide for mercy, despite the furious opposition of the city's foremost democratic leader, Cleon. The example set by Diodotus makes one blush for Socrates.

In later antiquity, when Plato's writings had made Socrates a cult hero and a secular saint, some writers must have wondered why — at least at critical moments — Socrates did not place his gifts at the service of his city. Fact and fiction were often mingled in ancient history and biography. Writers were notorious for inventing engaging incidents to enliven the accounts of their heroes. Perhaps they felt that these stories had an apocryphal truth, that they *should* have happened if these heroes had lived up to their reputations.

There are two such dramatic but imaginary incidents of Socratic good citizenship, one in the biographer Plutarch and the other in the historian Diodorus Siculus. Both stories were written half a millennium after the trial of Socrates. Both writers were moralizers, fond of tales that inculcate virtue. The story in Plutarch concerns the great naval disaster at Syracuse, one of Athens' worst setbacks in the Peloponnesian war. Plutarch seems to have wondered whether Socrates' *daimonion,* his private inner voice or familiar guardian spirit, did not warn him about this coming disaster, and why Socrates did not pass that warning on to his fellow citizens. That kind of speculation seems to be reflected in Plutarch's biography of Nicias, one of the Athenian generals in charge of the expedition against Syracuse. Plutarch, who was superstitious, says there were many omens of the coming disaster. "To Socrates, the wise man, also," Plutarch wrote, "his divine guide [*daimonion*], making use of the customary tokens for his enlightenment, indicated plainly that the expedition would make for the ruin of the city." Socrates "let this be known to his intimate friends," Plutarch continued, "and the story had a wide circulation."[16]

No such warning by Socrates is mentioned in Thucydides or any other ancient writer before Plutarch. Bernadotte Perrin, in his commentary on the *Nicias*, says the story "bears all the marks of inferential invention."[17] Had there been such a warning, we would have heard about it from Xenophon or Plato. Actually Socrates did not need a warning from his *daimonion* to worry him about the Sicilian expedition. One of its principal movers was his favorite, Alcibiades, and the project had that strategic brilliance but dangerous *hybris* characteristic of Alcibiades; he totally lacked that virtue of *sophrosyne,* or moderation, which Socrates emphasizes in Plato's *Republic.* But there is no evidence that Socrates ever turned up in the assembly to warn that the expedition was more grandiose than prudent.

This reference to moderation recalls the second imaginary incident in the literature about Socrates. It concerns his relations with an ill-fated Athenian political leader named Theramenes. He was the leader of the moderate faction in two oligarchic conspiracies that overthrew the democracy, first in 411 B.C. and then again in 404 B.C. in the wake of the Athenian defeat in the Peloponnesian war about five years before the trial of Socrates.

On both occasions Theramenes was a leader of those who wanted to replace the democracy with a moderate oligarchy and on both occasions he broke with the aristocrats when they drove their middle-class allies into opposition by establishing a tight little oligarchy instead — the so-called Four Hundred in 411, the Thirty in 404 B.C. Critias, the leader of the Thirty and Theramenes' rival, had him executed when he dared to oppose their dictatorship.

Some might have thought that Theramenes, who certainly tried to practice *sophrosyne,* would be a hero to Socrates and Plato. But in the pages of Plato, where Critias often appears as a glamorous figure, there is no mention of Theramenes. Nor does he appear in Xenophon's account of Socrates and the Thirty in the *Memorabilia.* The oligarchic aristocrats regarded Theramenes as a turncoat. But he is treated with approval by Aristotle in his *Constitution of Athens,* where he seems to figure as the embodiment in action of the Aristotelian Doctrine of the Mean, a statesman who sought a middle course between too narrow an oligarchy and too complete a democracy.

Diodorus Siculus, writing of the period in his history, apparently felt that Socrates must have sympathized with Theramenes, the moderate. Diodorus provides a fictitious account of what he *thought* should have happened when Theramenes — as attested by Xenophon's contemporary account in the *Hellenica* — was dragged out of an angry confrontation with Critias to be excecuted. Diodorus says that when Critias' bully-boys seized Theramenes, "he took the disaster courageously" because "he had gone a long way in exploring philosophy with Socrates." No other writer except Diodorus identified him as a pupil of Socrates. Diodorus embellished his story with a dramatic scene. He says that of those who saw Theramenes being dragged away, "In general, the crowd were distressed at Theramenes' fall, but did not venture to intervene in view of the force of armed attendants" mustered by Critias but "Socrates the philosopher and two of his circle, ran up to try to impede the officers" of the dictator.

Theramenes thereupon begged them not to resist. "He applauded their loyalty and courage" but said "it would cause him great grief" if their attempt to save him would make him responsible "for the death of men who felt like that towards him." So "Socrates and his associates," Diodorus concludes his rather wooden account, "in view of the lack of support from any of the others and the growing intransigence of the authorities, retired."[18]

No such incident is reported by Xenophon in his account of Theramenes' death in the *Hellenica*. Nor is it to be found in the speeches of Socrates' friend, the orator Lysias, our fullest contemporary source for what happened during the dictatorship of the Thirty. Nor is it in the account of Aristotle, a generation later.

Socrates' nonparticipation was extraordinary. Except for one quiet act of civil disobedience under the Thirty, which we will discuss later, it is as though he wasn't there in the city's hours of greatest need. Some public expression of protest would have gone far to dispel the suspicion that began to envelop Socrates after these terrible events within little more than a decade before his trial. There was a great need to make his position clear. For the overthrow of the democracy in 411 B.C. was initiated by his favorite, Alcibiades, and the overthrow in 404 B.C. was led by Critias and Charmides, who appear as associates of Socrates in the dialogues of Plato, a cousin of Critias and a nephew of Charmides. Critias and Charmides drew their supporters — their bully-boys and storm troopers — from the same circle of aristocratic pro-Spartan youth Aristophanes had described in 414 B.C. in his *Birds* as "Socratified."[19]

There is a link — too often overlooked — between the tragic end of Theramenes and that of Socrates himself. The most influential of the three accusers of Socrates at his trial — a man named Anytus — was a lieutenant of Theramenes. Anytus was one of the middle-class moderates who fled Athens after the execution of Theramenes, joined the democrats in the exiled opposition, and became one of the generals who led the coalition of moderates and democrats which overthrew the Thirty and restored the democracy. Anytus must have held it against Socrates that he had joined neither the moderates nor the democrats in opposition to the Thirty.

Socrates was sensitive to the charge that he had always stood apart from the political life of the city. At his trial — according to Plato's *Apology* — he cited two instances of participation in politics, once against the democracy, once against the dictatorship of the Thirty. These were, by his own account, the only occasions on which he took an active part in the affairs of his city. In both cases participation was forced upon him under circumstances not of his own free choice. But when confronted by duty, he acted justly and with courage.

The first occasion, in 406 B.C., came during the trial of the generals who had commanded the Athenian fleet at the battle of Arginusae. They were accused of failing to pick up survivors and the bodies of the dead after the battle. The generals claimed that rescue was made impossible by stormy seas. Socrates was a member of the *prytaneis,* the board of fifty that presided at the trial. These were chosen by lot. The issue which put Socrates' mettle to the test was whether the generals had a right to be tried separately.

To try them together was manifestly unfair. Each individual commander had a right to be judged on the basis of what he himself actually had done under the specific circumstances in the area of his own responsibility. The Athenian *boule,* or council, in preparing the case for trial by the assembly, had given in to public indignation against the generals and decided that they were to be tried together. But when the trial opened before the assembly, a resolute dissenter challenged the mass trial as invalid under established Athenian law and procedure.[20]

Such challenges were brought by a motion called a *graphe paranomon,* which was equivalent to what we would call a motion charging unconstitutionality. Normally — so far as can be determined in the rather scanty legal records of the fifth century B.C. (as distinguished from the many reported cases of the fourth) — the trial of the generals would have been delayed until this motion was debated and voted upon. But the populace was so angered by the thought of postponing the trial that it forced the presiding committee to brush aside the motion of "unconstitutionality" and instead allow an immediate vote on a resolution to try all the generals together. While the other members of the presidium were intimidated by threats from the floor, Socrates alone held out to the last against this illegal and unjust procedure. But unanimity was not required for a ruling of the presidency, and the majority prevailed. The way was cleared for a mass trial.

In relating his role at the trial of the generals, Socrates admits in the *Apology* that this was the one and only occasion on which he had held any public office in the city. "I, men of Athens," Socrates says, "never held any other office in the state but . . . it happened that my tribe held the presidency when you wished to judge collectively, not severally, the ten generals who had failed to gather up the slain after the naval battle; this was illegal, as you all agreed afterwards. At that time," Socrates continues, "I was the only one of the [presiding officers] who opposed doing anything contrary to the laws, and although the orators were ready to impeach and arrest me, and though you urged them with shouts to do so, I thought I must run the risk to the end with law and justice on my side, rather than join with you when your wishes were unjust, through fear of imprisonment or death."[21]

But Socrates, despite the fears he confessed, was not punished for resisting the majority. Indeed, when the moment of repentance came, they "all agreed afterward," as Socrates said, that what they had done was illegal. So he must have received credit for bravely doing what was right.

The second occasion on which Socrates was compelled to confront his duty as a citizen involved a wealthy *metic,* or resident alien, Leon of Salamis, under the rule of the Thirty. So narrow was the public support for the dictatorship that it could hope to survive only through the intimidating presence in Athens of a Spartan garrison. To pay the expenses of the garrison, it proceeded to "liquidate" rich resident noncitizen traders, and then expropriate their estates to pay the Spartan occupiers.

"After the oligarchy was established," Socrates tells his judges in Plato's *Apology,* "the Thirty sent for me with four others to come to the rotunda and ordered us to bring Leon the Salaminian . . . to be put to death." The Thirty did not need a citizens' posse for the arrest. The Thirty had bully-boy squads with whips and daggers to terrorize the citizenry. These could easily have seized Leon. Why did they want Socrates to take part? "They gave many such orders to others also," Socrates explains, "because they wished to implicate as many in their crimes as they could." Socrates, as we recall, knew the leaders of the Thirty well. Critias and Charmides, who led the dominant aristocratic faction, were part of the Socratic circle.

What did Socrates do? Socrates resisted, but minimally, not so much as a political but as a private act. Instead of protesting the order, he simply left the rotunda and quietly went home, and took no part in the arrest. This, when stripped of his boastfulness, was the substance of his own account. "Then I, however, showed again, by action," Socrates says, "not in word only, that I do not care a whit for death if that be not too rude an expression, but that I did care with all my might not to do anything unjust or unholy. For that government, with all its power, did not frighten me into doing anything unjust, but when we came out of the rotunda, the other four went . . . and arrested Leon, but I simply went home."[22]

Socrates did not — like his accuser, Anytus — leave the city and join the exiles who were already planning the overthrow of the dictators. He would have been a welcome and inspiring recruit. He "simply went home." Was that fulfilling his civic duty against injustice? Or was he merely avoiding personal complicity and, as he expressed it, saving his soul?

This was one of several reasons Socrates gave for his lifelong abstention from politics. Socrates says in Plato's *Apology* that he abstained from politics in order to take care of his soul, to keep it from stain. The implication was that civic affairs were somehow dirty and, as Christians were later to say, "sinful." In fact this is exactly how the later desert monks felt when they withdrew from the world to a collective or solitary life of their own. Had there been monasteries in classical Greece, Socrates and his followers would have been drawn to them. The Socratic teaching on the subject of the soul strikes a note that became characteristic of medieval Christianity, but was alien to the bright sunlight and joy — earthly and bodily as well as spiritual — of classical Greece.

Body and soul were united in the classical view. The Socratics and the Platonists divided them, demeaning the body and elevating the soul. A healthy mind in a healthy body — *mens sana in corpore sano* as the Roman poet Juvenal later phrased it in his famous Tenth Satire[23] — was the classical ideal.

A new strain appears with Socrates, and perhaps earlier with the Pythagoreans, who were among his admirers and devotees, as we can see from the discussions with them in his prison cell on the last day of his life in the lovely pages of Plato's *Phaedo*. The Pythagoreans or the related movement of the Orphics are supposed to have originated the saying — a pun on the words *soma* (body) and *sema* (tomb) — that the body was the tomb of the soul. Abstention from the life of the city soon shaded off into abstention from life itself. We can see this tendency most strongly in Antisthenes and the Cynical philosophy he derived — and exaggerated — from one aspect of Socratic teaching. Socrates not only practiced abstention from the affairs of the city but preached it. This was, he tells his judges in the *Apology,* his mission. "I go about doing nothing else," Socrates says, "than urging you, young and old, not to care for your bodies but for the protection of your souls."[24] Burnet's commentary on this passage in the *Apology* says, "Socrates appears to have been the first Greek to speak of the *psyche* (soul) as the seat of knowledge and ignorance, goodness and badness. It followed that the chief duty of man was to 'care for his soul' and this was fundamental to the teaching of Socrates."[25]

This, in the Greek and the modern view, begs the question. How does a man perfect his soul? By withdrawing from life, or plunging into it and fulfilling himself as part of the community? The classic ideal was to perfect oneself in perfecting the city.

Aristotle was closer to the classic ideal. He developed his politics and his ethics, as we have seen, from the premise that virtue was not "solitary" but political or civic. He saw the soul as the animating principle of all living things, plants and animals alike. "The soul and the body," Aristotle says, "make a living creature."[26] The individual soul, in Aristotle, disappears with the body. Aristotle brings back the question of "soul" from theology to physiology, from mysticism to science.

In the Athenian view, acting justly in the case of Leon of Salamis had two aspects. The one Socrates stressed was acting justly as an individual. This was essential and admirable, but only one half of a man's duty. The other half was to do his best to make the law and conduct of the city measure up to the standards of justice. He could not simply "go home" and wash his hands of responsibility. He was responsible as a citizen for what the city did. If it did wrong, he shared the blame unless he did his best to prevent it.

Injustice was rife under the dictatorship of the Thirty. They began by expelling the poor, the democrats, from the city. Socrates could have left with them, to show his concern for justice. Or he could have joined the second wave of the emigration when middle-class moderates like Anytus also left and allied themselves with the democrats to overthrow the dictatorship. Socrates would have won a place of honor in the restored democracy. His past associations with Critias would have been forgiven. Anytus would never have brought his charges. There would have been no trial.

Nor did his experience under the Thirty, when it was dangerous to speak out, give him a new appreciation for the free institutions of Athens. There was no sign of any change in his disdain for democracy. Instead, as we shall see, there was some ground to fear that his teachings might inspire a new generation of willful and violent youth in another attempt to overthrow it.

Chapter 9

THE PREJUDICES OF SOCRATES

୰ଽଵଌ୰ଽ

O NCE, BUT ONLY ONCE, does Socrates advise a disciple to enter politics. The unusual advice was given, oddly enough, to Charmides, Plato's uncle, who became the chief lieutenant of Critias in the regime of the Thirty. In Xenophon's *Memorabilia* Charmides, then a promising young man, is urged by Socrates to enter public life by joining in the debates of the assembly.

Charmides is reluctant to do so. Socrates then puts to Charmides the same question that might well have been addressed to Socrates. "If a man were to shrink from state business, though capable of discharging it with advantage to the state and honor to himself," Socrates argues, "wouldn't it be reasonable to think him a coward?"

Charmides confesses that he is shy about appearing in public. Socrates says he has often heard Charmides give excellent advice to public leaders in private conversation. Charmides replies that "a private conversation is a very different thing from a crowded debate."

Socrates, chiding him, then discloses the depth of his own contempt for the Athenian assembly. "The wisest do not make you bashful," he says to Charmides, "yet you are ashamed to address an audience of mere dunces and weaklings."

An unmistakable social snobbery lurked behind Socrates' scornful dismissal of Athenian democracy. Who are these people, he asks Charmides, who make you feel too bashful to address them? Then he calls the roll of the common and — in his view — vulgar occupations represented in the assembly.

"The fullers or the cobblers or the builders or the smiths or the farmers or the merchants," Socrates ticks them off disdainfully, "or the traffickers in the market-place who think of nothing but buying cheap and selling dear? . . . You are shy of addressing men who never gave a thought to public affairs."[1] Why then did they take time off from their occupations to show up in the assembly at all? This is the kind of social prejudice — and of mere ranting — one would not expect from a philosopher. It is made all the stranger by his own class background.[2]

Socrates was not a wealthy aristocrat. He was of the middle class. His mother was a midwife. His father was a stone-cutter, perhaps also a sculptor — the distinction between craftsman and artist was blurred in antiquity. Even the most distinguished artist was still a man who worked with his hands and depended on his earnings.

How did Socrates earn his bread? He had a wife and three sons to support. He lived to the age of seventy. But he never seems to have had a job or practiced a trade. His days were spent in leisure, talking. Socrates derided the Sophists for taking payment from their pupils. He prided himself on never asking a fee from his own disciples. How did he support his family? This natural question is never answered in the Platonic dialogues. In the *Apology,* Socrates describes himself as a poor man, and he was certainly poor by comparison with wealthy aristocrats like Plato so prominent in his adoring entourage. But he was never so poor that he had to take a job or practice a trade.

The answer seems to be that he lived on a small inheritance left him by his father, who did well at his trade of stone-cutter. The income seems to have been meager. His poor wife, Xanthippe, the unsung heroine of the Socratic saga, is pictured as a scold and a shrew, perhaps because she had a hard time raising the children on the money available. But it was enough to allow him leisure.

His income may have been less than that of the craftsmen he regarded with condescension. There are varying accounts of how much Socrates inherited. Our earliest estimate is in Xenophon's dialogue the *Oeconomicus,* or *How to Manage an Estate.* There in a conversation with his wealthy friend Critobolus, Socrates jokingly calls himself the richer man of the two, because Socrates' wants are so few. It is too bad that the harassed Xanthippe was not allowed in on that dialogue.

Socrates, challenged to give an estimate of his own estate, replies, "Well, if I found a good buyer, I think the whole of my goods and chattels, including the house, might readily sell for five minae. Yours, I feel sure," Socrates says to Critobolus, "would fetch more than a hundred times that sum."[3] Two later sources provide a larger estimate of Socrates' estate. Plutarch tells us that "Socrates owned not only his house, but also seventy minae,"[4] which he lent "out at interest to Crito," the close friend in the Platonic dialogue of that name. A similar estimate of the Socratic estate is given by the fourth-century-A.D. orator Libanius; in his *Apology,* Socrates says that he inherited eighty minae from his father but lost it through bad investments.[5]

The clearest indication of his own social status is given by his military service. He did not fight in the cavalry with aristocrats like Alcibiades. Nor was he enlisted with the poor in the light-armed infantry or at the oars of the navy. Socrates fought as a *hoplite,* a heavy-armed foot soldier. An Athenian had to provide his own military equipment. Only the middle class of craftsmen and merchants could afford the heavy armor of the *hoplite.* In describing the assembly, Socrates was sneering at his own social peers. The various trades and businesses he names were those of the middle class.

With the achievement of democracy, the Athenian middle class had won political, though not social, equality with the landowning gentry from which aristocrats like Plato and Xenophon came.

But as we know, sometimes the worst snobs are in the middle class. The snobbery of Socrates must have endeared him to the leisurely rich young aristocrats he himself describes in Plato's *Apology* as his followers. In talking to Charmides, Socrates was expressing the kind of disdain that an aristocrat felt for the "vulgar tradesmen" who had begun to make their appearance in politics, of "low birth" but sometimes of larger fortune than the aristocrats.

A private case pleaded by Demosthenes about half a century after the death of Socrates reveals that snobbish remarks about a person's humble origins or trade were then punishable in Athens under the law against *kakegoria* ("bad-mouthing"), which covered various forms of slander. In the private suit argued by Demosthenes, one of the complaints made against Eubulides, a minor official, was that he had sneered at the plaintiff's mother because she earned her living as a seller of ribbons and a wet-nurse; that was not much humbler than Socrates' own mother, who was a midwife. The plaintiff claims the right to sue "anyone who makes business in the market a reproach against any male or female citizen."[6]

Socrates' own attitude toward "traffickers in the market-place" may have played its part in provoking his chief accuser. Anytus was a master tanner. It seems from Xenophon's *Apology* that Socrates had insulted him by speaking disdainfully of Anytus' trade and criticizing him for bringing up his own son in the same vulgar occupation. Xenophon says Socrates, seeing Anytus pass by after his conviction, said, "There goes a man who is filled with pride at the thought that he has accomplished some great and noble end in putting me to death, because, seeing him honoured by the city with the highest offices, I said that he ought not confine his son's education to hides."[7]

Plato pictures a related encounter between Anytus and Socrates in the *Meno*. There Anytus warns Socrates that he may get into trouble for "speaking ill" (*kakegorein*) of Athenian statesmen. As Anytus stalks off angrily, Socrates comments unkindly that Anytus was offended because "he considers that he is one of them himself."[8] The Greek word *kakagorein* — to slander — used in the *Meno* is a verbal form of the same legal term applied to the snobbish remarks in Demosthenes.

In Plato's *Theaetetus* we see the Socratic snobbery pass over from the social to the philosophic plane. Plato has Socrates divide philosophers into two classes and explain how the superior type feels about the political institutions of Athens. Socrates says that he is speaking only of the "leading" philosophers, "for why," he asks, "should anyone talk about the inferior?" He says the superior philosophers, "from their youth up, remain ignorant of the way to the *agora* [the assembly]." They are oblivious of its very existence. They "do not even know," Socrates continues, "where the

court-room is, or the senate-house [the council chamber], or any
other public place of assembly. . . . As for laws and decrees,"
Socrates goes on, "they neither hear the debates upon them nor see
them when they are published."

Plato has Socrates reduce civic affairs to vulgar frivolity. "And
the strivings of political clubs for public offices," Socrates concludes, "and meetings, . . . and revellings with chorus-girls — it
never occurs to them [the philosophers of the better sort] even in
their dreams to indulge in such things." Politics are equated with
erotic dreams. Priggishness preserves the philosopher from them.
We are hardly surprised when he says of the true philosopher:
"Really it is only his body that has its place and home in the city;
his mind, considering all these things petty and of no account,
disdains them."[9] Here the Platonic Socrates, like the Aristophanic,
indeed has his head in the clouds.

Socrates is revered as a nonconformist but few realize that he
was a rebel against an open society and the admirer of a closed.
Socrates was one of those Athenians who despised democracy and
idealized Sparta.[10] The earliest reference to this is in Aristophanes,
in his joyous comedy, the *Birds,* produced in 414 B.C., when
Socrates was about fifty-five years old. Aristophanes portrays him
as the idol of the pro-Spartan malcontents in Athens. In his
exuberant inventiveness, the comic poet even coined two Greek
words to describe them.

In line 1281 of the *Birds* he describes them as *elakonomanoun* —
"Sparta-mad," as if from a verb *Lakono-maneo,* meaning to be
mad about Laconian or Spartan ways. In line 1282, Aristophanes
coins another word — *esokrotoun,* as if from a verb *Sokrateo,* to
imitate Socrates. These young men are described, in B. B. Rogers's
rollicking, somewhat Gilbert and Sullivanish translation, as:

> . . . *Laconian-mad; they went*
> *Long-haired, half-starved, unwashed, Socratified*
> *With scytales in their hands. . . .*[11]

The Spartans were legendary for their meager fare — we still
speak of a "Spartan diet" — and notorious for their avoidance of

refinement in dress, manners, and appearance. They wore their hair long and ill-kempt and didn't approve of bathing too often. The scytales in the last line of the passage just quoted is the word for the short clubs or cudgels that Spartans carried. So — according to Aristophanes — did their Athenian admirers.

That this was not too unfair a comic caricature may be seen from a passage in Plutarch's *Life of Alcibiades*. The latter, when in Athens, had been a fastidious dandy. But when he fled to Sparta to escape prosecution for parodying the sacred Athenian mysteries at a drunken aristocratic party in Athens, he won the hearts of his Spartan hosts by giving up his elegant Athenian manners, and adopting the Spartan mode of life.

"When they [the Spartans] saw him with his hair untrimmed, taking cold baths, on terms of intimacy with their coarse bread, and supping black porridge," Plutarch writes, "they could scarcely trust their eyes." Plutarch terms Alcibiades a "chameleon" and says that, "in Sparta, he was all for bodily training, simplicity of life, and severity of countenance."[12]

Plato was himself one of the disaffected Athenian aristocrats who admired and idealized Sparta. He adds another touch to the portrait of the Sparta-loving Athenians. Plato had a gift for comedy. There is an exchange in his *Gorgias* that dovetails with the description by Aristophanes. In that dialogue, after Socrates derides all the great statesmen of Athens, oligarchic as well as democratic, the climax of his tirade — as we mentioned earlier — is an attack on Pericles for making the Athenians "idle, cowardly, talkative and avaricious, by starting the system of public fees," i.e., pay for serving in the jury-courts. At this point Plato has his interlocutor Callicles comment sarcastically, "You hear that from the folk with battered ears, Socrates."[13] The "battered ears" is a reference to what we call "cauliflower ears" in boxing parlance.

This would have drawn an immediate chuckle from an Athenian audience but it requires a bit of explanation in our times. E. R. Dodds, in his commentary on the dialogue, explains this as a reference to "the young oligarchs of the late fifth century, who advertised their political sympathies by adopting Spartan tastes — one of which was, or was thought to be, the taste for boxing."[14]

The Socratic infatuation with Sparta is attested in both the Xenophontic and the Platonic portraits of him. The best-known evidence of this is in Plato's *Crito*. There his pro-Spartan bias is referred to in the imaginary dialogue between Socrates and the personified Laws of Athens.

Crito, one of Socrates' most devoted disciples, has come to see Socrates in his prison cell after the trial. Crito discloses that he and other friends of Socrates have been planning his escape. They have raised funds for the purpose and have already arranged to pay "some men who are willing to save you and get you away from here."[15]

Socrates refuses to be rescued. He says he will not requite evil with evil. He will not break the law even to save his life from a verdict he considers unjust. Socrates asks Crito to imagine what the Laws of Athens would say if they were now to appear in his cell and discuss the matter with him. In this imaginary conversation with the Laws, there is set forth the concept of law as a contract between the state and the individual citizen. This is probably the first appearance of the social contract theory in secular literature; the Bible implies a similar covenant between Jehovah and Israel.

The Laws argue that Socrates, after benefiting all his life from the Laws of Athens, would now be breaking that contract if he ran away instead of obeying a lawful decree simply because he considered it unjust. The argument, though lofty and weighty, is by no means conclusive. Here, as so often in the Platonic dialogues, Socrates is not forced to confront the full brunt of counterargument.

Crito, like so many of the Platonic interlocutors of Socrates, is no match for him. The real contradictions in the Socratic position have puzzled scholars ever since.[16] But this aspect of the imaginary debate, to which we shall return later, does not concern us here. What concerns us now is the reference which the Laws make to Socrates' pro-Spartan sympathies.

The Laws argue that at any time in his life Socrates had been free to leave the city, "if we did not please you and you thought the agreement unfair," but he had chosen to stay. The Laws say he might have emigrated to either of two other city-states whose laws he so much admired. "But you preferred neither Lacedaemon nor Crete," the Laws tell Socrates, "which you are always saying are well-governed."[17] Putting this remark in the *Crito* would be "pointless," Burnet noted in his commentary, "unless the 'historical' Socrates had actually praised the laws of Sparta and Crete."[18]

The Socratic admiration for Sparta and Crete, passed over with a joke in the *Crito,* is puzzling. Sparta and Crete were culturally and politically the two most backward regions of ancient Greece. In both, the lands were cultivated by serfs and the serfs were kept submissive (at least in Sparta, of which we know more than we do of Crete) by a secret police and a ruling military caste practicing an apartheid which reminds the modern reader of South Africa. The Socratic predilection for Sparta and Crete is confirmed elsewhere in Xenophon and Plato, both admirers of Sparta over their native city. In the *Memorabilia* Socrates calls the Athenians "degenerate" and compares them unfavorably with the Spartans, singling out for special praise their military training.[19] In the *Republic,* Plato has Socrates praise the "Cretan and Spartan constitutions" as the best form of government, preferable to oligarchy, which he ranks second, and of course to democracy, which he places third.[20]

We know that Sparta — and probably also Crete — restricted travel abroad by citizens, as do the Soviets and China. The purpose then as now was to prevent what Beijing has been assailing as the danger of "spiritual pollution" from foreign ideas. A similar Iron Curtain is a feature of Plato's *Laws,* where his spokesman is the "Athenian Stranger" (with views very strange indeed to Athens) and his interlocutors are restricted to a Cretan and a Spartan. The very cast of characters is as closed as the closed society all three agree upon. They all agree on an Iron Curtain to keep out foreign ideas and visitors, and to restrict the travel of their own citizens. They even propose to "debrief" the few allowed such travel, and decontaminate them of any dangerous thoughts, before allowing them to associate with the rest of the citizenry on their return.

The dialogue between Socrates and the Laws breaks off too soon. The Laws should have asked Socrates why he didn't emigrate to Sparta. The obvious answer, well known in antiquity, would have been embarrassing. Socrates was a philosopher, and philosophers were not welcome in Sparta. They flocked to Athens from all over Greece but never to Sparta or Crete. Neither was a market for ideas. Both regarded philosophy with suspicion.

Apparently the thought of Sparta as a refuge for Socrates never even occurred to Crito and the other devoted disciples who were planning the escape. "Wherever you go," Crito says, "they will welcome you." He even mentions backward Thessaly as a refuge, where Crito says he has friends "who will make much of you and will protect you,"[21] but makes no mention of the two places Socrates so much admired — Sparta or Crete.

Many pro-Spartan Athenians took refuge from time to time in Sparta. Socrates' disciple Xenophon spent the rest of his life there after his exile from Athens. Alcibiades, as we have seen, took refuge there for a time. But they were welcomed as military assets in Sparta's struggles with Athens. Xenophon had served the Spartans as a mercenary soldier. Alcibiades was met with open arms as a traitor to his own city. But Socrates was a philosopher. That was the difference. We never hear of a philosopher in Sparta or Crete. Plato fled Athens after the condemnation of Socrates. He traveled widely and visited Egypt; his admiration for its caste system is reflected in his *Laws* and the *Critias,* but there is no mention of his ever visiting Sparta or Crete.

Plato finally returned from a self-imposed exile to his native Athens. He founded his academy and spent the remaining forty years of his life there teaching antidemocratic philosophy unmolested, but without ever a word of appreciation for the freedom Athens afforded him.

It is easy to see why certain elements of the landowning aristocracy in Attica admired and idealized Sparta. In Sparta the middle class of craftsmen and merchants which played so dynamic a role in Athenian history was excluded from citizenship. They were *perioikoi* — "dwellers around" Sparta — with limited rights and low social status. But a heavy cultural price was paid for the military caste dictatorship required to stifle the rise of a middle class and to keep the majority of serfs or *helots* in submission.

Sparta was a military oligarchy where the ruling Spartiates lived a dour barracks existence under constant military training and discipline, the men taking their meals together at a common mess like soldiers in service. Their education was limited.

Sparta had no theater; there no tragic poets dwelt on life's mysteries; there no comic poets dared mock its notables. Music was martial; Sparta's one lyric poet, Alcman, seems to have been an Asiatic Greek slave. The most famous Spartan poet, Tyrtaeus, was himself a general and one of his surviving fragments "gives orders for tactical arrangements and is concerned with a siege."[22] As for philosophy, Sparta was a total blank and so was Crete. If Socrates had tried out his philosophic interrogations in Sparta, he would have been jailed or expelled. The philosophy of the Spartans was summed up centuries later in Tennyson's "Charge of the Light Brigade":

> *Theirs not to reason why,*
> *Theirs but to do and die.*

The anti-intellectualism of the uncouth Spartans was a favorite joke in Athenian comedy; some Athenians may have wondered how any philosopher could be enamored of a city so hostile to philosophy. Socrates in the *Protagoras* tries to counter such criticism with a jest: he claims that the Spartans are really what we might term closet philosophers.

Socrates does not deny that Sparta appears to be a closed society suspicious of all ideas. But he argues that this is not because the Spartans fear ideas or dislike philosophers. On the contrary, Socrates says, the Spartans close their doors to ideas and philosophic teachers because they do not want the outside world to discover how highly they prize them! The Spartan military ascendancy, Socrates even argues, is not due to their legendary arduous training and rigorous discipline, but to a secret addiction to philosophy.

"Philosophy," Socrates asserts, "is of more ancient and abundant growth in Crete and Lacedaemon than in any other part of Greece and sophists [here the word is used in a favorable sense] are most numerous in those regions."[23] This, of course, was nonsense; Greek philosophy first flourished in the cities of Asia Minor, founded by Ionian Greeks, as was Athens itself. The Spartans were Dorians.

The Spartans and Cretans "make pretense of ignorance," according to Socrates, "in order to prevent the discovery that it is by wisdom [*sophia,* in the sense of philosophy] that they have ascendancy over the rest of the Greeks. . . . They prefer it to be thought that they owe their superiority to fighting and valour, conceiving that the revelation of its real cause would lead everyone to practice this wisdom."

"So well have they kept their secret," Socrates continues, "that they have deceived the followers of the Spartan cult in our cities." The result, he says, recalling the similar exchange with Callicles in the *Gorgias,* is "that some get broken ears ["cauliflower ears"] by imitating them, bind their knuckles with thongs [like our "brass knuckles"], go in for muscular exercises, and wear dashing little cloaks, as though it were by these means that the Spartans were the masters of Greece."

Socrates even puts forward an ingenious explanation for Sparta's Iron Curtain. "The Spartans," Socrates says, "when they want to resort freely to their wise men and are tired of meeting them in secret . . . expel all resident aliens, whether they be sympathizers with the Spartan way of life or not, and converse with the Sophists unbeknown to any foreigners."[24] A. E. Taylor, one of this century's greatest — and most devout — Platonic scholars, commented on this passage: "It ought not to have to be said that this whole representation of Sparta and Crete, the least 'intellectual' communities of Hellas . . . is furious fun."[25]

When Socrates spoke of excluding aliens, he was alluding to the *xenelasia,* a law banishing aliens which the Liddell-Scott *Greek Lexicon* (an earlier version of the Liddell-Scott-Jones) explains as a peculiarity of Sparta. The Greeks were sailors, traders, and explorers. Hospitality to strangers is a virtue in Homer. Suspicion of them is a characteristic of savages like the Cyclops. Greek cities, especially Athens, were open to men and ideas. In this, Sparta and Crete were the exception. This was well known in Athens. In the

Birds Aristophanes makes fun of the Spartan paranoia about aliens. The eccentric astronomer Meton is warned to flee the realm of the Birds because its feathered rulers are in a frenzy of alien-hunting "as in Lacedaemon."[26] The Athenian spirit behind this joke is expressed in that passage of the funeral speech in Thucydides where Pericles boasts, "We throw our city open to all the world and we never by exclusion acts debar anyone from learning or seeing anything which an enemy might profit by observing. . . ."[27] Athens was proud of its freedom from the paranoia that has begun to infect our own society in the era of the national security state.

Sparta was the ancient prototype of such a closed society. Xenophon describes the Spartan anti-alien acts or *xenelasiai* in his treatise *The Constitution of the Lacedaemonians*. But Xenophon seems to have admired this anti-alien legislation. He writes in a tone of disillusion because the Spartans in the days of his exile there had begun to like foreign ways! "There were *xenelasiai* in former days, and to live abroad was illegal," Xenophon says, "and I have no doubt that the purpose of these regulations was to keep the citizens from being demoralized by contact with foreigners." But "now," Xenophon adds sadly, writing after Sparta's victory in the Peloponnesian war, when its generals enjoyed a lucrative rule over subject cities, "I have no doubt that the fixed ambition of those who are thought to be first among them is to live to their dying days as governors in a foreign land."[28] To understand this reference one must recall that while Athens quickly rebounded from its defeat in the Peloponnesian war, Sparta, corrupted by plunder, never fully recovered from its victory.[29]

There is a related and not at all humorous passage in Socrates' spoof in the *Protagoras* where he says that the Spartans "do not permit any of their young men to travel abroad to the other cities lest they unlearn what they are taught at home."[30] The Spartan Iron Curtain operated both ways: to keep foreigners out and citizens in. As we have just noted, this was one of the very features of the Spartan and Cretan constitutions that Plato adopted in the *Laws,* where travel abroad was restricted only to a few selected citizens, safely past the age of forty, and then only on public missions as heralds or ambassadors or on "certain commissions of inspection."[31] These sound like intelligence assignments. In this, as in other respects, notably strict state control of literature and the arts, Plato provides Leninist dictatorships with a precedent they cannot find in Marx or Engels.

It is significant that in the *Apology,* where Socrates blames the prejudice against him on the comic poets, he refers only to the *Clouds* of Aristophanes. He makes no reference to the pro-Spartanism alleged in the *Birds.* That play has a direct bearing on the charge in Socrates' indictment that he subverted the loyalty of the youth to Athens. The *Birds* supported that charge when it described the pro-Spartan "laconomaniac" youth of Athens as "Socratified."

Plato — writing the *Apology* years after the trial — was protecting himself as well as Socrates when he made no mention of the *Birds.* The foremost examples of those "Socratified" malcontents was Plato himself. In the fourth century B.C. he carried on the same intellectual assault against Athenian freedom and democracy that his master had launched in the fifth.[32]

PART II

THE ORDEAL

Chapter 10

WHY DID THEY WAIT
UNTIL HE WAS SEVENTY?

৻৶৵৻৶৵

T HE *CLOUDS* was produced a quarter of a century, the
Birds eighteen years, before Socrates was put on trial.
Aristophanes and the fragments of the other comic poets
show that his nonconformities — political, philosophical, and
religious — were notorious. Socrates was not operating under-
ground. He was no fearful dissident producing *samizdat* — as the
Soviets call it — for private circulation, or to be smuggled out for
publication abroad. His views could be heard "on any street-
corner": in the *palaestra* where the young athletes trained or the
marketplace. Wherever Athenians gathered, they were free to hear
him. No KGB — or, for that matter, FBI or CIA — had to tap his
telephone to learn his views. Though such institutions were
already known in other parts of ancient Greece, they did not exist
in Athens. Sparta, as we know from many sources, had a *krypteia*
or secret police, trained not only to spy out "uppity" *helots* but to
assassinate potential rebels and troublemakers among them.[1]

Political espionage seems to have developed early with the rise
of tyrannies in Greek city-states like Syracuse, where Plato at one
time hoped to turn his friend, the tyrant Dionysius II, into a model
"philosopher king." There, as Aristotle tells us, one of Dionysius'
predecessors, Hiero, used agents provocateurs as well as spies to
ferret out "any chance utterance or action" that indicated dissent.
Women called "sharp ears" were sent out "wherever there was
any gathering or conference." Their assignment was not only to
report dangerous utterance, but by their known or suspected
presence, to inhibit critics of the regime. "When men are afraid of
spies of this sort," Aristotle observes, "they keep a check on their

tongues."[2] Tongues wagged freely in Athens; none more freely than that of Socrates.

The Athenian equivalent of a free press was the theater. The comic poets were the "journalists" as purveyors of malicious and spicy gossip and as castigators of misdeeds in public office. Most of their prodigious output has disappeared. The only complete comedies that have survived are those of Aristophanes. Socrates figures in four of them, and we have fragments of four other comic poets that record the odd appearance and odd ideas of Socrates.[3] We know of one other lost play, the *Konnos,* by a comic poet named Ameipsias, in which Socrates was the main character. These are the only references to Socrates during his lifetime.

But the fact that Socrates was a favorite butt of the comic poets does not mean that he was in disrepute. On the contrary, it reflected his fame and popularity. The Athenians enjoyed their eccentrics. They also enjoyed jokes at the expense of their highest officials. The comic poets even took aim at the Olympian Pericles, with his intellectual girlfriend Aspasia and their circle of high-brows. But the lewd jokes and vulgar slapstick Pericles inspired did not keep the Athenians from reelecting him so often that Thucydides termed him a virtual monarch. Pericles' successor, Cleon, though a so-called *demagogue* or popular leader, was also a prime target. But that didn't keep him from being reelected, either.

Socrates himself, as we have seen, had a great sense of humor and often poked fun at himself. It is unlikely that he could not take a joke at his own expense. There is a story preserved in Plutarch's essays, the *Moralia,* that Socrates was once asked whether he was indignant over the way Aristophanes treated him in the *Clouds.* Socrates replied, "When they break a jest upon me in the theatre, I feel as if I were at a big party of good friends."[4] Indeed, in the *Symposium,* one of the loveliest of Plato's dialogues, we find Socrates and Aristophanes portrayed in friendly and convivial discourse.

Yet in the *Apology,* Socrates seems to attribute the origin of the prejudice against him to the comic poets. Almost at the very beginning of his defense, Socrates says that long before the charges he now faced in his trial, he had been beset by a swarm of slanderous accusations. Socrates says he had never been able to confront and refute them because these accusers were anonymous so that it was "not even possible to call any of them up here," i.e., to the rostrum before the court, "and cross-question him." So he was forced, Socrates complains, "to fight, as it were, absolutely with shadows and to cross-question when nobody answers." It was "not even possible," Socrates says, "to know and speak their names, except when one of them happened to be a writer of comedies." But this is ambiguous. It may be interpreted, as it usually is, as a reference to Aristophanes and the *Clouds*. But it could mean anyone "who happened to be a writer of comedies."

Socrates says that these early accusers "got hold of most of you in childhood."[5] This was no exaggeration. Children, too, attended the theater, and we know from the dates of production that the first parodies of Socrates came in 423 B.C., when many of his judges were indeed children. In that year at the annual city festival of the Dionysia, two comedies about Socrates made their debut, and both won prizes — the second prize to the *Konnos* of Ameipsias and the third to the *Clouds*.

We have only two fragments of the *Konnos,* but its jokes about Socrates may have been similar to those in the *Clouds* where Socrates presided over a *phrontisterion* — a "thinkery." The *Konnos* likewise had a chorus of *phrontistai* or "thinkers." Nobody is sure what the title *Konnos* meant, but there was a verb, *konneo,* that meant "to know." Like the *Clouds* it was a satire on intellectuals; perhaps it meant the "knower" or the "one who knows."

A similar joke seems to have been made by a third comic poet, Eupolis. In a surviving fragment there is a reference to Socrates which plays on the verb *phrontizo* — to think or contemplate. "Yes," Eupolis has one of his characters say, "and I loathe that poverty-stricken windbag Socrates who *contemplates* everything in the world but does not know where his next meal is coming from." We do not know the title or theme of the comedy of which this is a fragment. But Ferguson of Britain's Open University, to

whose sourcebook on Socrates we owe this translation, tells us
that an ancient marginal note on the *Clouds* says "that though
Eupolis did not often introduce Socrates [in his plays] he hits him
off better than Aristophanes in the whole of *The Clouds*."[6]

Plato's genius and love turned Socrates into a secular saint of our
Western civilization. But the bits and pieces that survive from the
Old Comedy, as it is called, of fifth-century Athens indicate that
to his fellow citizens he was long regarded as an odd — even
lovable — eccentric, a town "character." This is how his contemporaries saw him, and not as we see him in the golden haze of the
Platonic dialogues. The humor of the Old Comedy is rough and
bawdy; it is not for prigs or prudes. It is the ultimate ancestor of
Minsky's. Prototypes of the same skits and dirty jokes I remember
from youthful and semisecretive attendance at American burlesque
shows I have since found again in the pages of Aristophanes —
even the same lewd gestures, for example the middle finger jabbed
upwards.

But only a humorless pedant can believe that the joshing of the
comic poets led to the trial of Socrates. When Eupolis pictured
him as a man who "contemplated" everything but didn't know
where his next meal was coming from, it was crude and a little
cruel — as humor so often is — but hardly ground for a criminal
indictment. To blame Socrates' fate on the comic poets is like
blaming a politician's defeat today on the way he has been
"misrepresented" by newspaper cartoonists.

In the *Apology* Socrates makes two pointed references to the
way he is pictured in the *Clouds*. Socrates says that "in Aristophanes' comedy" his judges had seen "a Socrates being carried about
there, proclaiming that he was treading on air." But philosophers
all through the ages have often appeared to be "treading on air."
Socrates is exaggerating when he equates this with calling him "a
criminal and a busybody." Aristophanes was making a joke, not
filing an indictment.

Socrates also complains that his judges since childhood had been
led by comic poetry to see "a certain Socrates, a wise man, a
ponderer over the things in the air and one who has investigated

the things beneath the earth and who makes the weaker argument the stronger." These, Socrates says, "are my dangerous enemies."

But there is no record of anyone ever having been prosecuted in Athens because of what was said about him by comic poets. If their jokes had been taken seriously, most of the city's statesmen would have ended up in jail. This is true not only in the fifth century of Socrates but in the fourth century of Plato, when he too was a butt of contemporary comedy.

Plato has Socrates complain that his fellow townsmen think that those who ponder on "the things in the air" and "the things beneath the earth" are freethinkers who "do not even believe in gods."[7] Socrates says he had been brought into disrepute by such slander. But Athenian audiences, as we know from the Platonic dialogues, flocked — and paid well — to hear freethinking philosophers and "sophists" from all over Greece expound such radical views.

As for not believing in gods, the Athenians were accustomed to hearing the gods treated disrespectfully in both the comic and the tragic theater. For two centuries before Socrates, the philosophers had been laying the foundations of natural science and metaphysical inquiry. Their gigantic pioneering in free thought still awes us as we pore over the fragments of these so-called pre-Socratics. Almost all the basic concepts of science and philosophy may be found there in embryo. They first spoke of evolution and conceived the atom. In the process the ancient gods were not so much dethroned as demoted and bypassed. They were reduced to venerable fables or metaphorical personifications of natural forces and abstract ideas.

These philosophers were rationalists and rarely bothered with what we call "theology." The very term was unknown to them. Indeed it does not appear in Greek until the century after Socrates. The word *theologia* — talk about the gods — turns up for the first time in the *Republic* when Plato is explaining what the poets in his utopia will be allowed to say about the divine powers.[8] In his ideal society a Socrates would indeed have been punishable for deviating from the state-established *theologia,* but not in Athens.

The Olympian deities of Homer and Hesiod had dwindled in significance and stature beside the material forces and immaterial abstractions the pre-Socratics identified as the prime movers of the universe. The gods were relegated to a minor role in the cosmic drama. When some of these early freethinkers did touch on the nature of the gods, the results were shattering. In our Bible, God creates man in His image. But Xenophanes a century before Socrates turned this anthropomorphic conception right side up and declared that men create the gods in their own human image. Xenophanes observed that the Ethiopians had gods with "snub noses and black hair," while the Thracians worshipped gods with "gray eyes and red hair" like their own. He added that if oxen, horses, and lions had hands and could carve images, they too would worship gods of their own likeness. Xenophanes even dared criticize Homer and Hesiod, the twin "bibles" of traditional Greek religion. "They," he wrote, "have narrated every possible wicked story about the gods: theft, adultery and mutual deception."[9] This is much the same complaint made by Plato when he proposed to censor the poets.

Xenophanes himself seems to have been a kind of pantheist, while Plato consigned the Olympian gods to a shadowy and irrelevant existence somewhere between earth and the stratosphere of his eternal Ideas. But neither Xenophanes in the sixth century nor Plato in the fourth was ever haled into court for irreligious utterance.

Polytheism was, by its very pluralistic nature, roomy and tolerant, open to new gods and new views of old ones. Its mythology personified natural forces and could be adapted easily, by allegory, to metaphysical concepts. These were the old gods in a new guise, and commanded a similar but fresh reverence.

Atheism was little known and difficult for a pagan to grasp because he saw divinity all about him, not just on Olympus but in the hearth and the boundary stone, which were also divinities, though of a humble sort. One could in the same city and the same century worship Zeus as a promiscuous old rake, henpecked and cuckolded by Juno, or as Justice deified.

It was the political, not the philosophical or theological, views of Socrates which finally got him into trouble. The discussion of his religious views diverts attention from the real issues. Nowhere in the *Apology* does Socrates even mention the jokes about his pro-Spartan sympathies and the pro-Spartan youth who idolized and imitated him. Our problem is: What made these old political jokes suddenly begin to seem no longer funny?

Chapter 11

THE THREE EARTHQUAKES

ะ๛๛

THERE WAS no public prosecutor in Athens. Any citizen could file an indictment. If anonymous accusations and the comic poets had been building up prejudice against Socrates all through his lifetime — as he claims in the *Apology* — how is it that no one filed a complaint against him until he was seventy? The answer appears to be twofold. First, Athens must have been extraordinarily tolerant of dissident opinion. Second, something must have happened toward the end of his years to make it far less so.

What happened to turn old jokes sour? What converted prejudice into prosecution? The answer, I believe, lies in three political "earthquakes" that occurred in little more than a decade before the trial, shaking the city's sense of internal security and making its citizens apprehensive. But for these events, Socrates would never have been indicted even if twice as many comic poets had made fun of him.

The dates of those alarming events are 411, 404, and 401 B.C. In 411 and again in 404, disaffected elements in connivance with the Spartan enemy overthrew the democracy, set up dictatorships, and initiated a reign of terror. In 401 B.C., only two years before the trial, they were about to try again. The type of rich young men prominent in the entourage of Socrates played a leading role in all three civic convulsions.

Familiar characters parodied in the *Clouds* and in the *Birds* must have taken on a new and sinister significance. The spendthrift young aristocrat, Pheidippides, who took a course of instruction in the Socratic "Thinkery" of the *Clouds* no longer looked like a harmless fop. A chilling reality now colored his exultant little speech before thrashing his father: "How sweet it is to become acquainted with new clever ways, and be able to look down with disdain on the established laws."[1] The "Socratified" youth of the *Birds* with their Spartan-style clubs no longer looked dashing and cute. They had become the storm troopers with which the Four Hundred in 411 and the Thirty in 404 terrorized the city.

In the elegant and seductive phrases of his *Apology*, Plato does not allow these political events to obtrude on the reader, though they were fresh in the memories of the judges. Nor does he mention them anywhere else in his many dialogues.[2] Since one of Plato's main preoccupations was the achievement of a virtuous politics, this curious blank spot in his dialogues is itself a feat of selective political amnesia.

We have graphic contemporary descriptions of what happened. Thucydides is our authority for the events of 411 and Xenophon's *Hellenica* for those of 404. The first dictatorship — that of the Four Hundred — lasted only four months; the second — that of the Thirty — eight months. But each crowded many horrors into a short and unforgettable span.

The horrors were not accidental. All through history the narrower the base of a dictatorship, the more dreadful is the terror it feels necessary to maintain itself in power. In 411 and 404 democracy was not overthrown by a popular revulsion but by a handful of conspirators. They had to use violence and deceit and to work hand in glove with the Spartan enemy because they had so little support at home. It is against this background that we can better understand a curious denial entered by Socrates in Plato's *Apology*. There he says that all his life long he had avoided taking part in *synomosias*. This is translated as "plots" in the Loeb, and in Jowett.[3] But the word deserves fuller explanation if we are to get the significance of this denial. It derives from a Greek verb that means to take an oath together. It was applied to the more or less secret clubs or conspiracies in which aristocrats bound themselves by oath to help each other and to work against the democracy. These *synomosias*, Burnet explains in his note on this passage in the *Apology*, "were originally devised to secure the election to office of members of the oligarchical party and their acquittal when put on trial, and which had played so great a part in the revolutions at the end of the fifth century B.C."[4]

These aristocratic clubs were notorious. The earliest reference to them is in the *Knights* of Aristophanes where the Paphlagonian says, "I'll go this instant to the Council-board/And all your vile conspiracies [*synomosiai*] denounce."[5] The comedy won a first prize in 424 B.C., thirteen years before the first overthrow of the democracy.

Significantly, Socrates felt it necessary to deny membership in such conspiracies. There is no reason to doubt Socrates' denial of membership. But he and these *synomosiai* shared a common dislike for the democracy. Socrates' denial that he himself had ever joined a *synomosia* is the only point in the *Apology* where he touches — though ever so lightly — on what I believe to have been the real political issues behind his trial. But Socrates does not — and unfortunately could not — deny that some of his most famous pupils or associates had taken a leading part in these conspiracies.

The subversive strategy of the aristocratic clubs in normal times is frankly set forth by Adeimantus in the second book of the *Republic*. Adeimantus is usually identified as a brother of Plato. "With a view to lying hid," Adeimantus explains to Socrates, "we will organize societies [*synomosiai*] and political clubs [*hetaireias*] and there are teachers of cajolery who impart the arts of the popular assembly and the court-room. So that, partly by persuasion, partly by force, we shall contrive to overreach with impunity."[6]

Plato in the *Laws* provides the death penalty for anyone who would organize conspiracies or clubs to subvert his own ideal city.[7] But Athens was more tolerant. The right of association was safeguarded by an Athenian law that went back to the days of Solon. No legal action was ever taken against these aristocratic "clubs," although, as Gomme's monumental commentary on Thucydides points out, "only enemies of democracy needed secret organizations."[8] The first mention of *synomosiai* in Thucydides is in the famous affair of the mutilation of the Hermae just as an Athenian armada prepared to set out against Syracuse.[9] Statues of

Hermes, the patron divinity of (among other things) travel, stood in front of Athenian homes. In one night they were all mutilated. An oligarchic conspiracy (*synomosia*) was suspected behind this ill-omened affront against the god, calculated to bring bad luck on the expedition.

After the disaster at Syracuse, an aristocratic conspiracy was indeed set afoot. Thucydides tells us that a treasonable general Peisander began by reversing Athenian policy in the subject cities, abolishing the democracies Athens had fostered and replacing them with oligarchies. These revolutions in the subject cities soon provided troops of oligarchic sympathy for the overthrow of democracy in Athens itself in 411.

Thucydides relates that when they reached Athens the conspirators found that much of their "business had already been accomplished" by the aristocratic secret clubs. "Some of the younger men" in these clubs had organized squads of assassins to deprive the people of its leaders and to create an atmosphere of terror. They "secretly put to death a certain Androcles," the historian tells us, because he was "the most prominent leader of the popular party. Others opposed to their plans they secretly made away with in the same manner." Terror spread. People no longer "spoke against them, through fear and because it was seen that the conspiracy was widespread; and if anyone did oppose" them, Thucydides says, "at once in some convenient way he was a dead man." These were the prototypes of the death squads the military used in Argentina, El Salvador, and Chile in our time.

Domestic security broke down. "No search was made," the historian continues, "for those who did the deed, nor if they were suspected was any legal prosecution held." On the contrary, Thucydides observes, "The populace [the *demos*] kept quiet and were in such consternation that he who did not suffer any violence, even though he never said a word, counted that a gain." The terror had a multiplier effect. "Imagining the conspiracy to be much more widespread than it actually was," the democrats were "cowed in mind."

"All the members of the popular party," Thucydides explains, "approached each other with suspicion." This was not mere paranoia. There were unpredictable treacheries, as some switched sides from cowardice or opportunism. "There were among them men whom one would never have expected to change over and favour an oligarchy."

It was these turncoats, the ancient historian relates, "who caused the greatest distrust among the masses and rendered the most valuable service toward the few in securing their safety by confirming in the populace this distrust of their own people toward each other.[10] This was not ancient history to the Athenians when they put Socrates on trial.

There was a similar conspiracy after the Athenian surrender at the end of the Peloponnesian war. The Spartan general Lysander "sided with the oligarchical party," Aristotle tells us. So great was the fear of what the victors might do that the Athenian assembly itself voted to end the democracy. "The people," Aristotle explains, "were cowed and were forced to vote for the oligarchy."[11] So in 404 B.C. the Thirty came into power. Many of the Thirty were antidemocratic exiles. Some of them had fought on the Spartan side. The victors counted on such men to keep Athens firmly under the Spartan yoke. The legitimacy of the regime in the eyes of most Athenians was tainted from the first by these links to treason and defeat.

The Thirty depended on a Spartan garrison for their safety. In addition, they recruited a private army of young supporters to terrorize the citizenry. Aristotle says the Thirty enlisted "three hundred retainers carrying whips, and so kept the state in their own hands."[12] These young bullies must have reminded many Athenians of the "Socratified" and Sparta-mad youth derided by Aristophanes in the Birds. Socrates could not be held responsible for their conduct, but when he came to trial so soon after in 399 B.C. these bully-boys must have been remembered as just the kind of youth he was charged with turning against the democracy.

Indeed, Socrates himself seems to be answering such suspicions when in the Apology he tells his judges that after his death "Those who will force you to give an account will be more numerous than heretofore, men whom I restrained, though you knew it not; and they will be harsher."[13] This tantalizing remark appears in the third and final section of the *Apology* after the two crucial votes had been taken, the first on conviction, the second on the penalty, too late to affect either vote. Why did Socrates enter this claim so late? Evidence of this kind would have shown that while Socrates was opposed to the democracy, he never incited its violent overthrow. Such a plea, however, would have required him to admit that he was indeed a teacher, and that he did inculcate antidemocratic views. These are admissions Socrates resisted. He preferred to present himself as a man above the battle, withdrawn from politics altogether, and intervening only when the decision was forced upon him, and he chose resistance rather than participate in injustice, irrespective of the regime, as he had done in the trial of the generals under the democracy and the arrest of Leon under the Thirty.

To understand how the events of 411 and 403 must have changed popular attitudes toward Socrates, one need only recall how the democracy was twice restored. As in so many revolutions, like the fall of the czar and the kaiser in World War I, and the collapse of the Greek junta and the Argentine military dictatorship in the 1980s, the political overturn followed military disaster: For Athens in 411 it was the defeat at Syracuse; in 404, it was Athens' loss of its fleet — through treachery or unbelievable incompetence — at Aigospotomi and its surrender to Sparta.

In the wake of these defeats, there ensued not a struggle between rich oligarchs and poor democrats but a three-cornered class struggle. Those led by Critias represented aristocrats who had been organized in clandestine conspiracies waiting for an opportunity to overturn the democracy. A second faction spoke for the middle class, the third, for the poor, who provided the labor force and owed their achievement of political equality to the role they played as sailors and light infantry — the marines — in the navy on which the imperial power and trade primacy of Athens rested.

In 411 and in 404 the democracy was overthrown by a coalition of the aristocrats and the middle class against the poor, whom they disfranchised. But that coalition twice broke down when the aristocrats tried to disarm and disfranchise the middle class as well as the poor, and to establish a dictatorship rather than an oligar-chical or "republican" government based on a franchise limited to property owners. In 411 and in 404, the conduct of the aristocratic dictators proved cruel, rapacious, and bloody. Never in the history of Athens were basic rights and property as insecure as in those two interludes. Both times the middle class in its own defense had to form an alliance with the poor and restore democracy.

The restored democracy in 403 acquitted itself with magnanim-ity. Except for a few aristocratic leaders who lost their lives, the contending classes and factions were reconciled on the basis of a sweeping amnesty that won the admiration of antiquity. Aristotle, though he himself favored middle-class rule based on a limited franchise, paid his tribute to the restored democracy. "The Athenians," he wrote, about a half century after the overthrow of the Thirty, "appear both in private and public to have behaved towards the past disasters in the most completely honorable and statesmanlike manner of any people in history." In other cities the losers were often massacred and aristocratic landowners lost their estates to the landless. But the Athenian democrats, Aristotle notes with evident wonder, did not "even make a redistribution of the land."[14]

But Socrates, during those fateful conflicts and their humane resolution, did not take his stand with the aristocrats, or his own middle class, or the poor. The most talkative man in Athens fell silent when his voice was most needed. One possible reason is, simply, that he did not care enough. He seemed wholly to lack compassion. Nietzsche, who began as a classical scholar, once described the logic of Socrates as "icy." Gregory Vlastos, one of the foremost Platonists of our time, once wrote that while Jesus wept for Jerusalem, Socrates never shed a tear for Athens.

Socrates' lack of compassion is evident in Plato's *Euthyphro* if it is reread with a fresh eye. It is usually printed — along with the *Apology,* the *Crito,* and the *Phaedo* — as *The Trial and Death of Socrates.* But the *Euthyphro,* though it seems at first to promise much we would like to know, tells us disappointingly little of the prosecution. When it opens we meet Socrates on the portico of the *basileus archon,* or king magistrate, where he had been summoned for the preliminary examination before the trial. We look forward to hearing what happened there. Under Athenian law, as later in the European continental legal system, the preliminary examination before a magistrate fulfilled much the same function as the grand jury in Anglo-American law. The magistrate heard both sides and decided whether the case merited trial.

The accusers do not even appear in the dialogue. The opening scene turns out to be just a device for a dialogue that has almost nothing at all to do with the trial of Socrates. Instead we meet another plaintiff, Euthyphro, in an unrelated case. But in the course of it we do get inadvertent revelations about Socrates.

What makes Euthyphro's case unusual is that he has brought a charge against his own father as a result of a double slaying on his plantation on the island of Naxos. One of the family slaves had been killed in a quarrel by a hired laborer. Euthyphro's father threw the man, bound hand and foot, into a ditch while he sent off a messenger by ship to Athens to ask a religious adviser how to handle the killing of the slave. While waiting for the messenger's return, the laborer died of hunger and exposure. Euthyphro decided to file charges against his father for the death of the laborer.

Socrates utilizes the encounter with Euthyphro for another metaphysical — and semantic — wild goose chase. Socrates wants to know whether it is "pious" or "holy" for a son to bring such a charge against his own father. The dialogue is then devoted to a search for a definition of "piety" or "holiness."

Nowhere in the long, intricate, and sometimes tedious dialogue does Socrates ever utter one word of pity for the poor landless laborer. His rights are never mentioned. Was it "pious" or just to leave him exposed to cold and hunger while "the lord of the manor" decided in his own good time what to do with him? Had he no right to a day in court? The laborer might have shown that the quarrel in which he killed the landowner's slave was provoked, or that he acted in self-defense, or that the killing was accidental. All these pleas were known to Athenian homicide law. And now that the laborer had died of hunger and exposure did not justice require the trial of Euthyphro's father to determine whether his own conduct constituted homicide?

Socrates might say at this point that he was not arguing law or justice but logic. It might also be argued, however, that his lack of sympathy blinded him to a flaw in his logic and to the full dimensions of the case. The most agonizing question raised by it, the one that concerned Socrates most, is whether, under these circumstances, Euthyphro acted "piously" in bringing charges against his own father. But no definition of "piety" could really settle the matter. Euthyphro was caught in a classic conflict of obligations like those so frequent in Greek tragedy. He had a son's obligation to his father. He also had an obligation as a human being and a citizen to see that justice was done.

In the *Oresteia* of Aeschylus, similarly, poor Orestes is driven mad by just such a conflict of obligations. As a son, he had an obligation to avenge the murder of his father. But his father was murdered by his mother, Clytemnestra, to whom he also had a filial obligation. Which was more holy? In Aeschylus, Clytemnestra takes out her breast and puts the question in a terrifying gesture: How could her child plunge his knife into the breast that had suckled him?

The problem was not solvable by any syllogism based on a perfect definition of a moral or legal term. Aeschylus settled the matricide on a higher plane than law or logic. However justice was defined, it was unattainable under the dreadful circumstances. At the tragedy's end, the Athenian jury-court was deadlocked. Athena, the patron goddess of Athens, broke the tie by casting her vote for acquittal. Mercy had transcended justice.

But only pity clears our vision to see this. In the *Euthyphro,* you have to feel compassion for that poor laborer — we are never even told his name — to solve the deadlock in logic on which the dialogue ends. Euthyphro, like Orestes, was caught in a conflict — indeed a maze — of obligations, moral, legal, and political. These are unexplored in the arid semantics of the Socratic interrogation. Let us set forth the issues that Socrates overlooked:

1. True, Euthyphro had the obligation of a son to a father. But

even in this relationship he faced conflicting obligations. Of course it is appalling for a son to hale a father into court. But by Athenian and Greek standards, the father could not be cleared of guilt in the death of the laborer without undergoing a trial. In that trial he might be cleared of guilt or, if guilty, then cleansed by the court's penalty. If no one else would bring the landowner to this purgation by trial, was it not a duty for his son to take this painful task upon himself?

2. Euthyphro had the obligation of a citizen to bring the action even against his father. In Athens there was no public prosecutor. Every citizen had a right — and a duty — to bring an action when he thought the law broken; something like our legal doctrine of a "citizen's arrest," which allows any citizen to arrest when he sees a crime committed. In Athens the citizen not only could arrest but prosecute. This was in accord with the Athenian conception of participatory democratic government.

3. There was a third obligation, which would at once be apparent to the ancient Athenian observer. This obligation arose from a sense of common humanity and was both moral and political, when seen from the democratic point of view. This aspect of the case peeps out — inadvertently — but not until the very end of the dialogue. There Socrates says to a weary Euthyphro, that unless he clearly knew what was holy and unholy, "you would surely not have undertaken to prosecute your aged father for murder *for the sake of a servant.*"[15] Did it matter — in the eyes of the law, or of morality — that the dead man was only a servant?

There is a significant political difference between the English translation *servant* and the Greek word in the original. The Loeb translator chose the word *servant* for simplicity and because it does carry over the disdain in the original. But the Greek word Plato put into the mouth of Socrates was *thes,* a word with a special meaning in democratic Athens.

The citizenry of Athens had been divided for two centuries into four classes for purposes of taxation and to indicate their qualifications for public office. They were divided according to their wealth, or lack of it, in accordance with the assessed valuation of their property. The lowest and largest of the four classes, the *thetes* (the plural of *thes*) had little or none. They were free men, poor but not necessarily servants. Originally, even in Athens, they were not citizens at all. They did not "count" and they were not counted.

The word *thes* itself is as old as Homer, where it meant a hired laborer, as distinct from a slave.[16] There is a passage in the *Iliad* that comes to mind as one reads the *Euthyphro*. That passage reveals that a *thes* could be treated by his employer, the lordly Homeric landowner, as arrogantly as Euthyphro's father treated his hired hand.

In book twenty-one of the *Iliad,* Poseidon reminds Apollo of how shamefully they were cheated by the noble Trojan landowner Laomedon. Disguised as *thetes,* they had come down to earth — on the orders of Zeus — and served Laomedon "for a year's space at a fixed wage,"[17] building walls and herding his cattle. But when the time came to collect their wages, Laomedon not only refused to pay them but threatened to cut off their ears and sell them into slavery if they insisted on their pay. Homer says they traveled back to Olympus, unpaid and "with angry hearts." The lot of the hired laborer could be more precarious and less protected than that of the slave, who as property was taken care of, at least minimally.

This is one of the few places in the aristocratic world of Homer when we see the view from below. Here Homer, for a moment, was more sensitive to social justice than Plato's Socrates. In the *Euthyphro* the status of the free laborer on Naxos seems to have been little better than it was in Homeric times. Euthyphro's father was so angry over the loss of his slave that he had no concern for the rights of his hired hand, whom he threw into a ditch to die. By any definition, this treatment of the laborer could hardly be considered "holy." But this aspect of the case never enters the Socratic field of vision. To Socrates he was "a mere servant."

Euthyphro says to Socrates that the death of the hired man happened when "we," i.e., Euthyphro and his father, "were farming at Naxos" and "he was working there on our land."[18] What happened on Naxos could not have happened in Athens. Naxos was a fertile island in the Aegean that Athens liberated in the Persian wars and included in the Delian League under Athenian hegemony. It was one of the first to revolt against the burdensome Athenian yoke and when Naxos was subdued, its land was given to Athenian *cleruchs,* or colonists. The former owners — the luckier ones — became sharecroppers or hired laborers on the land they had once owned. When Athens lost the war with Sparta, Naxos was one of the subject states liberated and the Athenian colonists had to flee. The land was restored to its former owners. That is why Euthyphro speaks in the past tense of farming there.

The *thetes* on Naxos during Athenian ascendancy had neither the citizenship nor the rights enjoyed by landless laborers in Athens. In Attica the hired laborer would have had his day in court on a charge of murdering the slave. Had a landowner thrown the laborer into a ditch to die, friends or relatives of the dead man would have prosecuted the landowner for homicide. That is what Euthyphro is now doing on behalf of the luckless and friendless laborer.

Euthyphro is made fun of in the dialogue, as a kind of superstitious fanatic, but his attitude is more humane and enlightened than that of Socrates. At the very beginning of the dialogue, before he learned the facts of this unusual case, Socrates assumes that Euthyphro would not bring a charge against his father for murdering a "stranger" and asks whether the victim was a close relative. Euthyphro is surprised by this attitude.

"It is ridiculous, Socrates," he says, "that you think it matters whether the man who was killed was a stranger or a relative, and do not see that the only thing to consider is whether the action of the slayer was justified or not, and that if it was justified . . . and if not, one ought to proceed against him, even if he share one's hearth and eat at one's table."[19]

Euthyphro obviously felt this a duty transcending filial obligation and differences in status or class. Socrates brushes aside this aspect of the case. The idea of equal treatment under law, of social justice, is never discussed in the dialogue. But in 399 B.C., the time this discussion with Euthyphro is supposed to have taken place, on the very eve of Socrates' trial, the Athenian *demos* was sensitized to this very issue by its recent struggles against oligarchic repression in 411 and 404. The *thetes* class had been the main sufferer. It was deprived of the citizenship it had won two centuries earlier in the reforms of Solon. Its leaders had been killed. The poor had been driven out of Athens. They had lost their homes and their city. Had the overthrow of the democracy been consolidated, it would have become as easy in Attica as it was on Naxos for a landowner to take the law into his own hands as Euthyphro's father had done. The laborer would have had no rights.

The indifference Socrates shows to the fate of the hired laborer would have struck his contemporaries as on a par with the indifference he manifested to the fate of the *thetes* in 411 and 404. They could have concluded that his lack of sympathy reflected his own contempt for democracy. This would explain why he had not left the city under either dictatorship and had taken no part in restoring the democracy. He showed no interest in the rights of the poor, nor in social justice. Euthyphro's was the democratic attitude.

It would have provided a powerful argument for the defense at Socrates' own trial if he had been able to demonstrate that his followers were not all antidemocratic aristocrats like Critias and Charmides, but that there were democrats among them, too. It is revealing that at the trial he was able to name only one.

Plato certainly realized the importance of this because in the *Apology* he had Socrates single him out and make a point of that disciple's pro-democratic record. He was a man named Chaerephon. He could not be called as a witness at the trial because he was already dead.

"You know Chaerephon, I fancy," Socrates says to the judges. "He was my comrade from a youth and the comrade of your democratic party, and shared in the recent exile and came back with you."[20]

Notice that Socrates does not say "our," or even "the," democratic party but "your," as if clearly to dissociate himself from the dominant political view of his jurors. Note also that he does not say — as he might have, were it true — that despite the political prejudice against Socrates quite a few of his followers were of the people's party and then cite Chaerephon as one of them; evidently he was the exception. He is the only pro-democratic disciple mentioned anywhere in Plato or Xenophon. Most of the followers, as Socrates himself describes them, were "the young men who have the most leisure, the sons of the richest men."[21]

Socrates hurt his own cause when he said Chaerephon "shared in the recent exile and came back with you." "Observe," Burnet notes sadly in his commentary on the *Apology*, "that Socrates himself remained in Athens" and, Burnet adds, "it was a good deal more imprudent to remind the judges of that than it was advantageous to recall the democratic opinions of Chaerephon."[22] The reference to Chaerephon only emphasized how unlike him were Socrates and the rest of his disciples, including Plato, who also stayed in the city during the days of the Thirty.

When democracy was restored, to have "stayed in the city" became a badge of dishonor, as we know from many references in Lysias and other fourth-century orators. The amnesty that followed the overthrow of the Thirty did not wipe out the stigma on those who had taken no part in the resistance. Under the amnesty, once the leaders had been tried, no one could be prosecuted for any violations of the law he committed under the dictatorship or before it. The slate was wiped clean to solidify the civic reconciliation. Nor could anyone sue for recovery of property confiscated by the dictators and sold to meet their expenses or to enrich them. Many wealthy middle-class citizens and resident aliens had suffered such expropriations. But under the amnesty they lost the right to sue for recovery.

But in other types of litigation after peace was restored, the odium against defendants or plaintiffs who had "stayed in the city" was often utilized to influence the courts, as is evident in the orations of Lysias, who had been a friend of Socrates. Lysias was the most famous "lawyer" in the period just after the restoration. These advocates did not appear in court but prepared speeches for litigants. They were called *logographoi,* or professional writers of legal pleadings.

Lysias came of a distinguished and wealthy family of resident aliens. His father, Cephalus, presides as the host over the discus-

sions in Plato's *Republic*. The family of Lysias, like other rich
resident aliens, was a victim of the rapacious dictators, "partly on
the ground of their democratic sympathies," the *Oxford Classical
Dictionary* says of Lysias, "but chiefly because of their wealth."
Lysias saved his life by fleeing from Athens but his brother
Polemarchus, an interlocutor of Socrates in the *Republic,* was
executed. Their properties were confiscated. Lysias joined the
exiles who soon overthrew the Thirty. He returned to Athens as
a hero of the resistance.

From the orations of Lysias we know that litigants were often
questioned or attacked about their conduct under the Thirty. In
one case a defendant turned the tables on his accuser by an
unexpected revelation that must have won the sympathy of the
judges. He admitted that he had indeed stayed in the city, but he
revealed that his own father had been executed by the Thirty and
that he himself was only thirteen years old at the time. "At that
age," he said indignantly, "I neither knew what an oligarchy was,
nor would have been able to rescue" his father.[23] Another,
obviously an aristocrat — for he had served in the cavalry — was
mistakenly listed in the troops under the Thirty; he proved that he
was abroad during the dictatorship.[24]

Socrates could have been asked at his trial why he did not leave
the city, particularly after the execution of Leon of Salamis had
shown him the injustice of the regime. Was that not enough to
demonstrate — as it had to moderate oligarchs like Theramenes —
that democracy was at least a lesser evil, safer and more just than
a narrow oligarchy?

But Socrates was protected by the amnesty, too. He could not
be prosecuted for anything he had said or done before the
restoration of the democracy nor for having been a teacher or
associate of Critias and Charmides. Had the indictment covered
these earlier activities, it would have been attacked at the trial as a
blatant violation of the amnesty and we would have heard about
this from Plato and Xenophon.

The indictment, to be valid, could cover only the activities or
teachings of Socrates in the four years between the overthrow of
the Thirty and the trial. Socrates must have resumed the same

teachings, and attracted and inspired the same kind of following as before the Thirty. And his accusers may well have feared that these youths might again attempt the overthrow of the recently restored democracy. Just such an attempt was threatened in 401 B.C., only two years after the amnesty and two years before he was put on trial.

The Athenians had thought their troubles over in 403 when their opposing civic factions made peace. But there was a loophole in the amnesty agreement, and this was to cause fresh conflict. Some of the aristocrats who had supported the Thirty refused to be reconciled. Rather than renew the civil war and subdue them by force, the Athenians agreed to let them withdraw to the nearby town of Eleusis and establish a separate and independent city-state of their own.

The bitter-enders seem to have prepared for just such a contingency with characteristic foresight and ferocity. When the growing armed resistance to the Thirty won its first foothold in Attica by capturing a hilltop border stronghold at Phyle, Critias and his supporters decided to prepare a refuge where they could fight to the end should they be forced out of Athens. They picked Eleusis, but found the townspeople hostile. They took control of Eleusis by force, and executed three hundred of its males — probably the whole citizenry of this small town.

This massacre — quite in the style of Critias — is attested by two contemporary sources, one pro-democratic, the other anti-democratic. The former is Lysias[25] and the other Xenophon. They agree on Critias' motive and the number killed is supplied by Xenophon in his fuller account. Xenophon's *Hellenica* describes the trickery by which Critias seized the three hundred and then intimidated an Athenian assembly into giving the executions a semblance of legality by voting a mass death sentence without trial.[26]

This climactic horror of the doomed dictatorship prepared the way for the events of 401, which poisoned the atmosphere of Athens with fresh suspicion and — I believe — finally triggered the prosecution of Socrates.

Not long after the massacre in Eleusis, Critias and Charmides were slain in battle with the growing forces of the resistance. The dictatorship began to fall apart and the path was cleared to reconciliation. When peace was made, the minority of bitter-enders withdrew to Eleusis. The Athenians thought their troubles were over. But such men do not give up easily. The unreconciled came from the ranks of the wealthiest Athenians, with ample funds to hire mercenary soldiers. Hardly two years had passed when Athens learned that the Eleusinians were preparing to attack the city.

Xenophon tells us that the Athenians at once mobilized "their whole force against them," killed the commanders, "and then, by sending to the others their friends and kinsmen, persuaded them to become reconciled." So the civil conflict finally ended. "And, pledged as they were under oath, that in very truth they would not remember past grievances," Xenophon writes, "the two parties even to this day live together as fellow-citizens and the commons [demos] abide by their oaths" not to take revenge.[27]

That was in 401 B.C., just two years before the trial of Socrates. I believe there never would have been a trial had he, too, demonstrated his own reconciliation with the democracy, had he paid some tribute — as Xenophon did — to the magnanimity of the majority in the peace settlement. Had any such change in his attitude taken place, he would have allayed fear that a new crop of "Socratified" and alienated youth might emerge from his follow-ing to unleash civil war again within the city.

But there is no evidence, either in Plato or Xenophon, of any such change in Socrates after the overthrow of the Thirty. Socrates resumed his antidemocratic and antipolitical teachings. His tone had been more offensive than his doctrine. Neither was altered. The sneer barely below the surface of his irony was still there. He remained unreconciled. He seems to have learned nothing from the events of 411, 404, and 401.

It is as if he continued to live apart from the city, in the clouds above it, still looking down on it with disdain. He shows no awareness — either in the Platonic or the Xenophontic accounts — that his fellow citizens had reason to be concerned.

Chapter 12

XENOPHON, PLATO, AND THE THREE EARTHQUAKES

ເຈົ້າຈະ

XENOPHON AND PLATO were in their teens when the dictatorship of the Four Hundred was established in 411 B.C., old enough to be politically aware but too young to take an active part either in the overthrow of the democracy or its restoration. When the dictatorship of the Thirty was set up seven years later, both were in their middle twenties, but there is no record of their participation on either side. So far as we know they did not leave the city with the democrats — that would have been unthinkable for young men of their aristocratic background. Neither is mentioned in connection with the events of 401. Xenophon left Athens that same year to take up service as an officer commanding mercenaries in the Persian army. He never returned to Athens again. "It was probably in 399 B.C., the year of Socrates' death, and a time of difficulty for Socratic associates," the *Oxford Classical Dictionary* says, "that Xenophon was formally exiled." He spent the rest of his life in Sparta.

Plato, unlike Xenophon, was present at the trial of Socrates, as we know from the *Apology,* but seems to have fled the city before the execution. Perhaps he feared some action might be taken against him, too. The *OCD* biography of him says that "along with other Socratics" he first took refuge in nearby Megara. He stayed away for twelve years, voyaging as far as Egypt.

Xenophon's *Hellenica,* written in his Spartan exile, aims to complete the history of Thucydides, which breaks off in 411. Xenophon carries the story down to 400 B.C. Whatever his political upbringing and sympathies, he writes with admirable objectivity and his account of the debate between Critias and

Theramenes before the latter's execution is on a level with the
great debates in Thucydides. Xenophon's treatment of Critias is
remarkably different from Plato's. Critias is a glamorous figure in
the Platonic dialogues but a repellent despot, albeit a coldly logical
one, in the *Hellenica*.

Xenophon in his *Memorabilia* makes Socrates appear to be more
of an oppositionist to the Thirty than he is in Plato. In the *Apology*
his one act of defiance is his refusal to take part in the arrest of
Leon of Salamis, but his revulsion was not great enough to lead
him into active opposition. In Xenophon's *Memorabilia,* Socrates
did on one occasion publicly criticize the dictatorship. "When the
Thirty were putting to death many citizens of the highest respect-
ability and were encouraging many in crime," Xenophon writes,
Socrates turned a favorite analogy against the Thirty. "It seems
strange enough to me," Socrates said, "that a herdsman who lets
his cattle decrease and go to the bad should not admit that he is a
poor cowherd; but stranger still that a statesman when he causes
the citizens to decrease and go to the bad, should feel no shame nor
think himself a poor statesman."[1]

Considering the circumstances, this little homily seems a rather
tepid protest. According to Xenophon's *Hellenica,* Critias and
his associates murdered fifteen hundred Athenians during their
brief eight months of rule, "almost more" than the Spartans had
killed in the final decade of the Peloponnesian war.[2] That same
figure is reported by Aristotle in his treatise on the Athenian
constitution. Aristotle says that after getting rid of the democrats,
the Thirty turned against "the better classes" and "put to death
those of outstanding wealth or birth or reputation" to get potential sources of opposition out of the way and plunder their
property.[3]

Xenophon says Socrates' remark was reported to the dictators
and led to a confrontation in which Socrates had a chance to show
himself a more outspoken critic of the regime. He was summoned
to appear before Critias and Charicles, the two members of the
Thirty assigned the task of revising the laws of Athens for the new
regime. They showed him the text of a new law forbidding the

teaching of the *techne logon,* or art of reasoned discourse, "and forbade him to hold conversation with the young."

They were not just forbidding random conversation with the young but telling Socrates he could no longer go on with the characteristic mode of philosophic teaching that Socrates had initiated, and on which at least two of the Thirty, Critias and Charmides, had once sharpened their wits as his students. The stage was set for an eloquent defense of his rights as a teacher and a citizen, and for Socrates to tell them what he thought of their lawlessness.

Instead, Socrates asked, "May I question you, in case I do not understand any point in your orders?"

"You may," said they.

"Well, now," said he, "I am ready to obey the laws. But lest I unwillingly transgress through ignorance, I want clear directions from you. Do you think that the art of words [*techne logon*] from which you bid me abstain is associated with sound or unsound reasoning? For if with sound then clearly I must abstain from sound reasoning: but if with unsound, clearly I must try to reason soundly."

"Since you are ignorant, Socrates," said Charicles in an angry tone, "we will put our order into language easier to understand. You may not hold any converse [*dialegesthai*] whatever with the young."

"Well, then," said Socrates, "that there may be no question raised about my obedience, please fix the age limit below which a man is to be accounted young."

"So long," replied Charicles, "as he is not permitted to sit in the Council, because as yet he lacks wisdom. You shall not converse with anyone who is under thirty."

"Suppose I want to buy something, am I not even to ask the price if the seller is under thirty?"

"Oh, yes," said Charicles, "you may in such cases. But the fact is, Socrates, you are in the habit of asking questions to which you know the answer: so that is what you are not to do."

Socrates wants to know whether he must keep off his favorite subjects of "Justice, Holiness and so forth?"

"Indeed, yes," said Charicles, "and cowherds, too: else *you* may find the cattle decrease."[4]

So on that veiled threat this somewhat less than heroic confrontation ended.

What we have here is a mini-trial before two key members of the Thirty, the analogue of Socrates' trial four years later before the democracy. The contrast in the demeanor of Socrates is striking. There is none of the defiance he showed before the court of the restored democracy.

Xenophon is trying hard to show that Socrates was no supporter of Critias and the Thirty. It would have strengthened the case to be able to say that, at least secretly, Socrates went on teaching the young, and fulfilling his mission, despite the Thirty.

We are not told whether this confrontation occurred before or after Socrates refused the order to take part in the arrest and execution of Leon of Salamis. We are not told whether it occurred before or after the execution of the moderate leader Theramenes.

But the regime was marked from the beginning by lawlessness, and lynch mob methods of repression. We have no reason to believe that Socrates in any way approved the illegality and cruelty of the regime. But it is disappointing that he did not speak out forcefully against them, nor use his influence with his old friend and pupil Critias to bring him back to the paths of virtue. If Socrates had done so, he would have become a hero of the resistance and there would have been no trial.

But all we have in Xenophon's apologetic account is Socrates asking the dictators whether he must abstain from talking about "Justice, Holiness and so forth." Amid so many instances of injustice and "unholiness," all that seems to concern Socrates is his familiar search for absolute definitions of his favorite topics. He stayed in the city to the end. He who was prepared to die in his animosity to democracy was only lukewarm in his opposition to the Thirty.

We are still left, however, with a puzzling question: Why doesn't Plato in his *Apology* have Socrates cite the law against the teaching of the *techne logon* to prove that he was himself a victim of repression by the Thirty?

There is of course no way to answer that question with certainty. But some reasonable surmise is possible. In the first place, Xenophon's account of how the law came to be enacted by Critias sounds like gossip of a very low order. Xenophon says Socrates — in the pederastic society of Athens — provoked the enmity of Critias before the days of the dictatorship by criticizing the way Critias was wooing the youth Euthydemus.

Socrates said Critias' behavior was "unbecoming in a gentleman," and when Critias paid no heed, Socrates "exclaimed in the presence of Euthydemus and many others, 'Critias seems to have the feelings of a pig: he can no more keep away from Euthydemus than pigs can help rubbing themselves against stones.' " Such was the chitchat of the Athenian jet set.

According to Xenophon, Critias "bore a grudge against Socrates for this; and . . . when drafting laws" with Charicles, "he . . . inserted a clause which made it illegal" to teach the *techne logon*. "It was," Xenophon says, "a calculated insult to Socrates."[5]

Perhaps. But a more reasonable view is that the Thirty were doing their best to limit the rights of citizenship to as few as possible. They tried even to keep this narrow electorate from any real power. They must have felt — much like their Spartan protectors and the patricians later in republican Rome — hostile to teachers of rhetoric, argument, and philosophy. They did not want the citizenry to learn arts which would equip them for participation in government. They hated popular assemblies and the arts of public debate. They must have seen the *techne logon* as potentially subversive, and outlawed it.

That would have made it an all the more effective point for the defense in the trial of Socrates. It would have established a bond of sympathy between the restored democrats and the nonconformist philosopher, as common sufferers under the despotism.

Why does Plato leave it unmentioned? Perhaps it would have been embarrassing for Plato to make a point of this ban on the *techne logon* when he himself in the *Republic* also severely restricted the teaching of the dialectic in his own sketch of an ideal society. And for the very same reason: to keep power absolute and in the hands of a very few "philosopher kings."

Plato was about twenty-five when the Thirty seized power. But no lessons are drawn from their regime in the Platonic dialogues; it is never discussed or even mentioned. Perhaps it was too painful a memory. Critias, as we know, was his cousin and Charmides his uncle. There is only one brief reference to the Thirty in the entire Platonic canon, and that turns up in the *Seventh Letter,* the most interesting of them and the one most often attributed to Plato himself.

The letter purports to be written many years later and says that some of the Thirty were "relatives and acquaintances," but does not mention Critias or Charmides by name. It does say that they "invited me at once to join them, thinking it would be congenial." There is no explanation of why they thought it would be congenial to Plato, but the letter says the Thirty had established themselves "as absolute rulers" (*autokratores* or autocrats).

"The feelings I then experienced, owing to my youth," Plato explains, "were in no way surprising; for I imagined that they would administer the State by leading it out of an unjust way of life into a just way." This implies that he was at first inclined to join them.

Plato says he was soon disillusioned. "I saw how these men within a short time caused men to look back on the former government as a golden age."[6] Actually the original does not say golden age but "golden *politeia,*" i.e., polity, or political system.

This final phrase, and this startling admission, may indicate that the letter was not written by Plato. For there is no evidence anywhere else in the Platonic canon that the terrible events under the Thirty made him think more kindly about the restraints which democracy imposed on rulers, or led him to doubt the virtues of absolutism.

Certainly those events cast no shadow over his recollections of Critias and Charmides. They appear in the Platonic dialogues surrounded by a kind of golden haze. Nowhere are political lessons drawn from their brief season of power. Charmides — in the dialogue which bears his name — appears as a beautiful and gifted youth whom an enchanted Socrates interrogates to see whether his soul is as lovely as his body.

Critias is an honored figure in the same dialogue. Its goal is a perfect definition — as usual, unattained — of *sophrosyne,* moderation, a virtue as it turned out in which both men needed instruction. Socrates, ever so delicately, may be hinting as much at the very end of the dialogue when he warns the young man that "if once you set about doing anything and use force, no one will be able to withstand you."[7] But Theramenes, the real paragon of moderation in Aristotle's account of 411 and 404 and a hero in Xenophon's history, never appears in the Platonic canon, almost as if Plato could not bear even to mention his name.

Critias is a revered figure in three other dialogues of Plato — the *Protagoras,* the *Timaeus,* and the *Critias* — and in a fourth and inferior dialogue, the *Eryxias,* now generally regarded as the work of some follower of Plato. Whether genuine or not, it shows that Critias continued to be seen through reverent eyes in the Platonic schools.[8]

That reverence for Critias — so unlike the general abhorrence of him and the Thirty in the fourth century B.C. — must have been fostered in Plato's academy by two of the most beguiling dialogues of Plato's old age, the *Timaeus* and the *Critias.* In these utopian fantasies, the name of Critias is invested with antique venerability, as if they were an exercise in political rehabilitation.

In the *Timaeus* we encounter for the first time the legend of Atlantis, a fabulous vanished land in the Atlantic ocean beyond the pillars of Hercules. The story may have been developed by Plato from some earlier folktale. The story it tells is Plato's version of the Creation, and its mystic visions fascinated medieval Europe, where it was the only work of Plato really known (in a Latin abridgment by Chalcidice) until the fall of Constantinople to the Turks brought Greek scholars as refugees to Western Europe, and with them the whole of the Platonic canon.*

---

* Another exception among the dialogues may be the *Meno,* which seems to have become known in the West during the twelfth century.

But we are not concerned here with the still enchanting theology of the *Timaeus* but with its political purposes. Just as Critias had set out to transform the nature of Athenian society, so Plato in the *Timaeus* and the *Critias* set out to transform Greek history and Athenian political ideology. In this endeavor Plato used a Critias as a mouthpiece. The dictator's name was linked with a new myth designed to accomplish in ideology what Critias had failed to achieve in action. This was Plato, the philosophic revolutionary and master propagandist, at work rewriting history.

Plato's purpose was twofold. Athenian democracy drew inspiration from two legendary victories. One was its role in saving Hellenic civilization in the Persian wars, represented in Herodotus and in Aeschylus as the victory of free men over despotism, a tribute to the energizing value of democracy in stimulating martial valor, by giving men something worth fighting for.

The other was the ancient Athenian tradition, preserved by Plutarch in his *Life of Theseus,* about the founder of Athens, that he was already, even in that archaic time, a democrat. According to Plutarch, Theseus succeeded in uniting the scattered independent towns of Attica into the one city-state of Athens by mobilizing both the *demos* as well as the landowners against the petty "kings" who had ruled them, by promising the aristocrats "government without a king" and the common people the right to participate in the government. "The common folk and the poor," Plutarch relates, "quickly answered to his summons."[9] Theseus proposed that "he should only be commander in war and guardian of the laws, while in all else everyone should be on an equal footing."

This was political mythology. Democracy in any real sense was not won until centuries later. The Athenian democrats also liked to cite the famous Catalogue of Ships in Homer to show that in the expedition against Troy, the Athenians — and they alone — were already referred to as a *demos,* with the connotation of a self-governing people.[10]

In the *Timaeus* and the *Critias,* Plato came forward with an authoritarian substitute for these democratic myths. Plato's spokesman is a character named Critias. But scholars are still debating whether this is the same Critias who ruled Athens under the Thirty or the grandfather for whom he was named. Perhaps Plato, a master of subtlety and ambiguity, deliberately left the identification vague. He was writing in the fourth century B.C., when Critias was regarded as a monster, and readers might be startled to hear him introduced as an elder statesman. A touch of obscurity was politic.

Socrates, in introducing Critias, says it is beyond his own powers to describe how such an ideal state could be brought into being. He says this requires a statesman and invites Critias to take up this task since "as all of us here know" Critis is "no novice" either in the theory or the practice of politics.[11]

The conversation in the *Timaeus* is presented as a sequel to the *Republic*. The myth of Atlantis as told by Critias is intended to invest that sketch of an ideal society with a halo of antiquity. It was to make the Republic appear not as a fundamental break with Athenian tradition but as a reincarnation nine thousand years later — the number itself had a mystic Pythagorean significance as a millennial square of the number 3 — of a hitherto unknown Golden Age of Athens. Plato's political fantasy was thus portrayed as the true Athens reborn.

The legend of Atlantis is told as a story handed down in a distinguished and aristocratic family — the family of Plato's mother — from a grandfather named Critias, who heard it from *his* grandfather Critias, who heard it from his father, Dropides. And Dropides, according to the *Timaeus,* heard it from Solon, to whom it was revealed by the priests of Egypt when Solon visited that already ancient land.

This final touch linked Plato's ideal of an authoritarian caste society to the name of Solon, whom Athens revered as the founder of democracy. This was a master stroke of propaganda for Plato's New Order. Critias says that Solon might have tried to apply in Athens what he learned in Egypt. But Solon, Critias says, was forced to lay these revelations "aside owing to the seditions and all the other evils he found here [i.e., in Athens] on his return."[12]

It was this rigid caste structure in the Golden Age of Athens, Critias explains, that enabled Athens to save Hellenic civilization from subjugation by Atlantis. This was the Platonic substitute for the epic of the Persian wars in which Athens, because of its democracy, was able to save Greece from Persian dominion.

As an antidote to this political fairy tale, we may turn again to the sober pages of Aristotle's *Constitution of Athens*. There we learn the reason for the "seditions," as Critias stigmatizes them, which greeted Solon on his return to Athens from Egypt. The poor of Attica had literally become the slaves of the rich through debt peonage. Under the existing mortgage law, borrowers could impose servitude on the persons and families of defaulting debtors. Aristotle relates that Solon, to restore social stability and establish a modicum of social justice, wiped out the existing debt and forbade debt peonage. Had Solon been impressed by what he saw in Egypt, debt peonage would have provided an opportune means for establishing a similar serfdom in Attica. Critias lost his life in an effort to put the Platonic ideal into practice.

The counterpart of the Atlantis story is another of Plato's myths, the most famous of them all: the "noble lie" of the *Republic*. This, too, is antidemocratic. Its purpose was to inculcate a sense of ineradicable inferiority in the lower and middle classes and "program" them, as we would now say, for submission to the philosopher kings. What Critias tried to do by terror, Plato sought to achieve by "brain-washing," to adopt another neologism.

In the great debate over the use of terror between the hard-liner Critias and the moderate Theramenes in Xenophon's *Hellenica*, Critias defends terror with pitiless logic. When his council shows signs of being swayed by Theramenes' argument for moderation, Critias argues coldly: "If anyone among you thinks that more people than is fitting are being put to death, let him reflect that where governments are changed these things always take place."

This has been the complacent alibi of all dictators in our time from Mussolini to Mao Tse-tung. But Critias, with unusual candor and objectivity, took the argument a step farther. Critias said there were so many executions during his rule in Athens because the enemies of the dictatorship were so numerous. Not only, he said, was Athens the most populous of the Greek city-states but its common people "have been bred up in a condition of freedom for the longest time."[13]

How to disarm and disfranchise an Athenian citizenry accustomed for two centuries to equality and free debate, without widespread and ruthless liquidations? This was the icy question with which Critias sought to justify not only what he had done to the democrats but now the execution of his moderate colleague and rival Theramenes. This was the debut of totalitarianism.

Plato, seeking for a transformation fully as fundamental, tried to figure out in the quiet of his academy how a free citizenry might be inured to a new bondage. His solution was an elaborate system of state-imposed ideological indoctrination by which the "masses" from childhood would be accustomed to think of themselves as inferior. They were to be taught that they were born — and must remain — unfree and unequal. They would then, Plato theorized, willingly obey their self-appointed betters.

This is the noble lie, which Plato broaches through the mouth of Socrates in the third book of the *Republic*. His candor matches that of Critias. "How, then," Socrates asks, "might we contrive one of those opportune falsehoods of which we were just now speaking, so as by one noble lie to persuade if possible the rulers themselves, but failing that the rest of the city?" Plato assumes that the rulers, being philosophers, may gulp at their own propaganda but that the *hoi polloi* might eventually be brought to swallow it. His noble lie is that men are intrinsically divided into four classes: the philosophic ruling few, the military caste that enforces their will, the middle class of traders and craftsmen, and — at the bottom — the common laborers and tillers of the soil.

Plato's Socrates says that while they are in fact brothers, born of the same mother earth, they must be led to think of themselves as made of different metals. "While all of you in the city are brothers," Socrates explains, "we will say in our tale, yet God in fashioning those of you who are fitted to hold rule mingled gold in their generation, for which reason they are the most precious." The noble lie will teach that the "Guardians," or military caste, are also compounded of a precious metal, though of lesser value —

silver. The main body of the citizenry, the many, will be seen as made of base metal, iron and brass.[14]

The casual reader may miss an important point here, especially in the Loeb. This is an admirable edition, richly annotated, but colored by the devout Christian Platonism of its translator, the great American classicist Paul Shorey. In the passage just quoted, his translation speaks of the Guardians or military caste as "the helpers." The Greek word Plato used is *epikouroi*, which can indeed mean "helpers." But in its common military usage *epikouroi* meant mercenary troops *as distinct from citizen soldiers*.

Plato's purpose would have been obvious to an ancient Greek. The basis of democracy in the *polis* was the citizen soldier. The citizen in arms not only defended the city's freedom but could use his arms to defend his own.*

In Athens in 411 and in 404, the antidemocratic party disarmed both the poor and the middle class in order to enforce its rule. Critias himself depended largely on a garrison of Spartan occupation troops. They were his *epikouroi*. It was to pay these troops that Critias expropriated rich resident aliens like Leon of Salamis. The purpose of a military caste in Plato's *Republic,* as in ancient Egypt, was to keep the people disarmed and unable to resist their masters.

In another passage Socrates calls the military caste *phylakes,* or guardians, and says they are to act "as guardians in the full sense of the word, watchers against foemen without and friends within, so that the latter shall not wish and the former shall not be able to work harm" to the ideal state.

Note that the "watchers" are to act against discontent within as well as enemies without. The *phylakes* or *epikouroi* would be not only an occupying army but the internal enforcers of a police state. This is the dark side of Plato's utopia. Here his theorizing and Critias' practice converge.

This is not the only point at which they agree. Plato did not stop

---

* This idea lives on in the United States Bill of Rights, which guarantees the right to bear arms. This provision is abused today by the gun lobby but it reflected an experience still fresh in the mind of those who had made the Revolution. It was the private possession of arms that enabled the American colonists to defy the British crown.

at organized deception — "indoctrination." He was as ready as his cousin to use force in his dream of creating a New Order, and a New — and more submissive — Man.

In the *Republic* and the other Platonic utopias, if the recalcitrant refused to be persuaded — or at least pretend conformity — they were to be eliminated just as ruthlessly as was the opposition under Critias. The Platonic canon offers three examples. The first is from the *Statesman,* where Plato's ideal is absolute monarchy. In this dialogue of Plato's later years, Plato speaks — as he does again later in the *Laws* — through the mouth of "A Stranger," obviously Plato himself. The Stranger puts forward the Socratic analogy of the physician as "one who knows" and therefore has a right to rule in his relation to his patient. He draws a remorseless lesson in government from it.

The Stranger says that the physician cures us whether "against our will or with our will, by cutting us or burning us," whether "by written rules or without them," "purging us or reducing us in some other way." The word *purging* here seems to have some of the sinister connotation it has taken on in our time.

The Stranger says the physician can inflict pain so long as he operates "by art or science" and makes his patients "better than they were before." The ideal king is to rule in the same fashion and by the same rationale. The Stranger calls this "the only right definition of the rule of the physician *or of any other rule whatsoever.*"[15] The meaning is that the only true rule is absolute rule, requiring absolute submission.

This passage defining "the only true rule" seems to be the only place in the Platonic dialogues where we are told that we have finally achieved an "only right definition." Such exact and absolute definition is the only true form of *episteme,* or true knowledge. Plato feels he has proven that absolutism is the only legitimate form of government. Since it is the one and only legitimate form of rule, it has the right to kill or banish its subjects "for their own good."

Of course, like all arguments from analogy, this has its fallacies. The physician is not the absolute ruler of the patient. If the patient thinks his treatment harmful, he can get himself another physician.

If he feels that he has been harmed, he can sue for malpractice. The physician then and now was also subject under the Hippocratic oath to opprobrium and loss of professional standing for improper conduct. The physician, unlike the absolute ruler, was not his own judge and jury, ready to decide that whatever he did was *ipso facto* scientific.

As for justice, where was the balance to be struck between what was good for the state or community and what was good for the individual? Law, throughout the ages, has mingled in its delicate scales concern for both. But for Plato — the archetypal theorist of totalitarianism — it was the state, the abstraction, that mattered. It was this which justified the killing or banishment of individuals whose only crime was that they did not fit into the New Order.

This comes out strongly in our second example of Plato's ruthlessness in the pursuit of perfection: the striving for racial or caste purity in the eugenics of the *Republic,* along with its bizarre proposal for community of wives and children by the Guardians.[16]

Plato would breed human beings as one breeds animals. To improve "the herd of the Guardians," their procreation was to be strictly regulated by the state and their mating arranged, presumably, by lot. But the lot was secretly to be "fixed" by the philosopher kings for eugenic purposes so "that the best men cohabit with the best women in as many cases as possible and the worst with the worst in the fewest . . . if the flock is to be as perfect as possible."[17]

How could this be kept secret? How could it be enforced against the sexual jealousies it would provoke? What is to keep rebellious Guardians, who alone have the arms, from ousting the philosopher king or kings? None of these practical questions are addressed. Here utopianism escalated to lunacy.

Another example is, if anything, even more Mad Hatter. It appears at the end of the seventh book of the *Republic,* and it could have been an uproarious scene in a satire on Plato.

Cousin Critias exiled first democrats and then moderates in an effort to remake Athens. Plato goes him one better. Plato has Socrates suggest that "the best and speediest way" to pave the way for the ideal city is to exile everyone over the age of ten, and leave the children to be remolded by the philosophers.

Socrates is anxious to prove that the ideal he has been unfolding "is not altogether a day-dream. It is," Socrates says, "in a way possible," when "genuine philosophers, many or one," become "masters of the state" and "regarding justice as the chief and the one indispensable thing" proceed to "reorganize and administer their city."[18] His bedazzled interlocutor asks what this way is.

"All inhabitants above the age of ten," Socrates replies, "they will send out into the fields, and they will take over the children, remove them from the manners and habits of their parents, and bring them up in their own customs and laws which will be much as we have described."

Socrates terms this the speediest and easiest way such a city could be established "and bring most benefit to the people." His compliant interlocutor readily agrees that this is indeed "much the easiest way." No hard questions are raised. It is amazing how little dialectic there is at such crucial moments in Plato.

An easy method? How would a handful of philosophers nurse-maid a small army of children? Only a bachelor like Plato who never diapered a baby could possibly envisage this as a serious prospect. How to prevent anguished and enraged parents from coming back at night from "the fields" — as Plato delicately phrases it — to kill these philosophic loonies, and recover their children and their city? How could Plato's Socrates speak in one breath of justice as "the chief and the one indispensable thing" and then propose to overturn a whole city and condemn a whole generation to such suffering, without their consent and against their will?

Was Plato grossly misrepresenting the real views of his teacher? Or was there an umbilical link between it and the Socratic disdain for democracy? Did Plato feel it developed logically from the Socratic view of the human community as a herd, to be "thinned out" for its own improvement by its wise shepherd and natural king, "the one who knows"?

Most devout Platonic commentators avert their eyes from this passage in the *Republic*. Alan Bloom, one of the few who dare to

confront its egregious absurdities, takes refuge in the theory that
it is really a satire by Plato on his own utopianism! This might be
a plausible explanation were it not for the fact that in the *Statesman*,
the *Laws*, and the *Timaeus-Critias* one finds similar blueprints for
the ideal state. Plato could hardly have spent his life spoofing
himself.

The final horror in any anthology of Platonic statesmanship is
the "clean slate" metaphor in the sixth book of the *Republic*. Plato
prepares us for it by having Socrates paint a glowing portrait of
the qualities that legitimize the philosopher's claim to absolute
kingship. Socrates describes a true philosopher as "the man whose
mind is truly fixed on eternal realities." He thus "has no leisure to
turn his eyes downward upon the petty affairs of men" but "fixes
his gaze on the things of the eternal and unchanging order" to be
discerned in the heavens and the movements of the stars. Thus the
philosopher "will himself become orderly and divine in the
measure permitted to men."[19] Being godlike, the philosopher
may, if he is so minded, resume the work of Creation and fashion
a New Man.

Socrates puts all this in the form of a question to his interlocutor.
"If then," Socrates asks, "some compulsion is laid upon him to
practice stamping on the plastic matter of human nature in public
and private the patterns that he visions there [in the heavens], and
not merely to mould and fashion himself, do you think he will
prove a poor craftsman of sobriety and justice and all forms of
ordinary civic virtue?"[20]

This is the kind of question which in any court of law even the
sleepiest judge would strike from the record as leading and loaded.
An irreverent bystander might have asked Socrates at this point
whether a man who had no time "to turn his eyes downward upon
the petty affairs of men" was an ideal choice to rearrange those
affairs and decide how to refashion them. But the Platonic
interlocutor, of course, reverently assents. What should have been
challenged, and tested by argument, is simply assumed.

Socrates follows up with another loaded question, this one
pointed toward an instant conversion of the democrats to his
celestial visions. "But if the multitude become aware," Socrates

asks, "that what we are saying of the philosopher is true, will they still be harsh with the philosophers, and will they distrust our statement that no city could ever be blessed unless its lineaments were traced by artists who used the heavenly model?"

Socrates explains that the philosopher king or kings "will take the city and the characters of men, as they might a tablet, and first wipe it clean," but Socrates admits this is "no easy task." Indeed, "to wipe the slate clean" is what Critias tried to do with Athens, and the difficulty of the task was his excuse for the cruelties that his revolutionary goal compelled him to commit.

Socrates does not tell us nor is he asked to explain how the difficulties are to be surmounted. "But at any rate you know," Socrates adds, "that this would be their [the philosopher kings] first point of difference from ordinary reformers that they would refuse to take in hand either individual or state . . . before they either received a clean slate or themselves made it clean." Their power must be absolute and unquestioned.

Plato's Socrates seems to think all this might be made acceptable to the Athenians. Are we making an impression, he asks, on those who "were advancing to attack us with might and main? Can we convince them, that such a political artist of character and such a painter exists and are they now in a gentler mood when they hear what we are saying?" The answer? Again without argument, "Much gentler."[21]

It was fortunate for Socrates that at the time of his trial the *Republic* had not yet been written and could not be read to the judges. If this was indeed Socratic teaching, or its effect on a gifted youth like Plato, it would have been even harder to convince the court that Socrates had not turned some of its most gifted youth into dangerous revolutionaries. The fresh memory of the Thirty would have been a reminder of what inhumanity lurked behind that bland phrase about "wiping the slate clean."

Chapter 13

THE PRINCIPAL ACCUSER

༥༜Ꮇ

O F THE THREE ACCUSERS of Socrates, the only prominent in Athens was Anytus. The other two, Meletus and Lycon, were obscure men of whom little is known beyond what Socrates himself tells us of them in the *Apology*. Socrates asserts that Lycon joined the prosecution on behalf of the orators, Meletus for the poets, and Anytus for the craftsmen and political leaders.[1] That, if true, meant that all the leading citizens of the city were lined up against Socrates. Of the three accusers the only one who counted was Anytus. Lycon himself was not known as an orator nor Meletus as a poet. But Anytus was a wealthy tanner who had played a leading role in the armed resistance which overthrew Critias and restored the democracy. Yet in the *Apology* we hear only from Meletus, who proves a bit dim-witted and an easy pushover for Socrates.

We never hear from Anytus in the *Apology*, and Critias is never mentioned, but they are contrapuntal figures behind the trial. Critias, though dead, was in a sense the chief witness for the prosecution, the foremost example of what association with Socrates had done to "corrupt" the gilded youth of Athens and turn it against the democracy. The high repute of Anytus and the bad repute of Critias were the chief obstacles to an acquittal.

Anytus is sometimes portrayed as a fanatical democrat. Indeed, that invaluable work, the British Open University's *Source Book on Socrates*, even describes Anytus as "evidently a left-wing politician."[2] There might have been some excuse for describing

Anytus as an extremist democrat before Aristotle's *Constitution of Athens* was dug up out of the hot and preserving sands of Egypt in 1880. But there Anytus is listed not as a democrat at all but as a lieutenant of the moderate leader Theramenes, who in both 411 and 404 favored the disfranchisement of the poor but turned against the oligarchic extremists in both revolutions when they began to disfranchise — and disarm — the middle class as well as the *demos*. Anytus was one of those rich middle-class leaders who disliked full democracy but soon found it preferable to a narrow aristocratic dictatorship — and much safer for life and property.[3]

It should have been clear even before Aristotle's lost treatise was discovered, that Anytus was a leading moderate. This was already evident in Xenophon's *Hellenica*. There in the great debate between Critias and Theramenes before the latter's execution, Theramenes twice cites Anytus as an example of the wealthy moderates whom Critias was driving into opposition.

Anytus suffered heavy losses when his property was seized by the dictators after he went into opposition. After the restoration of the democracy, Anytus won respect because he did not use his political influence to sue for recovery of these lost properties. Such suits were barred by the amnesty, and Anytus abided honorably by its terms. The evidence of this is in a case about two years before the trial of Socrates where the orator Isocrates declared that "Thrasybulus and Anytus, men of the greatest influence in the city, although they have been robbed of large sums of money [under the Thirty] and know who gave in lists of their goods [to the dictators], nevertheless are not so brazen as to bring suit against them or to bring up old grudges against them; on the contrary, even if . . . they have greater power than others to accomplish their ends, yet in matters covered by the covenant [i.e., the amnesty] at least they see fit to put themselves on terms of equality with the other citizens."[4]

Anytus himself was not just a master tanner who suddenly became a general in the resistance. Anytus was already a general in the Peloponnesian war; we know he was sent with thirty triremes in 409 B.C. to take the Spartan stronghold of Pylos — the modern Navarino — but bad weather thwarted the expedition.[5]

There is a legend that Anytus came to a bad end. It turns up for the first time about five centuries after the trial of Socrates in the *Lives of the Philosophers* by Diogenes Laertius. He reports that after the death of Socrates "the Athenians felt such remorse" that they turned on his accusers, executed Meletus, drove Anytus and Lycon into exile, and erected "a bronze statue" of Socrates.

Diogenes embellishes the tale. "Not only in the case of Socrates," Diogenes insists, "but in very many others, the Athenians repented in this way." This is how they acted (so he says) after fining Homer fifty drachmas as a madman![6] This alone is enough to mark the whole story as invention. Had such an event occurred, had the poet been so treated in the most cultivated city of Greece, the scandal would have reverberated in the literature of antiquity. And if Athens had repented and erected a statue to Socrates, we would certainly have heard about it from Plato and Xenophon.

Insofar as Anytus is concerned, Diogenes gives two different versions of his fate, one in his life of Socrates, the other an equally engaging but contradictory account in his life of Antisthenes. There Diogenes says Antisthenes, the oldest disciple of Socrates, "is held responsible for the exile of Anytus and the execution of Meletus." He says that Antisthenes, some time after the death of Socrates, "fell in with some youths from Pontus whom the fame of Socrates had brought to Athens." Antisthenes "led them off to see Anytus, whom he ironically declared to be wiser than Socrates. Whereupon these youths "with much indignation drove Anytus out of the city."[7] In the other version Anytus was exiled by the Athenians, and later driven out of Heraclea of Pontus when he went there seeking refuge. To this the fourth-century-A.D. orator Themistius added a piquant detail of his own. He said the people of Heraclea were so furious over the execution of Socrates that they stoned Anytus to death on arrival.[8]

These legends reflect the awe with which Plato's genius had invested the memory of his master by the time of the Roman empire. The fact is that we know from an unimpeachable contemporary source that more than a decade after the trial of Socrates Anytus was still a leading figure in Athenian politics and had been elected to one of the most important offices in the city. The evidence appears in an oration by Lysias called *Against the Corn-Dealers.* Lysias was himself a friend of Socrates.[9]

The speech was delivered at a trial that took place about 386 B.C., some thirteen years after the trial of Socrates. The corn dealers were accused of violating laws that protected the supply and price of grain from price-fixing conspiracies. The laws were enforced by municipal inspectors known as *sitophylakes,* or guardians of the grain. The Athenians were not blind to the realities of a "free market." The inspectors were included among the *archons,* or leading magistrates of the city, and as one of the inspectors Anytus testified for the prosecution.[10]

I, too, believe that there should have been a revulsion against the verdict that condemned Socrates. But there is no sign of it in the surviving literature of the century after his death. Socrates did not become a cult figure outside the Platonic academy until long after his death. There is no cult of Socrates in Aristotle. He has many references to Socrates, but they are rather astringent and he makes no mention of the trial.

The theater was the chief barometer of popular sentiment in Athens. But one searches in vain among the many fragments of the tragic and comic plays after the trial for any note of sorrow or vindication. There is one fragment of a lost play by Euripides called *Palamedes* in which he is supposed — by Diogenes Laertius — to have upbraided the people of Athens for what they did to Socrates. It says, "Ye have slain, have slain, the all-wise, the innocent, the Muses' nightingale." But Socrates is not mentioned by name and, whatever his other virtues, he was hardly a nightingale of the Muses — an appellation for a lyric poet. Even Diogenes notes regretfully that Philochorus, the most famous of the fourth-century Athenian chroniclers, "asserts that Euripides died before Socrates,"[11] so the fragment Diogenes cites must have referred to someone else.[12]

Nor is there any reference to the trial in the works of Demosthenes, the century's greatest defender of what we would call civil liberties. The first and earliest surviving reference to the trial in the century after it, except for Plato and Xenophon, is in a famous speech — *Against Timarchus* — by the orator Aeschines, the rival of Demosthenes. The speech was delivered during a trial in 345 B.C. as part of the lifelong bitter duel between the two leading orators. In it Socrates is mentioned briefly in passing.

Timarchus, the man Aeschines was prosecuting, was a protégé of Demosthenes. Aeschines cited the verdict against Socrates, not as a dreadful example of civil liberty violated, but as a salutary precedent to be followed in the case of Timarchus. Aeschines said an Athenian jury "put to death Socrates the sophist . . . because he was shown to have been the teacher of Critias, one of the Thirty who put down the democracy."[13] Aeschines won his case. The speech of Aeschines shows that a half century after the trial of Socrates the popular view was that the old "sophist" got what he deserved because he was the teacher of the hated Critias. Otherwise it would have been impolitic for Aeschines to cite the verdict against Socrates as a precedent.

Something other than politics seems to have aggravated relations between Anytus and Socrates, a disagreement over the education of Anytus' son. According to Xenophon's *Apology*, Socrates believed that Anytus had initiated the prosecution because "I said that he ought not to confine his son's education to hides" (i.e., to the family's tanning business). Tanning was a vulgar occupation in the eyes of Athenian aristocrats like Xenophon and Plato. But it was unlikely that a middle-class political leader like Anytus would have confined his son's education "to hides," as Socrates put it, for that would have made it impossible for the son to follow in the father's footsteps and take a leading part in civic affairs.

It appears that there was a rivalry between Socrates and Anytus for the younger man's devotion. "At one time," Socrates reveals in Xenophon's *Apology*, "I had a brief association with the son of Anytus, and I thought him not lacking in firmness of spirit."[14] Socrates does not tell us what broke off the brief association.

In the *Meno* Plato describes an angry confrontation between Socrates and Anytus. Socrates — who usually sneers at the sophists — now defends them. Apparently Anytus in the *Meno* considers Socrates just another "sophist." When Anytus appears, Socrates and Meno are discussing the education in virtue of the sons of famous men, and Socrates challenges Anytus to name one famous man who had proved a good teacher by transmitting his virtues to his sons. "Give us a name," Socrates says, "anyone you please."*

"Why mention a particular one?" Anytus replies. "Any Athenian gentleman, he [the son] comes across, . . . will do him more good, if he will do as he is bid, then the sophists . . . or does it not seem to you that we have had many good men in this city?"[15] He breaks off the discussion with a warning. "Socrates," he says, "I consider you are too apt to speak ill of people. I, for one, if you will take my advice, would warn you to be careful: in most cities it is probably easier to do people harm than good, and particularly in this one."[16] It sounds like a threat.

In Xenophon's *Apology,* after the trial Socrates displays his own animus with a bitter prophecy. "I predict," Xenophon quotes him as saying, "that he [the son of Anytus] will not continue in the servile occupation that his father has provided for him." Socrates goes on to predict that "through want of a worthy adviser" the son of Anytus "will fall into some disgraceful propensity and will surely go far in the career of vice." "In saying this," Xenophon goes on, Socrates "was not mistaken; the young man, delighting in wine, never left off drinking night or day, and at last turned out worth nothing to his city, his friends or himself. So Anytus, even though dead," Xenophon triumphantly concludes, "still enjoys an evil repute for his son's mischievous education and his own hard-heartedness."[17]

---

* Is it unfair to add that none of Socrates' three sons ever amounted to much either?

This shows that Xenophon's *Apology* was written after the death of Anytus. Had Anytus been driven out of Athens by a remorseful citizenry after the trial and met his death at the hands of an indignant mob in a city where he sought refuge, Xenophon would certainly have mentioned it.

One might add that Anytus was not unreasonable in withdrawing his son from Socratic tutelage. Anytus had reason to fear that his son might have been turned by Socrates against his father, taught to despise the family business, and converted by his aristocratic associates into a pro-Spartan snob and a supporter of the Thirty.

Chapter 14

HOW SOCRATES DID HIS BEST
TO ANTAGONIZE THE JURY

I N AN ATHENIAN criminal trial, the jury voted twice. The
first vote was on conviction or acquittal. Then if the verdict
was for conviction, it voted again on the penalty. The biggest
surprise at the trial of Socrates was how closely the jury was split
on the first and basic question. Despite the fresh memory of the
Thirty, the prestige of the chief accuser, and the growing realiza-
tion of how antidemocratic were the teachings of Socrates, the
jury seemed to have great trouble in making up its mind. A mere
shift of six percent on the jury and Socrates would have been
acquitted.

Socrates himself, as Plato tells us in the *Apology,* had expected
his conviction. That, in itself, Socrates told the jury, "was not a
surprise." What did surprise him was that so many voted for his
acquittal. It was not the mathematics of a mob verdict. Socrates
pointed out that "if only thirty votes had been cast the other way,
I should have been acquitted."[1] If a shift of thirty votes would
have meant acquittal, the 500–man jury must have been 280 votes
for conviction, 220 votes for acquittal. That would be a majority
of sixty. Thus if thirty jurors had shifted their vote from conviction to acquittal, the jury would have been split evenly with 250
votes on each side, and in Athens a tie vote was resolved in favor
of the accused.

Why was Socrates so surprised by the close vote for conviction?
The question is not answered in Plato's *Apology*. But if we turn to
Xenophon's *Apology* we get a clue. Xenophon says Socrates
wanted to be convicted and did his best to antagonize the jury.
Unfortunately the testimony of Xenophon's *Apology* is often

obscured by a mistranslated word. The word is *megalegoria,* which appears three times in the opening paragraph. Confusion is compounded because for reasons of stylistic grace and euphony translators tend to render the word differently each time.

To show what we mean we will take two standard translations. The older is the lovely eighteenth-century English version by Sarah Fielding, in her *Socratic Discourses.*[2] The second is the Loeb translation by O. J. Todd. The word *megalegoria* is compounded of two Greek roots, *megal* (as in our word *megalomania*), meaning big or great, and the verb *agoreuo,* to speak or address an assembly, an *agora.* There are two ways of understanding *megalegoria.* One is uncomplimentary: as "big talking," boastfulness, and arrogance. The other is complimentary: as a synonym for eloquence.

Both translators chose to read the word as complimentary. But this is inconsistent with the very point Xenophon was trying to make. He begins his account of the trial by saying that people were surprised by the *megalegoria* Socrates displayed in addressing his judges. The word, as we have said, appears three times in the opening passage. Sarah Fielding translated the word as (1) "wonderful courage and intrepidity," (2) "the loftiness of his style and the boldness of his speech," and (3) "the sublimity of his language." Todd in the Loeb version has (1) "the loftiness of his words," (2) "his lofty utterance," and (3) "the sublimity of his speech."

These complimentary translations are open to challenge from two points of view. One is consistency to context and the other is the use of the same word elsewhere in Xenophon and in Greek literature. We will begin with the first. The careful reader who goes back to this passage in any one of these translations will see its inconsistency with the context. Xenophon says that all those who had written about the trial of Socrates were struck by his *megalegoria* before his judges and thought it was *aphronestera.* The Liddell-Scott *Greek Lexicon* translates this as "senseless, witless, crazed, foolish." Again, both our translators agree. Fielding renders the word as "unbecoming and imprudent"; Todd, as "rather ill-considered."

But how could anyone describe *megalegoria* as *aphronestera* if *megalegoria* meant sublimity of expression or loftiness of discourse? Why would it be senseless or "imprudent" to speak in lofty terms to an Athenian jury — notoriously susceptible to eloquence? Xenophon insists that Socrates' *megalegoria* was not senseless at all but deliberate and calculated to achieve his purpose, which was to provoke rather than conciliate the jury.

Xenophon was not in Athens at the time of the trial. He says he based his account on what he was told later by Hermogenes, one of Socrates' closest disciples, who told Xenophon that he pleaded with Socrates to prepare an eloquent defense because the juries were so susceptible to oratory. "Do you not observe," Hermogenes asked Socrates, "that the Athenian courts have often been carried away by an eloquent speech and have condemned innocent men to death, and often on the other hand the guilty have been acquitted either because their plea aroused compassion or because their speech was witty?"

Socrates replied that he had twice tried to write such a speech but each time his *daimonion,* or guiding spirit, had intervened and dissuaded him. Socrates told Hermogenes that this divine inner voice advised him that it was better to die now before the ills of old age overtook him. That is why, Xenophon argues, his *megalegoria* was not at all "senseless." It would have been *aphronestera* only if he wanted an acquittal!

Socrates goes on to say, "If my years are prolonged, I know that the frailties of old age will inevitably be realized — that my vision must be less perfect and my hearing less keen, that I shall be slower to learn and more forgetful of what I have learned."

The Socratic strategy clearly was to lose not only the first vote on guilt or innocence but the second vote on the penalty. A conciliated jury, even if it found him guilty, might have imposed a fine, as asked for by the defense, instead of the death penalty demanded by the prosecution. Socrates wanted to die. "If I perceive my own decay and take to complaining," Socrates asks, "how could I any longer take pleasure in life?"

But how could Socrates — a philosopher — say there are no joys in one's declining years? That it is better to relinquish the gift of life because of old age's inconveniences? Socrates had a wife, children, disciples. Why was he so ready to abandon them? In the *Crito* and the *Phaedo,* his disciples raise much the same questions. Socrates' attitude seemed to them inexplicable and even unworthy, an abdication of moral responsibility. To reject the gift of life, unless in the throes of an incurable disease, seems the ultimate impiety.

Socrates even says that the trial is his opportunity to commit suicide pleasantly, by drinking hemlock, the Athenian mode of execution. Here are his own words as reported by Hermogenes to Xenophon: "If I am condemned now, it will clearly be my privilege to suffer a death that is adjudged by those who have superintended this matter to be not only the easiest but also the least irksome to one's friends."

"It was with good reason," Socrates concludes, "that the gods opposed my studying up my speech at the time when we held that by fair means or foul we must find some plea that would effect my acquittal."[3] Death was his choice, and he could obtain it only from an exasperated jury. He did not wish to charm them. The tone he adopted in his address to the jury was offensively boastful and arrogant. That is what *megalegoria* meant.

This reading of *megalegoria* is supported by a related Greek word that Xenophon uses near the close of his *Apology.* The word is *megalunein* — to exalt — and it is used there with the reflexive pronoun *eautos* — to extol oneself. Xenophon says, "And as for Socrates, by exalting himself before the court, he brought ill-will upon himself and made his conviction by the jury all the more certain."[4] So Xenophon's *Apology* ends on the same note with which it began.

That court of final judgment, the Liddell-Scott-Jones *Greek-English Lexicon,* defines *megalegoria* in Xenophon's *Apology* as "big talking" and couples this with a verse in Euripedes' *Children of Hercules* where the children have fled to Athens for asylum. When an arrogant herald from Argos demands their extradition, a chorus of "old men of Marathon" sings that Athens will not be frightened by the herald's *megalegoriaisi* (the dative plural), which LSJ translates as "haughtiness" but might also be "blusterings." The LSJ gives this pejorative connotation to other forms of the same term elsewhere in Xenophon and in other writers of his time. It defines the verb *megalegoreuo* as "to talk big, boast," citing three passages in other works of Xenophon and supplements these with a similar usage by Aeschylus in his *Seven Against Thebes*. It is not until half a millennium later, in Greek writers on rhetoric under the Roman empire, that *megalegoria* was used to mean elevated discourse or sublimity of expression.[5]

It is significant in this context that at two points in Plato's *Apology,* Socrates feels it necessary to deny that he is boasting. The Greek term he uses is a synonym for *megalegoria: mega legein.* The first word means big, the second to talk — to "talk big" or boast. That the *megalegorein* of Xenophon's *Apology* is synonymous with the *mega legein* in Plato was often pointed out in earlier schoolbook editions of the *Apology* when Greek and Latin here and abroad were more widely studied than they are today.

One of these schoolbook editions, W. S. Tyler's, in a note on this passage linked it directly to Xenophon's *Apology* and said, "*Mega legein* properly denotes boasting . . . it was the seeming *pride* and *arrogance* [italics in the original] of what he [Socrates] said, which, he feared, would give offence, and which did actually give offence to the judges." Tyler added that Xenophon "speaks of the *megalegoria* which all the *Apologies* ascribe to Socrates in his defense." Thus the Platonic account lends support to the Xenophontic.[6]

There is a significant word that turns up in both *Apologies* in connection with their references to Socratic boastfulness. That word is *thorubos*. It means a noise, especially the noise of a crowded assembly, whether as a murmur of approbation or as an angry "clamor, uproar, groaning" of disapproval.[7] Twice in both *Apologies* Socrates causes a *thorubos* — once when he claims that he, unlike ordinary men, possessed a private oracle or familiar spirit, his *daimonion,* and a second time when he says that the oracle at Delphi declared that there was no one wiser than Socrates.

In Xenophon's account Socrates offers proof of his private divine oracle. "That I do not lie," Socrates says, "I have the following proof: I have revealed to many of my friends the counsels which the god has given me, and in no instance has the event shown that I was mistaken."[8] Xenophon says that when the jurors heard this they "raised a clamor" (thorubos), some in disbelief, others in "jealousy at his receiving greater favours even from the gods than they." Socrates responded by provoking the jury even further, "so that those of you who feel so inclined may have still greater disbelief in my being honoured of the heavens." Then Socrates related that the oracle at Delphi had said of him "that no man was more free than I, or more just, or more prudent."

The reference to Delphi was hardly prudent. "The jurors, naturally enough," Xenophon says, "made a still greater tumult [thorubos] on hearing this statement."[9] Socrates looks more like a picador enraging a bull than a defendant trying to mollify a jury. Plato's account is subtler and more graceful. But it is in the end as boastful and provocative. In Xenophon's account, Socrates proclaimed himself the wisest man in Hellas, but not necessarily the only wise one. In Plato's revision, Socrates became the one and only really wise man. All the others, however eminent, the political leaders and the poets, which included the tragic poets, turned out to be dunces. This was no way to win votes for acquittal.

Socrates' determination to die is even more evident in the second stage of the trial when the jury, having voted his conviction, had to vote on the penalty to be imposed. Under Athenian law, the jury could not decide on a penalty of its own. It had to choose between the penalty proposed by the prosecution and the penalty proposed by the defense. It could not "split the difference" between them. The prosecution demanded the death penalty. One could have expected this to stir sympathy for Socrates, and swing over more votes to a lesser punishment. But again it was Socrates who helped the prosecution by provoking the jury even further. Both *Apologies* agree on this. Socrates' cogent argument against the death penalty in Xenophon's is made only *after* the jury had voted it, when his plea was too late. "Now of all the acts for which the laws have prescribed the death penalty," Socrates says, " — temple robbery, burglary, enslavement, treason to the state — not even my adversaries themselves charge me with having committed any of these. And so it seems astonishing to me how you could ever have been convinced that I had committed an act meriting death."[10] Socrates should have said that earlier. The best strategy for the defense was to focus on the enormity — if not, indeed, downright illegality — of a death penalty.

The prospects could not have been more favorable for a milder alternative — at the worst banishment from the city, at the best a fine reasonable enough to satisfy a hesitant and troubled jury. The prospect for such a counterproposal was especially favorable if put forward with a more conciliatory demeanor on the part of Socrates — not a humiliating abasement, not a demeaning plea for compassion, just a little less self-aggrandizement and a little more of the charm Socrates could so well exert.

We know that Athenian juries were notoriously susceptible to graceful rhetoric and to pity. There is a passage in the *Republic* where Socrates sneers at the Athenians for being so easygoing that men already convicted can often be seen walking unmolested around the city. It is extraordinary that under such circumstances Socrates set out instead to provoke the jury in the debate on the penalty, as we see in Plato's *Apology*.

It appears that the trial actually ended up with a larger majority for the death penalty than had voted for conviction. Diogenes Laertius says in his life of Socrates that there were eighty more votes cast for the death penalty than in the vote to convict.[11] So, if Diogenes Laertius is correct, the vote for the death penalty was 360 to 140. "We have no means of checking this," Burnet says in his commentary on Plato's *Apology,* "but a considerable turnover of votes would not be surprising in view of the attitude taken up by Socrates" in his counterpenalty proposal.[12]

Plato and Xenophon differ only on the counterpenalty Socrates proposed. Xenophon says simply that Socrates refused to suggest any counterpenalty: "When he was bidden to name his penalty, he refused personally and forbade his friends to name one." Socrates objected "that naming the penalty in itself implied an acknowledgement of guilt."[13] So, according to Xenophon, Socrates left the jury no alternative to the death penalty. Plato's account turns the debate on the counterpenalty into a dramatic episode. It delights the reader but must have infuriated the jury. Socrates treats the charges, the court, and the city with scornful amusement. He begins with what for the Athenians was a supreme gesture of *hybris*. He suggests as a penalty that he be declared a civic hero and as such given free meals for the rest of his life in the Prytaneum!

The Prytaneum was a place of honor. It was the city hall, the seat of the city's executive government. For some of us the term city hall conjures up a picture of a rather seedy place full of politicians and spittoons, but for the Greeks the Prytaneum had a sacred character. Just as every home was built around its hearth, deified as the goddess Hestia, so every city had a civic hearth in the Prytaneum where a perpetual fire was consecrated to its Hestia. If colonists went forth, they carried a flame from the mother city's hearth to light a new one in the colony.

The name *prytaneion*, Latinized as Prytaneum, was derived from *prytanis*, which once meant prince, ruler, or lord. In democratic Athens the executive was a council of fifty chosen by lot and the year was divided into ten "prytaneis" so that in a normal lifetime almost every citizen had a chance of serving in it. Even Socrates, who avoided all political activity and never held any other civic office, was chosen by lot to sit as a member of the council which presided — as the reader will recall — over the prosecution of the Arginusae generals.

Members of the council had to be on duty at the city hall every day during their term of office. In the Prytaneum there was a public dining table where the councilmen took their meals. Foreign ambassadors and citizens of unusual distinction were honored by a place at this table. Among them were winners at the Olympic games and men associated with great deeds in defense of the city and its democracy.

When Plato's Socrates suggested that his penalty be an invitation to dine at the Prytaneum for the rest of his life, he was risking some damaging associations in the minds of his judges. The most honored citizens who dined there were the descendants of two Athenian heroes named Harmodius and Aristogeiton. They gave their lives in an (ultimately successful) effort to overthrow the Peisistratid dictatorship late in the sixth century. Statues were erected to them and there were annual sacrifices to their memory. Their descendants were exempt from taxation and took their meals in the Prytaneum. Harmodius and Aristogeiton had given their lives to restore democracy. Socrates was associated through Critias and Charmides with its recent overthrow. A lawyer would have advised Socrates against inviting such a harmful comparison.

Plato's Socrates soon retracted his little joke, but the harm was done. Then he suggested a fine so small — one mina — that it must have been almost equally offensive. His own followers were alarmed. Plato tells us that his disciples — himself included — begged Socrates to suggest a more respectful sum as a fine. Socrates then amended his counterpenalty to a fine of thirty minas of silver. "Plato here," he tells the court, "and Crito and Critobulus, and Apollodorus tell me to propose a fine of thirty minas, saying that they are sureties for it."[14] The fact that four Socratic disciples joined to stand surety for the payment indicates that it was a substantial sum. Had the thirty-mina fine been proposed by Socrates originally, it might have seemed enough to a jury as closely divided as his was on the vote for conviction. But the first two counterpenalties offered by Socrates must have made the jury feel he was laughing at them, and treating the trial with contempt, as indeed he was. This must have made the final, and reluctant, offer of thirty minas too late to appease the jury.

Of course Socrates had a right to look down his nose at the prosecution and the court, but the price he paid was to win votes for an alternative which might otherwise have been regarded as much too severe. Socrates himself seems to put the hemlock to his lips.[15]

The same death wish reappears in the *Crito* after the trial and aggravates the disciples. The dialogue opens in the darkness before dawn. The faithful and wealthy Crito has been waiting at the prison for Socrates to awaken. He is eager to tell his beloved teacher of a new and dramatic development. Arrangements have been made for his escape.

"It is not even a large sum of money," Crito tells Socrates, "which we should pay to some men who are willing to save you and get you away from here." Funds have been raised by admirers of Socrates in other cities and preparations have been made to receive him on his escape. "Do not be troubled," Crito pleads, "by what you said in the court, that if you went away you would not know what to do with yourself. For in many other places, wherever you go, they will welcome you."

But Socrates is determined to stay and die. Crito argues that the course Socrates is pursuing "is not even right." Crito says Socrates is betraying himself "when you might save yourself," and begs Socrates to think of his children, whom he will leave orphaned in destitution. His wife is included in the escape plan along with his three sons, so that wherever he goes he can see to their education. Crito scolds Socrates and terms his refusal to save his life unworthy of his own teachings — "you who have been saying all your life that you cared for virtue." When Socrates still refuses to flee, Crito breaks into an extraordinary tirade, giving us the full measure of the exasperation felt by his disciples. "I am ashamed," Crito says, "both for you and for us, your friends."

He even complains that the case had been allowed to come before the court at all, "when it might have been avoided."[16] This cryptic remark still tantalizes us. How could the trial have been avoided? Crito never explains. Perhaps the question is left unanswered in Plato because it was so obvious to the Greeks of his time. A clue may be provided by Roman law. Under the Republic it was long assumed and later enacted into law that a citizen facing a capital charge could evade trial or a death penalty after trial by the option of *exsilium*,[17] or self-exile from the city. This recourse was available to the guilty as well as the innocent. There may have been a similar legal doctrine in Athens.[18]

Socrates might have suggested banishment as a counterpenalty in order to give Athens an opportunity for calmer reflection, in which it might reverse itself and recall him. Many famous Athenians — including Alcibiades — had been exiled or ostracized and later recalled to posts of honor and leadership in the stormy politics of the city. Socrates hinted at the possibility of such a change of heart when he said in the *Apology* that the one day of trial allowed him was not enough. "I believe," Socrates told the jury, "if you had a law, as some other people have, that capital cases should not be decided in one day, but only after several days, you would be convinced [of his innocence]; but now it is not easy to rid you of great prejudices in a short time."[19] An escape could have provided an opportunity for reflection and a recall to Athens.

No one can reread Plato's account of the last days of Socrates — as moving as the greatest of the Greek tragedies — without feeling that such an outcome would have pleased his disciples, seeking desperately to divert their beloved master from his stubborn course.

Crito criticizes "the way in which the trial itself was carried on." He concludes that people "will think, as the crowning absurdity of the whole affair, that this opportunity [to arrange his flight from prison] has escaped us through some base cowardice on our part, since we did not save you, and you did not save yourself, though it was quite possible." Crito even terms the refusal to escape "disgraceful" and "evil."[20] To counter this angry criticism, Socrates now offers a new reason for his determination to die. In an imaginary dialogue with the personified Laws of Athens, he lets himself be convinced that it is his duty to obey the court's verdict and die. This is a unique occasion for Socrates. Nowhere else does he acquiesce submissively to someone else's line of argument. The easy surrender is significant. He did not reject escape because the Laws won the argument. He let the Laws win the argument because he did not want to escape. Scholars are still trying without success to resolve the contradiction between his lifelong nonconformity and his sudden readiness to submit to a verdict that he sees — and so do we — as unjust.

The debate between Socrates and his disciples over his readiness to die is continued in the *Phaedo,* when they bid him farewell. That is indeed the main theme of this lovely mystical dialogue. There a new — and elaborate — reason for seeking a death penalty is offered to them. When his sorrowful disciples on the last day of his life argue that his submission is really suicide and question its morality, he replies by declaring that death for a philosopher is the final fulfillment, much to be desired, because it opens the door to true knowledge. The soul, freed from its bonds to the body, at last achieves undimmed and celestial vision.

A man who gives so many diverse and inconsistent reasons for refusing to save his life is desperately avoiding candor. Socrates simply wished to die.

But before we enter into the rapturous recesses of the *Phaedo,* the most moving of all Plato's dialogues, we must pause to note that it is marred by Socrates' cold and unfeeling attitude toward his devoted wife, Xanthippe. This has too long been passed over in silence by reverent scholars.

Xanthippe had a lifetime of trying to make ends meet and feed the children while he went around enjoying himself in philosophical discourse. Socrates' constant boast that unlike the Sophists he never took a fee from his pupils was a luxury for which his poor wife paid the bill. Yet there is not a trace of gratitude or tenderness when they part forever. Plato paints the scene with inimitable artistry but a cold eye.

When the dialogue opens, Socrates has just been released from his fetters, which apparently were put on at night to hamper escape. Phaedo describes the scene as the disciples were admitted. "We went in then," he recounts, and found "Xanthippe — you know her — with his little son in her arms."

"Now when Xanthippe saw us," Phaedo relates, "she cried out and said the kind of thing women always do say: 'Oh, Socrates, this is the last time now that your friends will speak to you or you to them.' "[21] Phaedo's tone is unkind and insensitive. Xanthippe did not express pity for herself but for Socrates and his old friends. She was moved to tears that this was to be the last of those philosophic discussions they loved. She showed an understanding that transcended her own grief.

Socrates did not take her in his arms to comfort her, nor express any sorrow of his own, or even kiss the infant son in her arms. His farewell was a curt dismissal. The womanly love and understanding of the wife broke through but was ungraciously brushed aside.

Socrates glanced at Crito "and said, 'Crito, let somebody take her home.' And some of Crito's people [i.e., his servants] took her away wailing and beating her breast."²² She is never referred to again in the dialogue.

Later that evening Xanthippe seems to have been allowed back in again before Socrates drank the hemlock. For we ́are told toward the end of the dialogue that after Socrates had bathed in preparation for the execution, "and his children had been brought to him — for he had two little sons and one big one — and the women of the family had come, he talked with them in Crito's presence and gave them such directions as he wished; then he told the women to go home and he came to us [i.e., his disciples]." Xanthippe is not even mentioned by name. She is just included among "the women of the family."

Contrast this with the tender passage in which Phaedo describes the grief of the disciples. While they waited, he says, they spoke among themselves "of the great misfortune that had befallen us, for we felt that he was like a father to us and that when bereft of him we should pass the rest of our lives as orphans."²³

No such sympathy is expressed for Xanthippe. Turn to Homer and compare this farewell with Hector's to Andromache in the *Iliad,* so vibrant with love and humanity, still as moving as if it happened yesterday, and we see that there was something missing in Socrates and in Plato. In the farewell discussions of the *Phaedo,* the philosopher and his disciples show themselves capable of deep feeling, but only for themselves. Here as elsewhere in the dialogues of Plato we find no compassion for the common man or the common woman, even when, like Xanthippe, they demonstrate a quite uncommon devotion.

The two main philosophical interlocutors of Socrates in the *Phaedo* are the two Thebans, Simmias and Cebes, who had brought funds with them to finance the escape. The terrible moral question that hangs over their entire discussion with Socrates is his justification of suicide.

Of course the true philosopher should face death with equanimity. In this sense, he should be "glad to die." But is it right to seek out death before one's time has come — to abandon one's mission, to leave one's family and disciples, and — to put it in terms that an old soldier like Socrates understood only too well — to run away from one's post in the battle?

Socrates says early in the dialogue that "philosophy is the greatest kind of music." In the *Phaedo,* Plato and Socrates do indeed "make music"* — but not sense, though it takes a little time to shake off their hypnotic charm.

Just before this remark, Plato prepares for it with a delightful touch. He tells us that Socrates — to pass the time away in prison — has been turning Aesop's fables into lyric verse.

Socrates admits that suicide is morally wrong for most of mankind, but suggests that this does not apply to philosophers. This odd notion is broached ever so gently. Simmias says that a friend, Evenus, has inquired about him. Socrates says, "Bid him farewell, and tell him, if he is wise, to come after me as quickly as he can." Simmias pricks up his ears at this apparent invitation to join Socrates in death. Simmias says he knows Evenus well enough to be sure "he will not take your advice in the least if he can help it."

"Why so?" asks Socrates. "Is not Evenus a philosopher?" Simmias replies, "I think so." Then, says Socrates, "Evenus will take my advice, so will every man who has any worthy interest in philosophy." So not only professional philosophers but all men with a "worthy interest" in philosophy will seek an end to life as soon as possible!

At the very brink of this absurdity, Socrates hastens to add, "Perhaps, however, he will not take his own life, for they say that is not permitted." So he stops short at an explicit advocacy of suicide; indeed, at another point, Socrates admits that "these human beings for whom it is better to die," i.e., the philosophers, "cannot without impiety do good to themselves," i.e., commit suicide, "but must wait for some other benefactor." By this standard, the Athenians were his benefactors!

* Here our word *music* has the same broad metaphorical sense as the Greek word *mousike* conveys in this passage. Though sometimes used specifically of lyric poetry — which was sung, of course, to the lyre — *mousike* usually covered all the arts the Muses inspire.

A little later Socrates seems to blur this fine distinction and make a curious admission. "Perhaps," Socrates suggests, "it is not unreasonable to say that a man must not kill himself until god sends some necessity upon him, such as is now come upon me."[24] He seems to be saying that at some point suicide is justifiable and that this justifies him in dying and rejecting any opportunity for escape.

Socrates was confronted not by a "necessity" but by two alternatives. He chose death over a renewed chance of life. The choice he made was voluntary, and therefore the equivalent of suicide. It is clear in the *Phaedo* that is how the disciples felt about it, though they were too respectful to put it quite so bluntly. But they do press him. When they do, Socrates argues that for a philosopher death is not just a misfortune to be faced with serenity but the very goal of his existence. "Other people are not likely to be aware," Socrates tells the disciples, "that those who pursue philosophy aright study nothing but dying and being dead."

"Now if this be true," he continues, with no effort — let the reader notice — to prove this weird assumption, "it would be absurd to be eager for nothing but this all their lives, and then to be troubled when that came for which they had all along been eagerly practising." This was too much for Simmias, despite his reverence for Socrates. "Simmias laughed and said, 'By Zeus, Socrates, I don't feel much like laughing just now, but you made me laugh. For I think the multitude, if they heard what you just said about the philosophers, would say you were quite right, and our people at home [i.e., in Thebes] would agree entirely with you that philosophers desire death, and they would add that they know very well that the philosophers deserve it.' "[25]

Socrates replies that they would be speaking the truth but without understanding what it really meant. Then he proceeds to develop a familiar Platonic doctrine which originated in an Orphic or Pythagorean saying — a mystical pun — that the body (*soma*) is the tomb (*sema*) of the soul. Death thus frees the soul from its tomb. So, Socrates says, the soul "thinks best when none of these things troubles it, neither hearing nor sight, nor pain nor any pleasure, but it is, so far as possible, alone by itself, and takes leave of the body, and avoiding, so far as it can, all association or contact with the body, reaches out toward the reality."

"Then," Socrates asks Simmias triumphantly, "the soul of the philosopher greatly despises the body and avoids it and strives to be alone by itself?" Simmias responds, whether dryly or dutifully, "Evidently."[26] It follows that the philosopher must yearn for death as liberation and fulfillment, and seek it as soon as he can, as the doorway to unblurred vision and — at last — true knowledge.

That is the message of the *Phaedo*. It is mystical rapture of a high order. But we cannot leave it without a commonsense observation. Its praise of death may or may not be Socratic doctrine but it is indubitably Platonic, as we know from his other dialogues and especially from the *Republic*. There he would limit the teaching of the dialectic to those who could abandon the eyes and the ears and the other senses and rise to *to on,* or pure being. But by these Pythagorean standards, only in death is this fully possible.

Even Plato did not take his mysticism seriously. Otherwise he would have followed the advice he puts into the mouth of Socrates and joined his master in death as soon as possible, to share those blissful celestial visions. Instead, like any sensible burgher, Plato fled Athens after the trial of Socrates lest he be caught in a wave of repression, returned when things quieted down, founded his academy, and spent forty happy years in Athens writing his dialogues.

Chapter 15

HOW SOCRATES EASILY
MIGHT HAVE WON ACQUITTAL

꽃೨ഌ

I
F SOCRATES had wanted an acquittal he had — I believe — an
easy way to get it. Despite the prestige of his chief accuser and
the fresh memory of the Thirty, the jury, as we have seen, was
reluctant to convict. The reason, I believe, is that this was a
prosecution which went against the grain of Athenian law and
tradition. All that we have marshaled against Socrates may be
impressive evidence of how deeply he disagreed with Athens. But
it fell short as a case for a criminal prosecution.

When Athens prosecuted Socrates, it was untrue to itself. The
paradox and the shame in the trial of Socrates is that a city famous
for free speech prosecuted a philosopher guilty of no other crime
than exercising it. To invoke the memory of our own American
lapses, Athens had no Alien and Sedition Laws. Athens had no
little Iron Curtain like the McCarran-Walter immigration act to
bar visitors with suspect ideas. Indeed, nothing would have been
more alien to Athens, as we can see from the proud phrases of
Pericles' funeral speech, which celebrated an open city and an open
mind.

Athens never had an un-Athenian Activities Investigating Committee. In prosecuting Socrates, Athens was un-Athenian, frightened by the three political earthquakes when the democracy was
overthrown in 411 and 404 B.C. and then threatened again in 401.
These events help to explain the prosecution of Socrates, but they
do not justify it.

The trial of Socrates was a prosecution of ideas. He was the first
martyr of free speech and free thought. If he had conducted his
defense as a free speech case, and invoked the basic traditions of his

city, he might easily, I believe, have shifted the troubled jury in his favor. Unfortunately Socrates never invoked the *principle* of free speech. Perhaps one reason he held back from that line of defense is because his victory would also have been a victory for the democratic principles he scorned. An acquittal would have vindicated Athens.

Let us begin our argument with a fresh look at the indictment. The indictment is known from three ancient sources. One is in Plato's *Apology,* where Socrates paraphrases it by saying, "It is about as follows: it states that Socrates is a wrongdoer because he corrupts the youth and does not believe in the gods the state believes in, but in other new spiritual beings."[1] Almost identical versions are given by Xenophon in his *Memorabilia* and by Diogenes Laertius in his *Life of Socrates.*[2] The latter says that the historian Favorinus had found the original still preserved in the archives of Athens during the reign of the Emperor Hadrian in the second century A.D.

The indictment's two counts are equally vague. No specific acts against the city are alleged. The complaints are against the *teaching* and *beliefs* of Socrates. Neither in the indictment — nor at the trial — was there mention of any overt act of sacrilege or disrespect to the city's gods or any overt attempt or conspiracy against its democratic institutions. Socrates was prosecuted for what he *said,* not for anything he *did.*

The weakest part of the case for the prosecution is that nowhere does it accuse Socrates of violating any specific law either for the protection of the civic religion or of its political institutions. This is very puzzling because in the rich literature of fourth-century-B.C. Athenian forensic oratory — our reports of cases in which Lysias, Demosthenes, and other "lawyers" wrote the speeches for one side or the other — we are given the text of the law under which the indictment was brought.

We know from a passage in the *Rhetoric* of Aristotle two generations after the trial that unwritten law or "higher law" or "equity" could be invoked by the defense as the embodiment of "justice that goes beyond the written law."[3] But except for the trial of Socrates I have been unable to find evidence that unwritten law could be the basis for a prosecution. Yet it is curious that neither Socrates nor his defenders advance this as an argument against the prosecution.

On the impiety charge, Socrates is as vague as the indictment. He never discusses the accusation that he did not respect or believe in — the Greek verb used, *nomizein,* has both meanings — the gods of the city. Instead, he traps the rather dim-witted Meletus into accusing him of atheism,[4] a charge he easily refutes. But there was no law against atheism in ancient Athens either before or after the trial. Indeed, the only place we find such a law proposed is in Plato's *Laws.* In this respect Plato was the exception to the tolerance that paganism showed to diverse cults and philosophic speculation about the gods. Since paganism saw gods everywhere and of every kind, it was by its nature tolerant and incapable of imposing a rigid dogmatism. It easily accommodated a wide range of theological interpretation. At one end of the spectrum was a simple anthropomorphic and literal faith in the gods. At the other end was their transformation by the pre-Socratic philosophers into mere personifications of — or metaphors for — natural forces or abstract ideas.

The gods disappeared into air, fire, water, and earth. Classical mythology invited this metaphysical metamorphosis by its very names for the aboriginal divinities — the primordial Chaos, Kronos (later identified with Chronos or Time), Uranus (the sky), and Mother Earth. From a theology of nature to a philosophy of nature was an easy transition, and it was difficult to draw a line between them.

It was monotheism that brought religious intolerance into the world. When Jews and Christians denied divinity to any god but their own, they were attacked as *atheos* or "godless." This explains how — to borrow Novalis's characterization of Spinoza — a "God-intoxicated" Jew and Christian like St. Paul could be called an "atheist" by pious and indignant pagans.

The very word *atheos* had a different ring to it in classical antiquity than in the later Christian era. The word does not appear in Homer or Hesiod. It does not appear until the fifth century B.C., in Pindar and Greek tragedy. There it means "godless" or "ungodly" in the colloquial sense that we still use those words for the lawless and immoral. The Greek word could also mean abandoned by the gods, or struck by their wrath.[5]

If Socrates was liable to prosecution for what we would call atheism, then he could have been prosecuted a quarter century earlier, in 423 B.C. That was when the *Clouds* of Aristophanes pictured him as a philosopher who taught that knavish common man Strepsiades, eager to cheat his creditors by imbibing the New Learning of Socrates, that there was no Zeus and that the real gods were "Chaos, Respiration and Air."[6] Hence he could break his oaths and refuse to pay his debts without fear of divine retribution.

If the Athenians were sensitive to aspersions on the gods, they would have carted off to jail not only Socrates but Aristophanes. Instead they awarded the latter a prize and laughed at that simple countryman Strepsiades when he challenged Socrates by asking, "If no Zeus, then whence comes the rain?" Finally enlightened, Strepsiades admits sheepishly that he had thought the rain was Zeus pissing down upon earth through a sieve! This language may shock the prudish modern reader, but it is the literal translation of *dia koskinou ourein* in line 373. The last word is cognate with our word *urinate* and *koskinon* was a sieve. Apparently the high god was using it by mistake for a chamberpot!

Aristophanes obviously used this as a sure-fire joke, calculated to make the audience feel superior in its enlightenment to an unsophisticated rural oaf like Strepsiades. That should be enough to show that Athens was not shocked either by disbelief or disrespect for the gods. If it had been, not only Aristophanes but the equally and seriously "impious" Euripides would have been in trouble too.

As for Socrates, the comedy ends when Strepsiades leads a mob in setting fire to the Thinkery in which Socrates has been teaching that there is no Zeus. Socrates is trapped in the flames and pleads for mercy, "I am suffocating." But Strepsiades cries out triumphantly:

For with what aim did ye insult the Gods,
And pry around the dwellings of the Moon?

He urges the mob on against Socrates and his pupils —

Strike, smite them, spare them not, for many reasons,
But most because they have blasphemed the Gods![7]

If Athens had been a city of bigots, the audience would have rushed from the theater to the home of Socrates and set it ablaze. Instead, the spectators — probably Socrates among them — emerged laughing. No one filed a prosecution for heresy, impiety, or blasphemy.

By trapping Meletus into calling him an atheist, Socrates evaded the actual charge in the indictment. It did not accuse him of disbelief in Zeus and the Olympian divinities, or in the gods generally. It charged disbelief in "the gods of the city."

This was in the ancient Greek sense a *political* crime, a crime against the gods of the Athenian *polis*. This is a crucial point too often overlooked. What did the indictment mean by "the gods of the city"? A clue is provided by Xenophon in his *Memorabilia*. Twice he recalls that Socrates, when asked how to act piously toward the gods, quoted a saying by the Priestess of Delphi: "Follow the *nomos* of the city; that is the way to act piously."[8] *Nomos* means custom or law. The *nomos* was established by tradition or, later, by legislative act. This was the standard Greek view. The city was the state, and the state determined which gods it specially venerated. It regulated religious practices — the rites, the temples, the sacrifices, and the festivals. Religion was a civic function, a reflection of its local ways and customs.

The indictment said that Socrates did not conform to the *nomos* of his city. But it does not specify the beliefs Socrates did not share. Neither Xenophon nor Plato give us a clear answer, perhaps because such an answer would have lent more substance to the charge and weakened their defense of Socrates.

A clue to "the gods of the city" problem is provided in the *Oxford Classical Dictionary* article on Hephaestus, the god of fire, and especially of the fire in the smithy. Hence, the *OCD* says, "he was for the Greeks a craftsman's god and himself a divine craftsman."

The pre-Socratic philosopher Xenophanes once observed that men made gods in their own image, the Ethiopians with crinkly hair, the Celts with red. The same tendency appeared in the various crafts. The smith created a god in his own image as his patron divinity. The distribution of the Hephaestus cult in the Greek city-states was determined by the progress of metallurgy and industry. His cult, the *OCD* goes on, was "practically confined to the most industrialized regions, being particularly prominent at Athens."

As a city with a large concentration of craftsmen, and a city dependent in large part for its livelihood on the products of the smithy and the kiln, Athens would naturally include Hephaestus among its "gods of the city." The prominence of Hephaestus as an Athenian god is shown, the *OCD* suggests, by his frequent appearance in Athenian vase painting "from the first half of the sixth century." It was in the same century that the craftsmen and traders began to win political equality. The cult of Hephaestus grew with the advance of democracy. The one unruined fifth-century temple, the so-called Theseion, was really a temple of Hephaestus. From a low hill it overlooked the agora.[9]

The patron goddess of Athens, the foremost divinity of the city, was Athena, the goddess of wisdom, born directly from the head of Zeus. Hephaestus appears on Athenian vases assisting — as a kind of male midwife — in the delivery.

There was a common worship among all the Greeks for the Olympian deities of Homer. But even the great gods were worshipped under different forms and appellations in different cities. These special appellations, like the minor gods, were the subject of special civic cults, which symbolized the character of each city. In Athens, for example, Pallas Athena was worshipped not only as the goddess of wisdom but in that capacity especially as a patron of the arts and crafts. For wisdom — *sophia* — originally meant not just wisdom in our sense but any special skill or knowledge, whether in forging metals or weaving cloth or treating the sick.

But Socrates speaks with disdain for the craftsmen and traders who had begun to play so large a part in the assembly and the other democratic institutions of the city. As we have seen, the kind of society he admired was the Spartan, where the warrior landlords excluded craftsmen and traders from citizenship. In the Greek city-states, as in the Roman, not to recognize the city's gods was to be disloyal to the city.

The *Oresteia* of Aeschylus provides a further — and, I believe, unnoticed — clue to what was meant in Athens by "the gods of the city." The *Oresteia,* last and greatest work of Aeschylus, and the only surviving Greek trilogy, was produced and won the prize in 458 B.C., two years before his death at eighty. That was half a century before the trial of Socrates. The trilogy is the Mount Everest of tragedy, ancient or modern. Even the worst translation cannot altogether hide its grandeur or fail to transmit some of its power.* It deserves a digression for readers not yet familiar with it.

The legendary story on which Aeschylus built his tragedy first appears in the *Odyssey* as a well-known tale.[10] There is no better way to see the cultural gulf separating the archaic age of Homer from the civilization of Athens than to look at the Homeric and Aeschylean versions side by side. The moral and political distance between them is immense.

The bare bones of the story, of course, are that Agamemnon, on his return to Mycenae from the war against Troy, is murdered by his wife Clytemnestra and her lover Aegisthus, who have been ruling during the king's long absence. Orestes, a son of Agamemnon, and the rightful heir, returns to avenge his father and take the throne by murdering his mother and her paramour. Homer is

* To read it in the original fully repays the hard work. It took me twelve weeks, five to six hours a day and seven days a week, to read the three plays. The first, the *Agamemnon,* I read with Eduard Fraenkel's monumental three-volume commentary. For the trilogy as a whole, I used with pleasure George Thomson's two-volume revised edition (Prague, 1966), second only to Fraenkel in its learning.

matter-of-fact in telling the story. The only moral judgment on Orestes is one of approval. In book one of the *Odyssey,* Orestes is even held up as a model of filial piety by Athena for avenging his father. That Orestes killed his mother to avenge his father is not alluded to until book three, and then only incidentally. Homer says that Orestes after killing the usurper Aegisthus made a funeral feast for his mother and her lover. The murder of the mother is taken for granted; she is dismissed, with one word, as "hateful." Having so easily disposed of the matricide, Homer takes several lines to dwell appreciatively on the ships laden with gifts that Uncle Menelaus brought to the funeral feast for his nephew Orestes. That is the happy ending of the story in Homer. No Furies come to haunt the son for killing his mother. For the bard and his audience it was simply a dynastic struggle for a throne, all too familiar in royal families. The lawful heir disposed of an "unwarlike" usurper; that epithet took care of him. In the ordeal of battle, the better warrior had won.

But what concerns us here is not morals or aesthetics but politics. It is the political aspect of the *Oresteia* that too rarely has been noticed. Aeschylus turned an ancient myth into a celebration of Athenian institutions. The ultimate hero of the *Oresteia* is Athenian democracy. The day Aeschylus fought for it against the Persians at Marathon was — if we are to believe the marvelous elegiac quatrain he is supposed to have written as his own epitaph — the proudest day of his life, the achievement for which he most wished to be remembered.*

That same love of his native city reverberates in his plays, and finds its highest expression in the *Oresteia.* In one archaic version of the legend, Orestes was finally tried by a court of the Olympian gods. But in the Aeschylean version, the agonizing conflict of obligations finds its resolution in trial by an Athenian *dikastery,* or jury-court, fifth-century style. Justice is to be achieved in free and orderly debate after contending arguments have been heard. The decision was left, as we would say, not to *vox dei* — the voice of

---

* "Aeschylus, son of Euphorion, an Athenian, now departed, lies beneath this memorial in Gela, rich in corn. The famous grove of Marathon could tell you of his valor, and so could the bushy-haired Medes who experienced it."

God — but to *vox populi,* the voice of the people. The jury split down the middle, and Athena herself had to step in and break the tie. She voted for acquittal, establishing the Athenian rule that a tie vote acquits.

For the Furies, who prosecuted Orestes at the trial, murder was murder; blood had to be atoned by blood. But an Athenian jury was accustomed to consider mitigating circumstances and to distinguish in homicide cases — as our law does — varying degrees of guilt and penalty from the accidental killing to the premeditated murder. This was justice as they knew and applied it. For the modern reader, at least, it would seem that the outcome was a vote for mercy. Orestes, caught in an unresolvable conflict of obligations, had suffered enough.

In the final scene the indignant Furies had to be appeased and reconciled to this civilized jurisprudence. Athena succeeds in persuading them to accept defeat. As their reward she offers them a new shrine on the slopes of the Acropolis and a new name. The Furies are to be transformed into the Eumenides — gracious, smiling, and kindly divinities. The play ends with a civic procession escorting them to their new shrine — "now no longer," in the words of the ancient synopsis of the play, "Spirits of Wrath, but Spirits of Blessing" upon the city.

The play ends by paying honor to two special divinities. This is the climactic political message of the *Oresteia.* Athena, the Olympian and universal Greek goddess, pays tribute for her victory over the Furies to two "gods of the city" peculiar to Athens. They are Peitho, or persuasion personified as a goddess, and the Zeus Agoraios, or the Zeus of the assembly, the tutelary divinity of its free debates. They embodied the democratic institutions of Athens.

Athena requires the Furies to recognize "the majesty of Peitho." So the proud and arrogant Furies, ancient and infernal powers, gods of the underworld who defied the authority even of the Olympian deities and regarded Night as their mother, were now to recognize and hold sacred a new divinity, Persuasion, as the symbol of their conversion. When they do so, Athena proclaims that this is also the victory of the Zeus Agoraios. This may cast new light on the meaning of "the gods of the city" in the indictment of Socrates. The first of these civic divinities, Peitho, was unknown to Homer.[11] The other is Zeus in a special guise that Homer's aristocratic audience would not have understood.

In fifth-century Athens, Peitho had developed into a civic goddess of democracy, a symbol of the transition to rule by popular consent and consensus, achieved by debate and persuasion. Her political stature was reflected in the Athenian theater. "The unique character of Attic poetry," C. M. Bowra wrote, came "from the Athenian democracy itself. Tragedy was performed with religious solemnity . . . before a vast, critical, amazingly intelligent audience. Such a performance was, in every sense, a public event."[12]

In their personification of Peitho as a civic goddess of Persuasion, the Athenians recast not only their religion but their mythology and history to suit the ideas of fifth-century democracy. They even claimed, according to that most famous of ancient travelers, Pausanias, that the cult of Persuasion was first instituted by Theseus, the mythical first king of Athens.[13] This venerable genealogy was, of course, quite unhistorical.

Perhaps the most striking references to Peitho in Attic theater are in the *Frogs* of Aristophanes, in 405 B.C., six years before the trial of Socrates. In that comedy Aristophanes staged a debate between Aeschylus and Euripides in Hades. Euripides and Aeschylus hurl one-line quotations at each other about Persuasion from their plays, some now lost. These must have been familiar, or the points made would not have been appreciated by the audience.

Euripides begins with a line from a lost play he wrote about Antigone. In it Persuasion is associated with *logos*, reasoned speech. Euripides says that Persuasion needs no shrine except *logos* and adds that her "altar is in the nature of man."

Aeschylus counters Euripides with a quotation from a lost play of his own, the *Niobe,* in which he said that death alone is impervious to Persuasion. Even Aristophanes who jokes about everything and makes Dionysus himself the butt of the coarsest humor in the same play, makes no jokes about Persuasion. That must have been the most extraordinary tribute of all to Peitho.

A generation later the two greatest masters of fourth-century oratory — Demosthenes and Isocrates — also list Peitho among "the gods of the city" and refer to annual sacrifices in her honor.[14] There was a statue of her near the Acropolis[15] and an ancient inscription[16] tells us that her priestess had a special seat of honor in the Temple of Dionysus. She was commemorated in sculpture by Praxiteles and Pheidias.[17] It could be significant that there is no reference to Peitho as a divinity anywhere in Xenophon or in Plato.[18] They could hardly have venerated a civic goddess of the democracy they rejected. The Platonic contempt for persuasion and oratory as practiced in a democratic polity is summed up by Phaedrus in the dialogue that bears his name. "I have heard," he says, "that one who is to be an orator does not need to know what is really just, but what would seem just to the multitude who are to pass judgment, and not what is really good or noble, but what will seem to be so," and he adds sardonically that "persuasion comes from what seems to be true, not from the truth."[19] Of course oratory can be misleading as well as enlightening. The same is true of philosophy itself. Else why would philosophers so often — and so bitterly — disagree? But what better way to winnow out the truth than by free debate?

How effectively the cult of Peitho — and of the Zeus of the assembly — could have been invoked by Socrates in his own defense! To punish a philosopher for his opinions was no way to honor the goddess of Persuasion or the Zeus who symbolized and fostered free debate in the assembly. These "gods of the city," if appealed to, could have protected Socrates, too.

The Zeus Agoraios was the tutelary divinity which stood in the *agora*, the assembly, where the ultimate decisions of government were made. The political significance of this tribute by Athena to the Zeus Agoraios has often been lost in translation. It is sometimes rendered as the Zeus of the marketplace. An example turns up — I am sorry to say — in Gilbert Murray's *Oresteia*. There it is

translated "Zeus, whose Word is in the Mart, prevailed."[20] But
the final victory in the *Oresteia* had nothing to do with the
marketplace. It had to do with the agora as the place of assembly.
The LSJ lexicon describes the Zeus Agoraios as the "guardian of
popular assemblies." The political inference is also supported by
Farnell in his *Cults of the Greek States,* where he says that the Zeus
Agoraios was "the god who presided over assemblies and trials; it
was he who, according to Aeschylus, awarded victory to Orestes
in his trial for matricide."[21]

The earliest reference to a Zeus Agoraios is in Herodotus, where
a despot was slain by his rebellious people even though he took
refuge at the altar of Zeus Agoraios, no doubt in the belief that
they would not violate the sanctity of a god who symbolized the
freedoms he himself had violated. *Agora,* of course, can mean
either assembly or marketplace. But even in Homer it already
meant place of assembly or trial.[22] The word took on the meaning
of marketplace later, presumably as a market grew up around the
place of assembly. Similarly there developed two different kinds
of gods termed *agoraios.* But the god of the assembly was a Zeus,
the god of the marketplace was a Hermes. The same distinction is
drawn in Chantraine's *Dictionnaire etymologique de la langue
grecque.*[23]

Athens also had a Zeus Boulaios as the tutelary divinity of its
boule or council. According to Pausanias,[24] this was flanked by
two other statues, one of Apollo, and the other of *Demos* or the
People, perhaps as a reminder of where the final authority lay.
Today in the colonnade of the Agora Museum in Athens there is
a relief showing Democracy crowning Demos — an elderly
bearded man seated on a throne. Under the relief is the text of an
inscription dated 336 B.C. which safeguards the rights of the people
against tyranny.

There are two other passages in Pausanias about a deified
Demos in Attica. One reference describes statues of "a Zeus and
a Demos" side by side. The other passage also refers to a statue of
Democracy itself.[25] Was democracy at one time also personified as
a civic goddess in Athens?

Neither Frazer's *Golden Bough* nor Roescher's *"ausfuehrliches"* —

and it is indeed "detailed" — German *Lexicon of Greek and Roman Mythology* mentions such a cult. But the *Kleine Pauly* under *Demokratia* says that in the latter half of the fourth century at least Democracy was deified in Athens and that its priest had a seat of honor in the theater of Dionysus next to the priest of Demos.[26]

WHAT SOCRATES
SHOULD HAVE SAID

ভোগ্রেটো

THERE IS a third but little known *Apology* that has survived from antiquity in which Socrates invoked his right as an Athenian to free speech.

There were, as we know from scattered references, many ancient *apologies of Socrates* beside those of Plato and Xenophon. The writing of Socratic apologies seems to have been a literary genre in antiquity. All but one of them, an *Apology* written by Libanius in the fourth century A.D., were lost.

Libanius, a famous statesman and orator in his time, was a close associate of the Roman emperor Julian, called by later Christian writers "the Apostate," in a quixotic and ill-fated venture. Julian as emperor abandoned the Christian faith and tried to restore paganism as the religion of the Roman empire.

Libanius wrote an *Apology* in which Socrates speaks like a modern civil libertarian. Perhaps Libanius as a cultivated follower of the old "pagan" philosophers was sensitized to the issue by conflict with the Christians who had used their newly won political power to attack freedom of worship and thought. The persecuted had become the persecutors.

Libanius has Socrates utilize the memory of the Thirty to turn the tables against his chief accuser. "You, Anytus, in a democracy," Socrates says, "are acting more harshly than any dictator."

In the same passage Libanius has Socrates say that Athens had free speech "so that, freed from all fear, we might exercise our spirits by learning" as we do "our bodies by physical exercise" — an analogy that might have appealed to the real Socrates, who spent so much of his time talking in the palaestra where the athletes trained.

Free speech is praised in Libanius' version as the very foundation of the city's greatness. This was still true even in the days of Libanius eight centuries later. Long after its political and military primacy had passed away, Athens remained what we would call a university town, the Oxford of the Roman empire. Libanius himself studied philosophy at Athens and his *Apology* reflects a deep feeling for the city's inspiring past.

"It was for this reason," Libanius has Socrates say, "that Athens is a fair and delightful sight, and men come here from all quarters by land and sea: some stay and others go away reluctantly, and it is not because we excel Sybaris in the excellence of our table [i.e., cuisine], nor that our land is particularly rich in wheat. Quite the opposite, because we owe our sustenance to imported goods."

"It is talk, sheer talk, and the joy of talking," says Socrates — the greatest talker of them all — "that is the prime attraction of Athens." "All this," Socrates says, "is worthy of the goddess on the Acropolis, and of those educated by the gods, and of Theseus and of our democratic constitution. This" — and here Socrates touches the nerve center of civic pride and Hellenic rivalry — "makes the city more pleasant than Sparta. Because of this those who revere wisdom are held in higher esteem than those who are dreaded in battle. This is what makes the great difference between us and the non-Greek peoples. And he who is now taking away our freedom of speech is also destroying the customs of democracy as surely as if he were gouging the eyes out of the body or cutting out the tongue."[1]

Socrates concludes by accusing Anytus of laying down "a law of silence" upon a city where free speech was its life breath. So, in the Libanius version, the accused could have become the accuser.

The trouble with the Libanius defense is that it put Socrates in a disingenuous role. It cast him as a civil libertarian. But it would have been too late, after a lifetime of antipolitical and antidemocratic teaching, to expect an Athenian jury to take such a posture seriously. This is particularly true of the passage in which Libanius has him disparage Sparta in praising Athens. His lifelong fondness for the rival city was too notorious. But Socrates had another, more candid line of defense open to him. It might, at first glance, have seemed paradoxical. But the Athenians were charmed by paradoxes, as Cleon complains in Thucydides.

"Men of Athens, fellow citizens," Socrates could have argued, "this is not a trial of Socrates, but of ideas, and of Athens.

"You are not prosecuting me for any unlawful or impious act against our city or its altars. No evidence of any such sort has been brought against me.

"You are not prosecuting me for anything I *did,* but for what I have said and taught. You are threatening me with death because you do not like my views and my teaching. This is a prosecution of ideas and that is something new in our city's history. In this sense, Athens is in the dock, not Socrates. Each of you, as my judges, is a defendant.

"Let me be frank. I do not believe in your so-called freedom of speech, but you do. I believe the opinions of ordinary men are only *doxa* — beliefs without substance, pale shadows of reality, not to be taken seriously, and only likely to lead a city astray.

"I think it absurd to encourage the free utterance of unfounded or irrational opinions, or to base civic policy on a count of heads, like cabbages. Hence I do not believe in democracy. But you do. This is your test, not mine.

"I believe — and I have often said — that the shoemaker should stick to his last. I do not believe in versatility. I go to a shoemaker for shoes not for ideas. I believe the man who knows should rule, and the others should, for their own good, follow his prescription, as they do their physician's.

"I do not claim to know but at least I know when I do not know. Such men as I — you may call us philosophers or star-gazers as you like — are a civic treasure, not a menace, guides to a better way of life.

"Your freedom of speech is based on the assumption that every man's opinion is of value, and that the many are better guides than the few. But how can you boast of your free speech if you suppress mine? How can you listen to the shoemaker's or the tanner's views when you debate justice in the assembly, but shut me up when I express mine, though my life has been devoted to the search for truth while you have tended to your own private affairs?

"You are proud that Athens has been called the school of Hellas. Its gates have been open to philosophers from all over Greece and even the outer barbarian world. Will you now execute one of your own because suddenly you cannot stand to hear an unpopular opinion? It is not I but you that will be disgraced forever by my condemnation.

"You accuse me of having been the teacher of Critias and Charmides, the leaders of the extreme oligarchs under the Thirty. But now you are acting as they did. They summoned me, as you know, and ordered me to cease teaching the *techne logon* — the art of reasoned speech and logical analysis — to those under thirty years of age. You are doing the same thing. You are preparing to sentence me for having taught this *techne* to the youth of Athens during my lifetime.

"You say my ideas have been corrupting the youth, and leading them to question the democracy. Critias feared I might lead them to question the dictatorship. How, then, do you differ from the dictator you so recently overthrew? You say that I was Critias' teacher. You are acting as if you had become his pupils. They feared my ideas. So do you. But at least they did not claim to be lovers of free speech.

"The Thirty were arbitrary, and did as they pleased. You claim to be men who live by law. Are you not acting the same way? Tell me, now, by what law of Athens do you seek to restrict philosophic teaching? Where can I find it among the city's statutes? When was it debated and voted? Who proposed such a monstrosity, as you yourselves — in calmer days and in your right minds — would have termed it?

"The test of truly free speech is not whether what is said or taught conforms to any rule or ruler, few or many. Even under the worst dictator, it is not forbidden to agree with him. It is the freedom to disagree that is freedom of speech. This has been the Athenian rule until now, the pride of our city, the glory on which your orators dwell. Will you turn your backs on it now?

"You say I have shown disrespect for the city's gods. Beware that you do not make yourselves guilty of that very offense in condemning me. How can you honor Peitho when persuasion is inhibited, and nonconformist thoughts prosecuted? Are you not disobeying the Zeus Agoraios, the very god of debate, when you restrict debate by condemning me?

"Ideas are not as fragile as men. They cannot be made to drink hemlock. My ideas — and my example — will survive me. But the good name of Athens will wear a stain forever, if you violate its traditions by convicting me. The shame will be yours, not mine."

Had Socrates invoked freedom of speech as a basic right of all Athenians — not just the privilege of a superior and self-selected few like himself — he would have struck a deep and responsive chord. Socrates would have been showing a certain respect for Athens instead of the amused condescension all too evident in the *Apology* of Plato. The challenge would also have been a compliment.

Chapter 17

THE FOUR WORDS

७৩২৫৩৬

C OULD A FREE SPEECH APPEAL have succeeded? Obviously Athenians enjoyed free speech. But did they think
of it as a basic principle of government, as we do?

Men must have spoken freely long before they formulated the
idea of free speech. Perhaps the idea itself was developed in
reaction against attempts to take it away from them — or in a fight
to regain it.

One way to get at the answer — and dig into the thoughts of a
vanished civilization — is to examine the words they used. A
thought or concept clearly held finds expression in a word that
embodies it. If it wasn't on their tongues, it wasn't in their minds.
The way to delve into their minds is to look into their vocabulary.

So in studying the trial of Socrates I set out at this point of the
investigation to discover whether the Athenians and the ancient
Greeks had a word for free speech. What I found were no less than
four words for freedom of speech — more, I believe, than in any
other language ancient or modern. Then I followed the trail of
these words and their usage into the surviving literature. I was
convinced by what I found that no other people in history prized
free speech more than the Greeks, and this was especially true of
the Athenians.

Except for Sparta and Crete, both ruled by warrior landlord
minorities amid intimidated serfs, the Greek city-states tended
toward democracy; Athens was its citadel. The Greeks coined the
very word for it which all men everywhere still use — *demokratia*,
rule by the *demos* or common people. Political equality rested on
an equal right to speak freely. Etymology and politics are linked in

the evolution of ancient Greek. With the struggle for democracy, more than two hundred compounds containing the word *isos* for equal were added to the language.[1] Two of the most important were *isotes* for equality and *isonomia* for equal treatment under the law. Two others, equally important, were words for the right of free speech, *isegoria* and *isologia*.

The earlier term, *isegoria,* appears for the first time in Herodotus. Its synonym, *isologia,* does not appear until the third century in Polybius, the historian of the last period of Greek freedom in the Achaean League. The league was the first successful experiment in representative and federal government, and Polybius attributes its survival for a century under the Roman shadow to the fact that it allowed freedom of speech — *isologia* — in its federal assembly as symbol and guarantee that its member city-states (unlike those in the earlier leagues organized by Athens and Sparta) enjoyed full political equality. The Framers of the United States Constitution looked back to the Achaean League as a model for their own federal union.

Isegoria is cited by Herodotus when he explains the heroic role the Athenians played in the Persian wars, where he attributes their valor to the achievement of *isegorie* (he uses its Ionic form) or an equal right to speak in the assembly. Herodotus says that the value of *isegoria* was proven by many instances of bravery in war, "seeing that while they were under despotic rulers the Athenians were no better in war than any of their neighbors, yet once they got rid of tyrants they were far and away the best of all." While "oppressed" the Athenians were cowardly and slack, much like slaves "working for a master, but when they were freed each one was zealous to achieve for himself."[2]

This is, of course, not the full complex story of how the ancient Greeks achieved victory over the Persians. The Spartans were equally brave, though under a different political system. As a ruling minority or master race, they could hold down their serfs and intimidate their neighbors only by subjecting themselves to the dour rigors and rigid discipline of a militaristic barracks way of life. But seen from within, Spartan society also offered a rough and comradely military egalitarianism and some features of internal democracy — annual elections of their *ephors* or overseers — though without freedom of expression. The Spartans nevertheless *felt* like free men, and as compared with the Persians they were, and they fought for Hellas as nobly as did the Athenians.

To understand how *isegoria* became a synonym for political equality we need only recall for a moment the story we told about Thersites from the second book of the *Iliad,* where that common soldier dared speak up in the assembly of the warriors and was beaten by Odysseus for his presumption. For the Athenians the right to speak in the assembly meant political equality.

We can see this clearly if we compare the procedure in the Athenian assembly with that in the Spartan assembly. There, as later in the Roman Republic, a formal but fictitious popular sovereignty cloaked the realities of rule by an astute oligarchy. There was no *isegoria* in either Sparta or Rome. There was a right to vote but not a right of free speech. In Sparta there were monthly meetings of the *apella,* the Spartan assembly. But only the two vestigial kings, the members of the council or Senate of Elders, and the *ephors* — the elected chief magistrates — had a right to address the session. It could vote only on proposals put to it by these officials. There was no debate. The assembly expressed its opinion by a *thorubos,* as in Homer, a roar of approval or disapproval, a *boa* or shout. Only on rare occasions was a vote actually taken even on a declaration of war, which theoretically had to be made by the citizens in assembly.[3]

In Rome the popular assemblies suffered from a similar impotence. "The ordinary voter in Rome," J. A. O. Larsen wrote, "never gained any greater right of initiative or of addressing the assembly than the common man had in Homeric times . . . he had no right either to address the people or to make motions."[4] In addition, the voting system in the Roman assemblies was rigged to give the wealthiest — the patrician senators and the well-to-do businessmen — a built-in majority.[5]

"Freedom of speech, in the sense that any citizen had the right to speak," Ch. Wirszubski of Jerusalem's Hebrew University wrote in his *Libertas As a Political Idea in Rome,* "did not exist in the Roman assemblies."[6] Latin had no word for *isegoria.* Roman law had no use for it.

For those who may dismiss this as "ancient history," it is worth recalling that the first struggle for free speech in the Anglo-American constitutional tradition centered on the right to speak freely in Parliament and later in Congress. Originally it was a struggle against the power of the crown, which made free speech in the House of Commons hazardous. In 1576, just two hundred years before the American Declaration of Independence, a brave young Puritan, Peter Wentworth, suffered imprisonment for daring to speak freely in the House of Commons. It took another century before the right to speak was firmly established, and freed from the fear of royal displeasure, by the British Bill of Rights in 1689.

This was the ancestor of the oldest free speech clause in our own Constitution. Few Americans realize that the earliest guarantee of free speech in the Constitution is not the First Amendment but the Free Speech and Debate clause in Section 6, Article I of the original Constitution. This declares that no member of the Congress can be sued or prosecuted in any court of law for anything he says "in any Speech or Debate in either House." Were it not for this clause, powerful corporate or other special interests — the "kings" of our own time — could harass members of Congress, and make freedom of debate precarious, by expensive and protracted libel suits or other legal actions. Debate in Congress on such matters as industrial pollution or the profiteering by arms manufacturers would soon be restricted by the threat of such litigation. In this sense *isegoria* is imbedded as a right in our own Constitution.

In the Athenian assembly any citizen was not only allowed but invited to speak. We know this from three sources. One is Socrates himself, in his snobbish reflections on the Athenian assembly where everyone could speak freely, whether "a smith, a shoemaker, a merchant, a sea-captain, a rich man, a poor man, of good family or of none."[7] From two other sources we know that in Athens the assembly was opened by a herald who asked, "Who wishes to speak?"[8] The floor was open and speech unrestricted. Anyone who had something to say did not have to be recognized by a presiding officer; that was *isegoria*. Socrates could not have invoked a more cherished Athenian concept.

It is no exaggeration to say that the theater enjoyed more free speech in fifth-century Athens than in any other period of history. It is not surprising therefore that it celebrated free speech as a basic principle. The two other words for free speech in ancient Greek first appear in the tragic poets, one in Aeschylus, the other in Euripides.

The earlier is in the *Suppliant Maidens* of Aeschylus, probably in 463 B.C., when Socrates was a child of six. This play introduces us to a compound term for free speech made up of two roots — *eleutheros* (free) and *stomos* (mouth).[9]

The play, set in archaic times, becomes a lesson in democracy — perhaps our earliest introduction to the idea that legitimate government rests on the consent of the governed. The suppliant maidens are the fifty daughters (no less!) of Danaus, fleeing their insistent, fortune-hunting suitors. The maidens have escaped from Egypt with their father to beg asylum in Greece.

In the *Suppliant Maidens,* as so often in Greek tragedy, there is a conflict of law and of moral obligations. An arrogant herald arrives from Egypt demanding the extradition of the fugitives. The Greek king recognizes that under the laws of the country from which the maidens fled, the suitors as next of kin had a right to marry them and keep their fortunes in the family. The principle of "original jurisdiction" apparently was as basic in international law then as it is now. The doctrine holds that the law of the country in which the case originated is binding on a foreign court.

The suppliants appeal to a "higher law" — their right to asylum as victims of persecution, a popular theme with the tragic poets: the Athenians were proud of their city's reputation as a haven for the oppressed. But to grant asylum in this case might provoke hostilities with Egypt. The king himself favors asylum but, like a fifth-century-B.C. Athenian leader, says he cannot risk war without consulting his people. He summons an assembly and in preparing to address it the king prays that Peitho (Persuasion) may attend his efforts.[10]

The king proposes that the appeal be granted and the people follow "the persuasive windings" of his speech, like Athenian aficionados of forensic oratory. "A forest of raised hands" records their approval, and the king announces the decision to the Egyptian herald as the product of *eleutherostomou glosses,* "of free-speaking tongues," a triumph of free debate.

No special word for free speech appears in Sophocles, but its importance is dramatized in the *Antigone.* This play is usually read as a tragedy revolving around the conflict between the law of the state and a higher law of moral obligation — a sister's duty, despite a tyrant's order, to bury her dead brother. But it can also be read as the tragic outcome of a willful monarch's disregard of the more humane opinions of his people. To them, as to the Athenian audience, the fiat of the king lacked moral validity.

This comes out in the debate between Creon, the king of Thebes, and his son, Haemon, the betrothed of Antigone. Haemon thinks his father was wrong in ordering that the body of Antigone's brother be left unburied and dishonored outside the city walls as a rebel. Creon insists that as a king his will must be obeyed in all things, great or small, right or wrong. Creon affirms that "there is no more deadly peril than disobedience" and insists on his right to punish Antigone for it. The exchange which ensues between father and son is a clash between the ideas of monarchy and democracy:

CREON: Is not Antigone a law-breaker?

HAEMON: The people of Thebes do not agree with you.

CREON: Would you have the city dictate to me what I should decree?

HAEMON: It's you who now speak like a boy. [A few lines earlier Creon had asked whether he was to be taught wisdom by his son.]

CREON: Am I to rule as others see fit, or as I do?

HAEMON: A polis ruled by one man is no polis at all.

CREON: Does not the state belong to him who rules it?

HAEMON: No doubt in an uninhabited desert you could rule alone.[11]

Democracy had the last word and it is the will of the people that the play celebrates. Too little attention has been paid this political lesson in the *Antigone*. Creon himself learns it too late to save his son and his queen from death with the defiant Antigone. The tragedy is the tragedy of blind and obstinate tyranny. The moral of the play is that the people not only have a right to speak but to be heeded: a ruler puts himself and his city in peril when he disregards their opinions.

Sophocles was a friend of Pericles and a loyal son of democratic Athens. He was twice elected *strategos* — the highest executive and military office of the city. He served as imperial treasurer and in the wake of the Sicilian disaster he was one of the ten *probouloi* or special councilors appointed to investigate it. Unlike Socrates in the fifth century and Plato in the fourth, Sophocles during a long life — he died at the age of ninety — was a full participant in the affairs of the city, an exemplary citizen.

Of the three great tragic poets, it was the youngest, Euripides, who had most to say about freedom of speech. A fourth Greek word for freedom of speech — *parrhesia* — is one of his favorite themes.

Aeschylus and Sophocles dealt with the kings and gods of archaic myth. In Euripides the common man — and, even more so, the woman, common and uncommon — make their proud debut. The emancipation of women begins in Euripides.

It is often said that in his plays the gods and goddesses speak like mortals; his men and women, as loftily as gods, in the language of philosophy.

In Euripides egalitarian democracy finds its fullest expression. There, perhaps for the first time and a century before the Stoics, the slave is proclaimed equal with the master, the bastard with the legitimately born. Noble birth is disparaged as compared with innate character. In his *Electra,* it is the humble peasant who shields that hunted princess and turns out to be truly noble — not in family tree but in spirit.

Euripides was the Walt Whitman of Athens. In this tragic poet, democracy found its bard. In the *Frogs* of Aristophanes, Aeschylus

and Euripides debate in Hades. In one passage Euripides boasts
that he taught the common people how to speak.

The fourth word for free speech in ancient Greek, *parrhesia,* first
appears in Euripides. An authoritative special German lexicon tells
us that it was a word of Athenian coinage and a focus of Athenian
pride.[12] It had two basic and related meanings. One was personal:
frankness or outspokenness. The other was political: freedom of
speech. It expressed the Athenian's idealized image of himself, as
a free man accustomed to speak his mind.

So Ion, in the play that bears his name, a foundling searching for
the secret of his birth, hopes that his mother will turn out to be an
Athenian so that *parrhesia* will be his birthright: "from my mother
may *parrhesia* be mine."[13] In the *Phoenician Maidens,* the queen asks
her fugitive and rebel son, Polyneices, what is worst about being
an exile. The worst, he replies, "is that the exile has no *parrhesia.*"
The queen observes sadly, "That is a slave's lot — not to be able
to speak one's mind."[14]

The same spirit is expressed in the *Hippolytus.* Phaedra, the
young wife of the aging King Theseus, founder of Athens, is
sickened by a guilty passion for her chaste and aloof stepson,
Hippolytus. She tells her chorus of handmaidens she would rather
take her own life than give way to her desires and bring disgrace
upon her children. She wants them to grow up "in glorious
Athens, flourishing on its free speech" (*parrhesia*).[15] The same
problem of free speech is viewed from an opposite angle in the
Bacchae.[16] There in an undemocratic society, the herdsman is
afraid to speak frankly to King Pentheus unless he is permitted
parrhesia; he fears the royal temper. The king, in permitting him to
speak, says, "We must not be angry with honest men." Those
who speak their minds contribute to the welfare of the realm.

In Euripides, as in democratic Athens, the right to speak was
coupled with a duty to listen. In the *Children of Hercules,* the dead
hero's persecuted children plead for asylum in Athens. A herald
from their persecutor, the king of Argos, threatens war if asylum
is granted. A chorus of Old Men of Marathon sings, "Who can
give judgment, who grasp arguments/Ere from both sides he
clearly learn their pleas?"[17] (Marathon was fought centuries later,

of course, but the Athenian audience wasn't bothered by such patriotic anachronisms.)

To hear both sides before giving judgment was the lesson the Athenians learned through experience in the jury-courts. It was often repeated in the theater. So Orestes in the *Andromache* of Euripides says, "Wise indeed was the lesson of him who taught mankind to hear the arguments of both sides."[18] When Orestes himself stands trial in Euripides' *Orestes,* he speaks in the same vein. "Let plea face plea,"[19] he says, so that the jury may decide fairly. This was the standard of a free and just society as the Athenians conceived it.

Euripides expressed his hatred for those who would destroy democracy. In a lost play, the *Auge,* of which only a few lines survive, Euripides had one of his characters cry out, "Cursed be all those who rejoice to see the city in the hands of a single man or under the yoke of a few men! The name of freeman is the most precious of all titles: to possess it is to have much, even when one has little."[20]

This democratic viewpoint also finds expression in the *Phoenician Maidens.* Eteocles, fighting his brother for the throne of Thebes, cries out passionately, "I would fight my way to the risings of the sun and stars, or if I could, plunge below the earth to seize Power [*tyrannida,* tyranny], greatest of all the gods."[21] But his mother, Jocasta, reproves her power-hungry son. She warns him that ambition is the worst of all divinities and the goddess of injustice. She praises *isotes* — equality — as a finer ideal. "Better far, my son," she says, "prize equality that ever linketh friend to friend, city to city, and allies to each other, for equality is man's natural law."[22] This was the voice of fifth-century Athens at its best. But Euripides must have known the city often failed to abide by its own basic principles in dealing with its allies and subject cities. One would like to believe Euripides wrote these lines as reproof and that this is how the audience heard it.

Before we leave Euripides, I must deal with an unfair attack on the poet by Plato in the third book of the *Republic.*[23] Plato calls Euripides the "wisest" of all the tragic poets, but he does so with manifest sarcasm. For he goes on to accuse Euripides of praising tyranny.

Paul Shorey in his edition of the *Republic* says in a footnote to this wry remark, "This is plainly ironical and cannot be used by the admirers of Euripides."[24] Similarly James Adam in his monumental commentary on the *Republic* calls it "a highly ironical and sarcastic sentence."[25]

Quoting Euripides as having called tyranny "godlike," Plato says he and the other tragic poets "praise" tyranny "in many other ways," and has Socrates conclude that their plays should therefore properly be barred from the ideal city. Plato could hardly have been more unfair to the whole tenor of Athenian tragedy.

Plato does not cite the play in which Euripides called tyranny "godlike," but there are two such passages. One is in the *Trojan Women* where Hecuba, the vanquished queen of Troy, bewails the murder by the victorious Greeks of her grandson, the infant child of Hector, her city's fallen champion. There is indeed a reference to "godlike tyranny" (*isotheou tyrannoou*).[26] But the Greek term *tyrannos* was used in two meanings, sometimes as a synonym for a legitimate king, and sometimes for a man who had seized power unlawfully. What Hecuba laments is that her infant child was cut down without ever having enjoyed youth or the pleasures of marriage or of the "godlike power" that would have been his someday as the successor to the throne of Troy. But this was a lawful monarchy; neither Hecuba nor Euripides was advocating tyranny.

The second passage is the one we have just quoted from the *Phoenician Maidens* where the power-hungry Eteocles did indeed call tyranny "the greatest of all the gods." But, as we have seen, his mother, Jocasta, rebuked him and held up *isotes,* equality, as the nobler ideal. Plato distorted the real message in Euripides.

When Milton wrote his *Areopagitica,* the noblest defense of free speech in the English tongue, he chose two lines from the *Suppliants* of Euripides to preface his appeal to Parliament against censorship — "This is true Liberty, when free born men/Having to advise the public may speak free."[27]

Clearly, the theater would have provided a civil libertarian defense of Socrates with a rich store of treasured sentiment with which to challenge and shame his judges.[28]

Chapter 18

THE FINAL QUESTION

ক্রিউটিউট্র

THERE IS A PASSAGE in the *Crito* where a civil libertarian argument is invited. There, in the debate between Socrates and the Laws, they declare "in war and in court and everywhere, you must do whatever the state . . . commands, or must show her by persuasion what is really right."[1] Socrates should have asked how could he persuade the Laws of "what is really right" if free speech were shut off?

Implicit in this debate is the notion of a contract between the state and the citizen. The Laws argue that if the citizen accepts the terms of the contract when it suits him, he must also accept the obligations of the contract when it goes against him. This, of course, was Socrates' argument for refusing to escape.

But the contract between the city and the citizen in a free society binds the state as well as the citizen. A very different, unequal relationship is implied by Plato at the very beginning of the debate. There the Laws ask Socrates, "Were you not our offspring and our slave?"[2] This is a fallacious analogy; the relationship of state and citizen is not that of an authoritarian parent to a child or of a master to a slave. Very few fifth-century Athenians would have spoken of themselves as the slave of the state. A basic rule of Athenian democracy, as we have seen, was that the citizen ruled and was ruled in turn. The slave does not change places with his master.

Basic to a free city was the right to speak back to the state, to criticize its actions in the assembly, the courts, the theater, or conversation. If the state suddenly interfered with that right, it was breaking its part of the contract. It was becoming a tyranny.

Socrates could have argued — and most of his judges, I believe, would have agreed — that if the Laws broke the contract by preventing free speech, they released the citizen from the obligation to obey them. When he lost the right to persuade, he won the right to resist.

It was on this very basis only four years before his trial, Socrates could have argued, that the *demos* and many moderates, including his most prominent accuser, Anytus, had taken up arms against the Thirty and overthrown them.

Socrates should have argued that the Laws, by denying him freedom of speech, were turning a citizen into a slave. This is how the argument should have been made in the *Crito,* and in the trial itself.

To understand why the argument did not take that course, and why Socrates did not use his best defense, one must take a fresh look at the attitude of Greek philosophers toward freedom of speech.

This can be divided into three periods. In the first, the era of the pre-Socratics, the philosophers so took their extraordinary freedom for granted that they did not bother to analyze it, much less defend it.

This is remarkable because these earlier philosophers were the first freethinkers. They shook the foundations of religion, modern as well as ancient, and their bold insights laid the foundations of philosophy for twenty-five hundred years to come. Yet their freedom of thought was not restricted.

In the second period, which we may call the Socratic and Platonic, the philosophers enjoyed their own freedom of speech, but would have denied it to others. Socrates in particular seems to have taken his freedom of speech for granted — it was his by virtue of his superiority, albeit masked by his "irony."

In the third period, with the extinction of political freedom under Macedon and, later, Rome, the ancient philosophers tended to retire into their private worlds, indifferent to political events, like the withdrawn and hence ever-blissful gods of Epicurus and Lucretius.

It is hard to find even a mention of the four words for freedom of speech in Socrates and his followers. It is as if they found even the terms for free speech distasteful. Of the four, only one, *parrhesia,* appears in the Platonic dialogues and only one, *isegoria,* in Xenophon.

The only discussion of free speech in Xenophon turns up in his *Cyropaedia,* where the rather priggish young Cyrus delivers a lecture on temperance to his grandfather, King Astyages, a heavy drinker. Cyrus is disgusted because his grandfather became too familiar with his cronies at a drinking party. "And all of you quite forgot," Cyrus says, "you, that you were king; and the rest, that you were their sovereign."[3]

Cyrus considered that a salutary lesson in the real meaning of free speech. "It was then," he tells his grandfather, "that I . . . discovered, and for the first time, that what you were practicing was your boasted 'equal freedom of speech' [*isegoria*]." In writing of Socrates, Xenophon does not invoke free speech at all; none of the four words appears in his *Memorabilia* or in his *Apology.*

Freedom of speech is not permitted in any of the Platonic utopias and it gets scant and scornful attention in the Platonic corpus. There are only four references to freedom of speech listed in the admirable analytical index to the sixteen hundred pages of the one-volume Bollingen edition of Plato's works as edited by Edith Hamilton and Huntington Cairns.

The only respectful reference is in the *Laws,* where Persia under Cyrus is held up as an example of an ideal kingdom. Since it is the only place in Plato where he says a good word for free speech, we quote it in full.

"When the Persians, under Cyrus," says the Athenian, Plato's mouthpiece in the *Laws,* "maintained the due balance between slavery and freedom [*eleutheria*], they became, first of all, free themselves, and, after that, masters of many others. For when the rulers gave a share of freedom to their subjects and advanced them to a position of equality, the soldiers were more friendly to their officers and showed their devotion in times of danger."[4]

Then Plato shifts from the military to the civilian sphere. "If there was any wise man amongst them, able to give counsel," he continues, "since the king was not jealous and allowed free speech [*parrhesia*] and respected those who could help at all by their counsel — such a man had the opportunity of contributing to the common stock the fruit of his wisdom. Consequently," Plato concludes, "at that time all their affairs made progress, owing to their freedom, friendliness and mutual interchange of reason."

It is a pity this "mutual interchange of reason" in the *Laws* itself was so restricted. No democratic spokesman appears in its cast of characters. The Athenian's interlocutors are limited to a Spartan and a Cretan, both representing closed societies.

But though Plato, writing the *Laws* in his old age, finally acknowledged some merit in free speech, he was unwilling to develop this passing reference and give it institutional embodiment. The ideal sketched in the *Laws* is a dour polity of strict thought control, enforced by an inquisitorial Nocturnal Council empowered to send nonconformists to ideological "rehabilitation" centers and impose the death penalty on the recalcitrant.

All the other references to freedom of speech in the Platonic canon are satirical and contemptuous. They turn up in the *Protagoras,* the *Republic,* and the *Gorgias.*

In the first of these three, as we have seen, Protagoras is allowed to set Greek mythology to a new democratic music. The myth propounded by Protagoras gives divine sanction to the common man's right to speak, but Socrates never confronts the issue. All the myth elicits from him, as we have also seen, is a snobbish tirade about the vulgar craftsmen and tradesmen allowed to speak in the Athenian assembly.[5] When the favorite Athenian term for free speech, *parrhesia,* is actually used in the *Republic,* Plato's Socrates treats it with the same kind of derision. Describing democracy in Athens, Socrates asks sarcastically, "Are they [the citizens] not free? And is not the city chock-full of liberty [*eleutherias*] and freedom of speech [*parrhesias*] and has not every man license to do as he pleases?"[6]

Socrates in another passage speaks derisively of democracy because political leaders must pay attention to the opinions "of the motley multitude in their assembly, whether about painting or music or, for that matter, politics."[7]

At one point Socrates seems to be on the verge of paying

democracy a compliment. There Socrates admits that "possibly" democracy "is the most beautiful of polities." But he goes on to compare it with "a garment of many colours, embroidered with all kinds of hues . . . decked and diversified with every type of character" and attractive to many "like boys and women" who like "bright-coloured things."[8] What looked like a compliment turns into a sneer. Socrates compares democracy to "a bazaar" and "a delicious entertainment" but not a form of government a philosopher could take seriously. He describes "the climax of popular liberty . . . when the purchased slaves . . . are no less free than the owners who paid for them."

Socrates says, "No one would believe how much freer the very beasts" are in such a city. The dogs become like their mistresses and "the horses and asses are wont to hold on their way with the utmost freedom and dignity, bumping into everyone who meets them and does not step aside. And so," he concludes, "all things everywhere are just bursting with the spirit of liberty."[9] The prejudice is venomous.

In the *Gorgias,* Socrates runs into trouble with Polus, a teacher of rhetoric, the "Sophist" whom he is interrogating. Polus does not wish to be limited to answering the loaded questions put by Socrates. He wants to express his views in his own way. He senses that the famous Socratic method can be a trap, and he revolts against it. "Why," he asks Socrates, "shall I not be at liberty to say as much as I like?"

Socrates replies with a little joke that is the closest he comes to paying his native city a compliment on its free speech. He says, "It would indeed be a hard fate for you, my excellent friend, if having come to Athens, where there is more freedom of speech than anywhere in Greece, you should be the one person there who could not enjoy it." But here Socrates avoids the four complimentary terms for freedom of speech and uses the phrase *exousia tou legein.* The LSJ lexicon translates *exousia* in this passage as "license," which makes it read "license in speaking." In Greek, as in English, "license" can be pejorative, so this compliment to Athens may be ironical rather than real.[10]

An unequivocal compliment might have mollified the jury. A

free-speech defense might well have won his acquittal. But the historical Socrates might have considered it beneath his dignity to invoke a principle he had so often derided. In any case, if we are to believe Xenophon's *Apology,* Socrates wanted to die. This is also what the disciples suspected in the *Crito* and the *Phaedo.*

But there still remains the curious fact that nowhere in the many dialogues that touch on the trial of Socrates does Plato have any of his characters make the obvious point that Athens was untrue to its own principles in condemning Socrates. Perhaps Plato disliked democracy so much that he would not demean himself to treat its principles seriously.

If we look at Plato for a moment as a dramatist, with Socrates as his tragic hero, we can see that it would have been out of character to write a scene in which Socrates invoked free speech and Athens honored its traditions by setting Socrates free. Plato's hero lived and died by his principles. The historical, like the Platonic, Socrates would have found it repugnant to plead a principle in which he did not believe; free speech for him was the privilege of the enlightened few, not of the benighted many. He would not have wanted the democracy he rejected to win a moral victory by setting him free.

His martyrdom, and the genius of Plato, made him a secular saint, the superior man confronting the ignorant mob with serenity and humor. This was Socrates' triumph and Plato's masterpiece. Socrates needed the hemlock, as Jesus needed the Crucifixion, to fulfill a mission. The mission left a stain forever on democracy. That remains Athens' tragic crime.

EPILOGUE
Was There a Witch-hunt in Ancient Athens?

❧

WAS THE CONDEMNATION of Socrates a unique case? Or was he only the most famous victim in a wave of persecutions aimed at irreligious philosophers?

Two distinguished scholars, both justly respected, have put forward the view in recent years that fifth-century Athens, though often called the Age of the Greek Enlightenment, was also — at least in its latter half — the scene of a general witch-hunt against freethinkers.

According to E. R. Dodds in his famous work, *The Greeks and the Irrational,* this witch-hunt began with the passage in Athens of legislation so terrifying that one wonders why so many philosophers dared to flock there and by what miracle Socrates managed to avoid arrest for thirty years after its passage.

Dodds wrote that "About 432 B.C. or a year or two later, disbelief in the supernatural and the teaching of astronomy were made indictable offenses. The next thirty-odd years witnessed a series of heresy trials. . . . The victims included most of the leaders of progressive thought at Athens — Anaxagoras, Diagoras, Socrates, almost certainly Protagoras also, and possibly Euripides."

Dodds said there were almost no acquittals. "In all these cases except the last," Dodds claimed, "the prosecution was successful: Anaxagoras may have been fined and banished; Diagoras escaped by flight; so, probably, did Protagoras; Socrates, who could have done the same, or asked for a sentence of banishment, chose to stay and drink the hemlock." The evidence "is more than enough to prove," Dodds concluded, "that the Great Age of Greek Enlightenment" was also marked by the "banishment of scholars, blinkering of thought and even (if we can believe the tradition about Protagoras) burning of books."[1]

A similar picture was drawn more recently by Arnaldo Momigliano in two essays he contributed to the fascinating but too little known *Dictionary of the History of Ideas*, one on "Freedom of Speech in Antiquity" and the other on "Impiety in the Classical World."[2] Any reexamination of the trial of Socrates would be incomplete if it did not deal with these dark views, from such respected sources.

I believe the evidence for all this is belated and dubious; that the witch-hunt fable originated, like some other notorious historical misconceptions, in Athenian comedy — in a lost play, fragments of which may someday turn up among new papyrus finds. These have added so much in the past century to our knowledge of classical antiquity.

No "evidence" of a witch-hunt appears any earlier than in writers of the Roman era, principally Plutarch, who wrote about five centuries after Socrates. Plutarch's distance in time from Socrates was as great as ours from Columbus, and the gulf in political outlook is as wide. The frequent expulsion of philosophers and other Greek teachers from Rome is well attested, and it was natural for writers of that time to assume that the Athenians were equally suspicious and intolerant. That also suited their contempt for democracy. The farther one turns back to the writers of Socrates' own lifetime and the two generations after, the more difficult it becomes to find evidence of such previous persecutions. Indeed, the strongest rebuttal may be inferred from Plato himself, although — and especially because — he was as ready as any Roman aristocrat to believe the worst of the vulgar many.

Let us begin with the law against "disbelief in the supernatural and the teaching of astronomy," which Dodds cited as the basis for this wave of prosecutions — a law sponsored by a man named Diopeithes.

So dramatic a departure from Athenian law and tradition should have provoked wide and bitter controversy. Yet the only mention of a law sponsored by Diopeithes is a solitary reference in Plutarch's *Life of Pericles*.

All we know earlier of Diopeithes comes from Athenian Old Comedy: he was a favorite butt of its poets and they pictured him as a religious fanatic and wacky oracle-monger. Diopeithes — but not his decree — is mentioned in three plays of Aristophanes.[3] The Pauly-Wissowa German encyclopedia of classical antiquity also lists references to him in four fragments from other writers of comedy. But nowhere is he encountered in serious literature, as one would expect if he was influential enough to put such an unprecedented enactment through the Athenian assembly.

Indeed the context in the *Life of Pericles* leads one to suspect that Plutarch was led astray by some recollection of another lost comedy that made fun of Diopeithes as well as Pericles. Plutarch's account is part of an extraordinary jumble that generations of scholars have failed successfully to unravel.

Plutarch links a prosecution of Pericles himself with charges of impiety against his brilliant mistress, Aspasia, and his philosophic mentor, Anaxagoras. Included is a titillating assertion that Aspasia ran a private "house of assignation" for Pericles, and finally the allegation that he started the Peloponnesian war to divert public attention and restore his power, though even Plutarch admits lamely that "the truth about it is not clear."[4]

Only one detail of Plutarch's story is attested by Thucydides. We know that Pericles in a moment of great dissatisfaction with his policies was once fined and temporarily removed from office by the Athenians. But this happened not before, but after, the Peloponnesian war began, when a second Spartan invasion of the lands around Athens and sufferings within the besieged city led to a demand for peace. Pericles paid a fine but soon rallied fresh support and was reelected to the leadership.[5]

So much was fact. Plutarch's description of the impiety prosecutions, however, is highly improbable. "About this time also," Plutarch wrote, "Aspasia was put on trial for impiety, Hermippus the comic poet being her prosecutor, who alleged further against her that she received free-born women into a place of assignation for Pericles. And Diopeithes brought in a bill providing for the public impeachment of such as did not believe in gods, or who taught doctrines regarding the heavens, directing suspicion against Pericles by means of Anaxagoras."

Plutarch says, "The people accepted with delight these slanders"; Pericles saved Aspasia "by shedding copious tears at the trial" but "he feared for Anaxagoras so much that he sent him away from the city" and "kindled into flame" the conflict with Sparta to divert attention from all the charges against himself and his friends.[6] Such a plot, at once philosophical and sexy, was made to order for the comic poets.

The telltale detail in Plutarch's account is his statement that the prosecutor was "Hermippus the comic poet." Of course a comic poet, like any other citizen, could initiate a prosecution under Athenian law. But we know of no other case in which a comic poet ever convicted himself of seriousness by taking his jokes and lampoons into court. In its article on Hermippus, the Pauly-Wissowa takes the Plutarchian account at face value and notes that Hermippus was the only comic poet who "did not limit his attacks on Pericles to the comic stage."

Hermippus, I believe, would have made himself a laughingstock in Athens if he had stepped out of his role as a comic poet and tried to translate his jokes into a legal indictment. Indeed, it is hard to see how he could have found the time even if he had the inclination. He was prolific in his profession. Forty plays are attributed to him; we know the titles of ten and have one hundred fragments. He would have cut a strange figure as a prosecutor of impiety, since one of his own lost plays "impiously" made fun of the birth of Athena and was, as the Pauly-Wissowa observes, "the oldest example of comic treatment of a divine birth," a genre much cultivated in later antiquity.

Pericles was one of his favorite targets. One of his plays — perhaps the one known as the *King of the Satyrs* — accused Pericles of "erotic insatiability." Perhaps that explains his joke in accusing Aspasia of providing a private brothel for her indefatigable lover! Plutarch's description of how Pericles saved his mistress from conviction is evidence enough that this stems from comedy, not history. The incongruous spectacle of the aristocratic and notoriously standoffish Pericles shedding copious tears to save his mistress would have delighted an Athenian audience.

As for Plutarch's suggestion that this may explain why Pericles started the Peloponnesian war, it is on a par with the joke that Aristophanes put forward in the *Acharnians*. There he suggested that it all began with a feud between two rival brothelkeepers. Some of Athens' gilded youth, more drunk than usual, stole Simaetha from a house in Megora — an ally of Sparta — and the Megarians in revenge "paid back the theft and rape of Aspasia's harlots two."[7] This seems to have been standard bawdy fare in Athenian antiwar plays.

In fact, the suggestion that the Plutarchan account originated in a lost play by Hermippus was pointed out at least as long ago as the 1927 edition of the *Cambridge Ancient History*, but in so inconspicuous a way that it attracted little attention. There, in volume 5, on Athens in its heyday, the great historian J. B. Bury contributed a chapter called "The Age of Illumination," which included a section on the "blasphemy trials" in Athens. In this section — except for a revisionist footnote on Protagoras to which we will return later — Bury also took at face value all the impiety trial stories.

But at the end of the volume in the *CAH* there is appended "Notes on Points Especially on Chronology." One of them, "The Attacks on the Friends of Pericles," says: "It is possible that Aspasia was prosecuted for impiety (as related by Bury on p. 383 of the *CAH* volume) but the statement that her accuser was the comic poet Hermippus, who added to it the charge of being the procuress for Pericles, makes us suspect that we have no more than a conflation of the belief in Aspasia's free-thinking and the scurrility of comedy. The charge of being a procuress was brought also by Aristophanes in the *Acharnians*."[8] The writer was F. E. Adcock, one of the three editors, with Bury and S. A. Cook, of the *Cambridge Ancient History*.

Adcock went on to note that the Plutarchan charge that Pericles started the war to divert attention from his troubles "was first brought by Aristophanes, ten years after the outbreak of the war, in the *Peace*," and was "clearly the invention of a comic poet who rejoices in his extravagant novelty." Adcock says it "was removed from its context and taken seriously by those who wished to blacken the character of Pericles."

But what of the possibility that the decree of Diopeithes was also taken out of the context of a lost comedy by Hermippus and treated seriously to blacken the reputation of democratic Athens? The question is still unanswered. Adcock concluded that "the decree of Diopeithes is, doubtless, historical fact." Adcock never explained why it was "doubtless."

An admirable recent work by Mary R. Lefkowitz, *The Lives of the Comic Poets,* reaches a different conclusion. "The story that Hermippus charged Aspasia with impiety," she wrote, "appears simply to replicate the plot of a comedy about her." She put the decree of Diopeithes in the same category, suggesting that "the notion of trials for impiety made particular sense" for later writers "because they offered precedents for Socrates' condemnation."[9]

Plutarch in his *Life of Nicias* gives a different version of the witch-hunt. Nicias was the superstitious general in command of the Athenian naval expedition against Syracuse in the final years of the Peloponnesian war.

A surprise night attack on the city had been planned, "but just as everything was prepared for this and none of the enemy was on the watch," Plutarch relates, there was an eclipse of the moon. "This was a great terror to Nicias and all those who were ignorant or superstitious enough to quake at such a sight." He called off the assault when it could have succeeded and the expedition eventually ended in the greatest Athenian disaster of the war.

Plutarch attributes this setback to a favorite theme — the superstitious character of the Athenian *demos,* and its hostility toward philosophical and astronomical speculation. Had the Athenians been more sophisticated they would not have been frightened off by an eclipse of the moon.

Anaxagoras, Plutarch says, "was the first man to put in writing" a rational explanation of the moon's eclipses, but his doctrine was not "in high repute" and was circulated in secret "among a few only." Discretion was necessary; because "men could not abide the natural philosophers and 'visionaries,' . . . they reduced the divine agency down to irrational causes, blind forces, and necessary incidents." As a result of these popular prejudices, Plutarch says, "even Protagoras had to go into exile, Anaxagoras was with difficulty rescued from imprisonment by Pericles, and Socrates, though he had nothing to do with such matters, nevertheless lost his life."[10]

Plutarch does not explain why Protagoras was driven into exile. But a century after Plutarch, in Diogenes Laertius, this story had taken on melodramatic details. According to his version, the first book from which Protagoras ventured to give a public reading in Athens was called *On the Gods*. In its preface Protagoras said, "As to the gods, I have no means of knowing that they exist or that they do not exist. For many are the obstacles that impede knowledge, both the obscurity of the question and the shortness of human life."

According to Diogenes Laertius, this threw Athens into a frenzy. "For this introduction to his book," he tells us, "the Athenians expelled him." They also "sent around a herald to collect" the book "from all who had copies in their possession" and "burnt his works in the market-place."[11]

A telltale incongruity should have disposed of this tale a long time ago. Diogenes Laertius says Protagoras gave his reading at the home of Euripides. The Athenians were accustomed in his plays to hearing not just a mild Protagorean skepticism but aspersions on the gods that were downright insulting, as in Ion's scornful remarks about the criminal lusts of the Olympians,[12] or downright atheistic, as in Hecuba's prayer where she wonders whether Zeus is not merely "the necessity implicit in nature or a figment of mortal minds."[13]

The conclusive answer to these Roman-era fables is provided by Plato himself, though the clue seems to have been overlooked until the great Scottish classicist John Burnet called attention to it in 1914 in his *Greek Philosophy: Thales to Plato*. All the nonsense about Protagoras in Cicero, Plutarch, and Diogenes Laertius should have been dissipated centuries ago by a passage in Plato's *Meno*. Socrates is speaking to his future accuser, Anytus, who has

attacked Sophists — and, by implication, Socrates, too — for corrupting the youth.

Socrates replies that one of these teachers, Protagoras, "amassed
more money by his craft than Pheidias — so famous for the noble
works he produced — or any ten other sculptors." And yet,
Socrates adds, "how surprising that menders of old shoes and
furbishers of clothes" could not go "undetected thirty days if they
should return the clothes or shoes in worse condition than they
received them" and would quickly starve to death, while for more
than forty years all Greece failed to notice that Protagoras was
corrupting his classes and sending his pupils away in a "worse
state than when he took charge of them!" Socrates concludes that
Protagoras had died at seventy and "retains undiminished to this
day the high reputation he has enjoyed."[14]

Burnet observed that this account in the *Meno* is "quite inconsistent" with the statement in Diogenes Laertius that Protagoras
"was prosecuted and condemned for impiety" in 411 B.C., only
twelve years before the trial of Socrates. "Plato represents
Sokrates," Burnet wrote, "as saying things which make it impossible to believe that Protagoras was ever prosecuted for impiety at
all." For Socrates in the *Meno* made "a special point" of the fact
that Protagoras' "good name remained unsullied down to the
supposed date of the dialogue, several years after his death."[15]

Burnet rejected as "absurd" the story of Diogenes Laertius that
the Athenian authorities collected and burned all copies of the
book in which Protagoras expressed some skepticism about
the gods. Burnet cited passages in the *Theaetetus* of Plato and in the
Helen of the fourth-century orator Isocrates that show "that the
work was widely read long after Protagoras died."[16]

But it is surprising that Burnet failed to see that the speech Plato
put into the mouth of Socrates in the *Meno* rebuts not only the
fables in Diogenes Laertius but also those in Plutarch. For if we go
back to this passage in the *Meno* and look again, we see that
Socrates did not limit his defense to Protagoras but extended it to
cover all the teachers whom Anytus stigmatized as Sophists.
Socrates ended his speech by saying that it was not only the "high
reputation" of Protagoras that had remained "undiminished to

this day" but "a multitude of others too: some who lived before him, and others still living." This is wholly inconsistent with the notion of a witch-hunt against freethinkers.

Socrates asks Anytus triumphantly, "Now are we to take it, according to you, that they wittingly deceived and corrupted the youth, or that they were themselves unconscious of it? Are we to conclude those who are frequently termed the wisest of mankind [sophistoi] to have been so demented as that?"

The reply made by Anytus to those new questions is also revealing. "Demented! Not they, Socrates," Anytus answers, "far rather the young men who pay them money, and still more the relatives who entrust young men to their charge; and most of all the cities that allow them to enter, and do not expel them, whether such attempt be made by stranger or citizen."[17] This complains that Athens — and other Greek cities — has been too tolerant of Sophists. What a strange reply if Athens had indeed only a few years earlier driven Protagoras out of the city, burned all copies of his book in the marketplace, and passed a "decree of Diopeithes" that initiated a general onslaught against philosophers.

But Burnet's acute inference from the *Meno* made too little impact on classical scholarship. Thirteen years later, in the *Cambridge Ancient History,* Bury retold all the old fables about Protagoras, though he added a footnote saying, "See Burnet's *Greek Philosophy* I, p. 111 sqq. for reasons for rejecting the story with which the present writer is disposed to agree."

But if Burnet's observations had been accepted and carried to their logical conclusion, then the "Age of Illumination" was not also — as Bury still insisted — an age of witch-hunting and "blasphemy trials." Even now, while Burnet's views about the case of Protagoras are generally accepted, the rest of the witch-hunt account is still treated by many scholars as historical fact. Scholars, like journalists, hate to give up a good story so long as it can be attributed to some source, however shaky.

Let us now turn to the other famous philosopher who was supposed to have fallen victim to an Athenian witch-hunt. Later centuries provide many diverse stories about Anaxagoras.

Our earliest surviving source for a trial of Anaxagoras is the historian Diodorus Siculus, who wrote in the days of Julius Caesar and the Emperor Augustus. He tells the same story told by Plutarch — that Pericles started the Peloponnesian war to divert attention from scandalous charges brought against some of his friends. Diodorus adds that "the sophist Anaxagoras, who was Pericles' teacher," was "falsely accused" of impiety in the same affair.[18] Diodorus takes it for granted that comedy could be read as history because he naïvely cites as proof, "Mention has been made of this even by Aristophanes," and quotes lines 603–6 from his antiwar play *Peace*. But actually Anaxagoras is mentioned neither in that play nor in the similar passages about the origins of the Peloponnesian war in the *Acharnians*. The Diodorus reference to Anaxagoras may have come from the same lost comedy by Hermippus that Plutarch seems to have echoed.

If there had been an impiety prosecution of Anaxagoras, one would expect some mention of it in Cicero, who wrote somewhat earlier than Diodorus. There are many references to Anaxagoras in Cicero's philosophical works, and in two of his essays on oratory Cicero credits the eloquence of Pericles to the teaching of Anaxagoras.[19] But nowhere does Cicero say that those teachings got either of them into trouble.

A rich crop of legends about Anaxagoras is harvested by Diogenes Laertius in the third century A.D. They provide a jumble of inconsistencies, chronological and otherwise, that scholars are still trying to disentangle.

"Of the trial of Anaxagoras," he writes, "different accounts are given." He supplies four. One had Anaxagoras convicted of impiety, but added that Pericles got him off with a fine and a decree of banishment. A second version held that he was convicted of treasonable connections with Persia and escaped the death penalty by flight. The third account said he was in prison awaiting execution, when Pericles made a pathetic speech declaring himself a pupil of Anaxagoras and begging the people to free his teacher, which they did — but Anaxagoras "could not brook the indignity he had suffered and committed suicide." A fourth version had Anaxagoras brought into court by Pericles "so weak and wasted" that he was acquitted "not so much to the merits of his case" but because the judges took pity on him![20] All but one of the authors cited by Diogenes are Alexandrians of the third century B.C. One of them, Satyrus, is notorious for using not only Attic comedy but Greek tragedy as fact, as he did in his *Life of Euripides*.

The most thorough examination of these and other ancient accounts, including details added by Church Fathers anxious to convict the pagans of intolerance, is to be found in an unusual but neglected work, *Anaxagoras and the Birth of Physics* by Daniel E. Gershenson and Daniel A. Greenberg, in which the late Ernest Nagel of Columbia assigned a physicist and a classicist to write what was to be the inaugural volume of a history of physics.

All the ancient references to his life and work down to the Aristotelian commentator Simplicius in the seventh century A.D. are there translated and analyzed. They conclude that "the trial . . . is a persistent historical myth based on plausible reconstruction . . . because of its spectacular nature in posing him as the earliest martyr of science, and as the forerunner of Socrates."[21]

Clearly, if the story was more than a later myth, this aspect of the case as a forerunner of that against Socrates would have been mentioned by those who had lived through the trial of Socrates or who wrote about it in the years following his death. But there is no reference to a prosecution of Anaxagoras in Thucydides, Xenophon, or Plato.

The silence of any one writer may have many possible explanations, but the silence of all the "contemporaries" cannot be so easily dismissed. The most striking is that of Thucydides. Pericles is the hero of his history, but he makes no mention of any cabal to strike at Pericles through friends like Aspasia and Anaxagoras. Nor as the first "scientific" historian does he lend any credence to the scandalous and sexy explanations of how the Peloponnesian war started.[22]

The silence of the pro-Periclean Thucydides is matched by the silence in the anti-Periclean Xenophon and Plato. Xenophon attributes to Socrates the same reactionary views about astronomy as those of Diopeithes. He even quotes Socrates as saying that "he who meddles" in the study of the heavenly bodies "runs the risk of losing his sanity as completely as Anaxagoras, who took an insane pride in his explanaton of the divine machinery."[23] But Xenophon never mentions any prosecution of Anaxagoras or any decree that would have made such astronomical speculation unlawful.

In Plato, Anaxagoras is discussed more often than any other philosopher, and there are many places where one would have expected some reference to his prosecution if it had really happened. In the *Phaedrus* Socrates credits Anaxagoras for Pericles' "loftiness of mind"[24] and skill in speaking but does not say that this association later caused Pericles political difficulties. In the *Gorgias* Plato had Socrates argue that Pericles was a bad "herdsman" as a statesman because he made his "herd" worse than he found it.[25] Socrates claimed that the Athenians in the later years of Pericles "all but condemned him to death" for embezzlement! Here Plutarch's story about the attack on Aspasia and Anaxagoras — if true — would have provided another dramatic illustration of how fickle and benighted the Athenian *demos* could be.

In the *Phaedo,* Socrates tells his disciples how thrilled he was as a youth when he first encountered in Anaxagoras the doctrine that mind rather than blind material forces set the universe in motion; he does not add that Anaxagoras, like himself, had become the victim of Athenian hostility to philosophic speculation.

In the *Crito,* the disciples could have argued that Socrates follow the example of Anaxagoras and flee Athens, reestablishing a school elsewhere as Anaxagoras did at Lampsacus.

The *Apology* is the place where one most expects mention of a prosecution of Anaxagoras. Burnet, to clinch his argument for disbelieving the story about the prosecution of Protagoras, says, "Further, there is no reference to any accusation of Protagoras in the *Apology,* though such a reference would have been almost inevitable if it had ever taken place. Sokrates has to go back to the trial of Anaxagoras to find a parallel to his own case. It is therefore safer to dismiss the story altogether."[26]

But this same inference from the silence of Socrates applies with equal force to Anaxagoras. Socrates nowhere mentions a trial of

Anaxagoras as "a parallel to his own case." Anaxagoras is indeed mentioned, but in quite a different connection and with a different purpose. His name comes up in the exchange between Socrates and his accuser Meletus. Socrates diverts attention from the actual language of his indictment by trapping the witless Meletus into accusing him of atheism. "Are you saying," Socrates asks Meletus, "that I do not honor or believe in the gods the city believes in but that I honor other gods" — the actual charge in the indictment — "or that I do not myself believe in gods at all and that I teach this unbelief to other people?" The unwary Meletus replies, "That is what I say that you do not believe in gods at all." Then Socrates says, "You amaze me, Meletus! . . . Do I not even believe that the sun or yet the moon are gods, as the rest of mankind do?" Meletus replies, "No, by Zeus, judges, since he says that the sun is a stone and the moon earth."

Socrates is delighted by that answer. He sees a chance to expose Meletus to the court as a benighted ignoramus. "Do you think you are accusing Anaxagoras, my dear Meletus," Socrates asks, "and do you so despise these gentlemen [i.e., the juror-judges] and think that they are so unversed in letters [*apeirous grammaton*] as not to know, that the books of Anaxagoras the Clazomenian are full of such utterances?"

Socrates goes on to say that the youth he is accused of leading astray with such irreligious ideas about the sun and moon can buy the book of Anaxagoras "for a drachma in the orchestra and laugh at Socrates, if he pretends they are his own, especially when they are so absurd!"[27] The word *orchestra* (*orxestra*) could mean not only the forepart of the theater where the chorus danced but also an open section near the *agora* where books and other wares were on sale.

This reference by Socrates conjures up a picture of Athens quite different from that in Plutarch — not of a bigoted city in which the works of a rationalistic philosopher were burned at the stake, but one in which such books were freely on sale and widely read. Socrates is paying his judges an implied compliment on their sophistication and open-mindedness.

If, on the other hand, Anaxagoras and Protagoras and other freethinkers had indeed been prosecuted for their views, such a compliment would have been unthinkable. He would have attacked the Athenians for their intolerance. He could not have spoken in so light a tone if Anaxagoras had also met a tragic fate.

The only credible parallel with the case of Socrates is that of Aristotle. In 323 B.C., when Alexander died, Athens rose in joyful revolt against its hated Macedonian occupiers and restored the democracy. Aristotle, a lifelong protégé of the Macedonian court, fled the city, fearing for his life. An ancient tale quotes Aristotle as saying that he fled because he did not wish Athens to sin a second time against philosophy.[28]

A parallel with the case of Socrates is drawn by Diogenes Laertius. He claims that Aristotle fled rather than face a charge of impiety. The charge was based on a poem Aristotle wrote supposedly paying divine honors to the memory of a minor tyrant who had once befriended him. The poem does not bear out the charge. Anton-Hermann Chroust, who made the most thorough study of Aristotle's flight, including Arabic sources, concludes that the most credible reason for the flight from Athens was the philosopher's close ties to the Macedonians.[29] According to Chroust, no formal charges had been filed and Aristotle left voluntarily, taking with him his personal property and servants. He withdrew to nearby Chalcis, probably in expectation of returning when Macedonian rule was restored, but he died there a year later. His school at the Lyceum was not closed down but remained in operation under Aristotle's chosen successor, Theophrastus.

Macedonian rule over Athens was soon reimposed. But sixteen years later there was a second uprising and then, for the first time in Athenian history, the assembly did pass a law restricting the freedom of its philosophical schools.

The uprising had ended ten years of rule by a philosopher, Demetrius of Phalerum, who had been installed as dictator by the Macedonian general Cassander. In 307 B.C. rebellious elements allied themselves with a rival general in overthrowing Cassander and restoring the democracy. Demetrius fled, along with a group of philosophers associated with him. One of them was Theophrastus, Aristotle's successor.

One of the first laws by the reconstituted democracy forbade any philosopher to open a school in Athens without the express permission of the assembly. Both the Platonic and the Aristotelian schools were tainted by the special privileges they enjoyed under Demetrius of Phalerum and they were regarded as sources of antidemocratic teaching and Macedonian influence.

The little-known story may be found in W. S. Ferguson's *Hellenistic Athens.* "Philosophy," Ferguson wrote, "had indeed been an aristocratic movement from its very inception. It had been recognized as dangerous to democratic principles from the time of Alcibiades and Critias, while 'the greatest crime in Athenian history' had been committed in defending democracy against the . . . teaching of Socrates."[30]

The new law would have ended academic freedom in Athens and subjected philosophic teaching to political regulation. But the law, though quickly passed, was soon attacked in the assembly. Democratic Athens never had a written constitution, but there was a special motion called a *graphe paranomon,* which was the equivalent of a charge of unconstitutionality. Any law passed by the assembly could be called up again within a year of passage for renewed debate and a vote to reconsider if it was attacked as *paranomon,* or contrary to fundamental law. If the assembly voted for the motion, the law was invalidated and its sponsor fined.

The law was obviously at odds with the free-speech traditions of democratic Athens. In the debate, the law was defended by a prestigious democrat, a nephew of Demosthenes named Demochares, who had led the revolt against Demetrius of Phalerum. Nevertheless, the assembly voted to repeal the law and fine its sponsor. Academic freedom was vindicated, and this laid the foundations for Athens' survival as a venerable university town to which students like Cicero came from all over the Roman empire.

Three centuries later we get a glimpse of the intellectual atmosphere in Athens from an unexpected source, the New Testament, in its account of St. Paul's travels as a missionary. Elsewhere Paul met with persecution, but when Paul preached in Athens he found an open city, still fascinated by new ideas. Though the city was "full of idols" and he dared argue against paganism in the *agora* "with those who chanced to be there," he met with intellectual curiosity rather than charges of impiety. Some of the "Epicurean and Stoic philosophers" met with him and took him to the Areopagus, the seat of the city's ancient aristocratic high court, not for trial but for philosophic discussion.

"You bring some strange things to our ears," they said; "we wish to know therefore what these things mean." The writer of *Acts* explains with evident surprise that "all the Athenians and the foreigners who lived there spent their time in nothing except telling or hearing something new."

So Paul preached on the Areopagus and received a mixed but not hostile reception. "Now when they heard of the resurrection of the dead," his most sensational doctrine, "some mocked; but others said, 'We will hear you again about this.' " They were willing to suspend judgment and take time for reflection. Paul made some converts, one of them even a member of the court — described as Dionysius the Areopagite. The humble Christians were proud of so aristocratic a convert. Paul left Athens unmolested.[31]*

That is the last glimpse that a meager history provides us of philosophical freedom in Athens until 529 A.D., when the Emperor Justinian closed down the Platonic academy and the other philosophical schools of Athens forever under the pressure of Christian intolerance and imperial avarice; their rich endowments were tempting.

So from the sixth century B.C. to the sixth century A.D., philosophy enjoyed freedom in Athens. That was twelve hundred years, or about twice as long as the period of free thought from the Renaissance to our own day.

---

* Some centuries later there was a memorable echo of Paul's visit. An otherwise unidentified Christian mystic used Dionysius the Areopagite as his pseudonym in writing the first synthesis of Christian theology with neo-Platonic philosophy. In medieval Europe he was identified with Paul's convert, and his treatises were treated as almost canonical; Thomas Aquinas was among those who wrote commentaries upon them.

The sad little story of how the schools were finally closed is told by Gibbon in chapter 40 of the *Decline and Fall*, of course with his unmatchable eloquence, but also with a tribute to democracy unexpected from an eighteenth-century source. "The studies of philosophy and eloquence," he wrote, "are congenial to a popular state, which encourages the freedom of inquiry, and submits only to the force of persuasion."[32] Pericles could not have wished for a finer epitaph on his city and the free traditions it preserved to the very brink of the Dark Ages.

NOTES

ෝඌ෧෩

Prelude

1. See *The Works of Plato* (London: Bohn, 1908), 6:236, which includes the biography by Olympiodorus.

2. It would be easy to drown in the existing Socratic literature. Some idea of its dimensions may be obtained from a double-volumed dissertation for the Sorbonne in 1952, which offered the most complete bibliographical survey up to that time: V. de Megalhaes-Vilhena, *Le Problème de Socrate* (The Socratic Problem) and *Socrate et la légende platonicienne* (Socrates and the Platonic Legend) (Paris: Presses Universitaires de France, 1952), which add up to more than eight hundred pages, much of them in close-packed, small-type footnotes. It would take another volume to cover the Socratic literature that has appeared since then.

3. These have been collected in translation by the British classical scholar John Ferguson, for Britain's Open University, in *Socrates: A Source Book* (London: Macmillan, 1970). I came across it many years ago while browsing at Foyle's in London. It has not been published in the United States. Even these mostly meager scraps fill 355 double-column pages. Ferguson's collection also makes available for the first time in English a little-known third surviving *Apology of Socrates* by the fourth-century-A.D. Greek orator Libanius.

Chapter 1: Their Basic Differences

1. Aristotle, *Politics*, 1.1.10.

2. Ibid., 2.1.9–10.

3. Ibid., 2.1.2.

4. Xenophon, 7 vols. (Loeb Classical Library, 1918–1925), *Memorabilia*, 3.8.10–11 (4:229).

5. Ibid.

6. Plato, *Republic*, 7.537D7ff.

7. Aristotle, *Politics* (Loeb Classical Library, 1932), 1.2.1 (3).

8. Ibid., 3.9.9.

9. Kurt von Fritz in the *Oxford Classical Dictionary*, edited by H. G. L. Hammond and H. H. Scullard, 2nd ed. (Oxford: Clarendon Press, 1970), on Antisthenes.

10. Athenaeus, 5.221d.

11. Diogenes Laertius, *Lives of Eminent Philosophers,* 2 vols. (Loeb Classical Library, 1925), 6.8 (2:9).

12. Plato, *Phaedrus,* 260C.

13. *Politics,* 3.7.2 (Loeb, 241–243 and note, 240).

14. Plato, 8 vols. (Loeb Classical Library, 1925–1931), *Gorgias* 516C, 517A (5:497–499).

15. Ibid., 521D (Loeb 5:515).

16. *Memorabilia,* 4.6.12 (Loeb 4:343–345).

17. Ibid., 3.9.11–13 (Loeb 4:229–231).

18. Ibid., 3.2.1.

19. *Politics,* 5.9.1.

Chapter 2: Socrates and Homer

1. Homer, *Iliad,* 15.558, 22.429.

2. Ibid., 1.263. Richard J. Cunliffe, *Lexicon of the Homeric Dialect* (London: Blackie & Sons, 1924).

3. Homer, *Odyssey,* 9.317.

4. Homer, *Odyssey,* 2 vols. (Loeb Classical Library, 1919), 9.40ff (1:305).

5. Ibid., 9.176.

6. Ibid., 9.252ff (Loeb 1:321).

7. *Politics,* 1.1.12 (Loeb 13).

8. *Odyssey,* 3.71–74.

9. Homer, *Odyssey,* edited by William B. Stanford, 2 vols., 2nd ed. (London: Macmillian, 1959), 1:357.

Chapter 3: The Clue in the Thersites Story

1. Plato, *Statesman,* 229B.

2. *Memorabilia,* 1.2.9–12 (Loeb 4:15–17).

3. Ibid., 1.2.56 (Loeb 4:39).

4. Translation by Dorothy Wender, *Elegies* 847–850, in *Hesiod and Theognis* (London: Penguin Press, 1976), 126.

5. Hesiod, *Works and Days,* 1.309.

6. Hesiod, *Works and Days* (Loeb Classical Library, 1956), 1.248–264 (21–23).

7. *Memorabilia,* 1.2.58 (Loeb 4:41).

8. *Iliad,* 2.203–206.

9. *Memorabilia,* 1.2.59 (Loeb 4:41).

10. *Iliad,* 2.216–219.

11. See the article on Thersites in *Der Kleine Pauly* (Munich, 1979). This five-volume abridged and modernized version of the huge ninety-volume *German Encyclopedia of Classical Antiquity* is familiarly known as the "Pauly-Wissowa" from the names of its chief editors.

12. Lucian, 8 vols. (Loeb Classical Library, 1960), *True Histories* 2 (1:325).

13. It is amazing how the prejudice stirred up against Thersites by Homer lives on to this day in classical scholarship. Typical is the snobbish treatment

given him in the *Oxford Classical Dictionary*, where he is described as "an ugly, foul-tongued fellow, who rails at Agamemnon until beaten into silence by Odysseus." The *OCD* adds, "Evidently, from his description, he is of low birth." The German equivalent of the *OCD* is even harsher. In *Der Kleine Pauly*, Thersites is described as a *Meuterer, Laesterer und Prahlhans* — mutineer, slanderer, and braggart. His attack on Agamemnon is termed a *Hetzrede* — the inflammatory speech of an unscrupulous agitator. Neither the German nor the British reference work in their articles on Thersites mentions this as the first time a commoner tried to exercise free speech in the assemblies of Homer. But in the *OCD*'s article on Democracy, the venerable Victor Ehrenberg traces "the germ of Greek democracy" back to the second book of the *Iliad*. "Beginning with Thersites," Ehrenberg wrote, "there were always movements against the rule of the noble and the rich, as the lower ranks of free people tried to win full citizenship."

14. Homer, *Iliad*, 2 vols. (Loeb Classical Library, 1925), 1.224–227 (1:19–21).
15. Ibid., 1.165–168.
16. Ibid., 14.80ff (Loeb 2:73).
17. *Gorgias*, 525E.
18. *Republic* 10.620C.
19. Plato, edited by Edith Hamilton and Huntington Cairns (Princeton: Princeton University Press, 1971), *Apology*, 41B (25).
20. Ibid., *Symposium* 174C (52).
21. Ibid., *Cratylus* 395A (433).
22. *Republic*, 3.389Cff.
23. Ibid., 3.390A (quoting the *Iliad*, 1.225).
24. Ibid., 2.383A.
25. *Republic*, edited by James Adam (Cambridge: Cambridge University Press, 1963), 7:522D.
26. Aeschylus, *Oresteia*, 1429–1443.

Chapter 4: The Nature of Virtue and of Knowledge

1. *Politics*, 1.1.8–11.
2. *Iliad*, 9.440ff.
3. *Memorabilia*, 1.6.1–15.
4. Kathleen Freeman, *Ancilla to the Pre-Socratic Philosophers* (Cambridge: Harvard University Press, 1970), 148, Fragment 14 Ox. Pap. translated.
5. Ibid., 147.
6. Kathleen Freeman, *The Pre-Socratic Philosophers: A Companion to Diels' Fragmente der Vorsokratiker*, 2nd ed. (Oxford: Clarendon Press, 1966), 401.
7. Aristotle, *The "Art" of Rhetoric* (Loeb Classical Library, 1926), 1.13.2 (141).
8. Plato, *Protagoras*, 319B–C (Loeb 4:125).
9. Ibid., 319D (Loeb 4:127).
10. Ibid., 322B–C (Loeb 4:133–135).
11. Ibid., 328D (Loeb 4:151).

12. Ibid., 361C (Loeb 4:257).

13. Ibid., 329A (Loeb 153).

14. Herodotus, 4 vols. (Loeb Classical Library, 1922–1931), 5.78 (3:87).

15. Aeschylus, *Plays,* 2 vols. (Loeb Classical Library, 1922–1926), 1:109.

16. Ibid., 1.241ff.

Chapter 5: Courage as Virtue

1. Aristotle, *Nichomachean Ethics,* 3.8.6–9 (Loeb Classical Library, 165).

2. Ibid., 3.8.1–5 (Loeb 163–165).

3. Here I am quoting Anna S. Benjamin's vivid and colloquial modern translation of Xenophon's *Memorabilia* (Indianapolis: Bobbs-Merrill, 1972), 4.4.9 (122).

4. For those who would like a guided tour through the intricate discussion in the *Hippias Major,* we can recommend a comprehensive commentary and excellent new translation by a scholar at the University of Texas, Paul Woodruff, *Hippias Major* (Indianapolis and Cambridge: Hackett Publishing Co., 1982).

5. Plato, *Greater Hippias* (Loeb 6:334).

6. Ibid., *Lesser Hippias* (Loeb 6:426).

7. Ibid., 376C (Loeb 6:475).

8. Plato, *Meno,* 99Eff (Loeb 4:369).

9. Ibid., 80A–B (Loeb 4:297–299).

10. Ibid. (Loeb 263).

11. Ibid., 80B.

12. Cicero, *Academia,* 1.4.16 (Loeb 19:425).

13. Cicero, *de Natura Deorum,* 1.5.11 (Loeb 19:15). It is curious that this quotation does not appear in the otherwise awesomely conprehensive *Socrates: A Source Book* compiled by John Ferguson (London: Open University Press, 1970).

14. St. Augustine, *Confessions,* 2 vols. (Loeb Classical Library, 1912), 7.20 (1:393).

15. St. Augustine, *Against the Academics,* 2.6.14 (Ferguson, *Source Book,* 312).

16. St. Augustine, *City of God,* 7 vols. (Loeb Classical Library, 1965) 8.2 (3:15).

17. Ibid. (Loeb 3:13).

18. *Memorabilia,* 1.2.12.

19. Ibid., 1.2.13–14 (Loeb 4:19, slightly revised).

20. Ibid., 1.2.15–16 (Loeb 4:19).

21. Ibid., 1.2.9 (Loeb 4:17).

Chapter 6: A Wild Goose Chase: The Socratic Search for Absolute Definitions

1. Aristotle, *Metaphysics,* 2 vols. (Loeb Classical Library, 1933), 1.6.2 (1:43, italics added).

2. Ibid., 1.6.3 (Loeb 1:43).

3. Plato, *Theaetetus,* 147B (Loeb 2:23).

4. Plato, *Phaedrus*, 260B (Loeb 1:515).

5. Diogenes Laertius, 6.18 (Loeb, 2:9).

6. *Phaedrus*, 260B–D (Loeb 1:515–517).

7. Thomas Hobbes, *Leviathan* (London: Penguin Press, 1968), 113.

8. *Metaphysics*, 8.9.22 (Loeb 2:249).

9. Plato, *Statesman*, 294A–C (Loeb 3:133–135).

10. Xenophon, *Apology*, 14–16 (4:497).

11. Plato, *Apology*, 21A (Loeb 1:81).

12. Xenophon, *Apology*, 16–17 (Loeb 4:651).

13. Plato, *Apology*, 21B (Loeb 1:81).

14. If I be too unkind in this judgment, I call Liddell-Scott-Jones, *A Greek-English Lexicon* (Oxford: Clarendon Press, 1940), as a witness. It defines *eironeia* as "ignorance purposely affected to provoke or confound an antagonist, a mode of argument used by Socrates against the Sophists . . . generally, mock modesty." Another equally authoritative witness is the Roman Quintilian, antiquity's most prestigious writer on rhetoric. He wrote that Socrates was called "ironical" because he "played the part of an ignoramus who revered others as sages" — and thereby made them look all the more foolish (*Education of the Orator*, 9.2.46). This quote is from Ferguson's *Source Book*.

15. Plato, *Apology*, 20C (Loeb 1:79).

16. Ibid., 23C (Loeb 1:89).

17. *Gorgias*, 515E (Loeb 5:495).

18. *Meno*, 94E (Loeb 4:351).

Chapter 7: Socrates and Rhetoric

1. Cicero, *Brutus*, 12.46 (Loeb 5:49).

2. Plato, *Apology* (Loeb 1:408).

3. *Gorgias*, 463A–B (Loeb 5:313).

4. Ibid., 502D–E (Loeb 5:451–453).

5. *Rhetoric*, 1.1.1 (Loeb 3).

6. Ibid., 1.1.11–13 (Loeb 11–13).

7. Cites the *Prior Analytic*, 70a10, and *Rhetoric*, 1355a6.

8. Here I am using Lane Cooper's translation (Norwalk, Conn.: Appleton-Century, 1950) (p. 12), which is clearer than the Loeb version in dealing with Aristotle's often tortuous Greek.

9. *Rhetoric*, 1.8.13 (Loeb 145–147).

10. Liddell-Scott-Jones, *Greek-English Lexicon* (hereafter LSJ).

11. *Nicomachean Ethics*, 5.10.6. (Loeb 317).

12. Quoted here from Ernest Barker's commentary and translation of *The Politics of Aristotle* (Oxford: Clarendon Press, 1946), 146n4. The Greek original of the oath was preserved in *Pollux* (8.122) — an encyclopedic and eccentric Greek rhetorical work under the Roman empire — as cited in W. L. Newman's indispensable four-volume commentary on Aristotle's *Politics: The Politics of Aristotle* (Oxford: Clarendon Press, 1887), 1:273n1.

13. *Statesman*, 294A–Bff (Loeb 3:133–135).

Chapter 8: The Good Life: The Third Socratic Divergence

1. *Politics*, 1.1.9–10. The Greek word used by Aristotle is *adzux* and has usually been translated in this passage as "isolated," which the *LSJ* recommends and the Loeb adopts. But I venture to suggest that this gives too narrow an interpretation to the metaphor. A piece isolated on the checkerboard is indeed defenseless, like a man without a city, but it may be "rescued" and brought back into a protected formation. The isolated piece is still part of the game. But a solitary checker piece is in no game at all. That is what Aristotle meant by a "cityless" (*apolis*) man, since he defines him as one who is without a city "by nature and not by *tyche*," fate or chance. The word *adzux* Aristotle then uses to describe him meant literally "unyoked" as applied to horses or oxen. It came also to denote unpaired, unmarried, isolated, or single, and hence seems best rendered in this context as "solitary."

2. Plato, *Apology*, 29E (Loeb 1:109).

3. *Politics*, 1.2.15–16 (Barker, 7).

4. Aristotle, *Athenian Constitution* (Loeb Classical Library, 1961 reprint), 8.5 (31).

5. Plutarch, *Parallel Lives*, 11 vols. (Loeb Classical Library, 1959–1962, reprint), *Life of Solon*, 20.1 (1:457).

6. Thucydides, 4 vols. (Loeb Classical Library, 1920–1928), 2.40.2 (1:329).

7. Plato, *Apology*, 30E (Loeb 111–113).

8. Ibid., 32A (Loeb 116).

9. Ibid., 31C–D (Loeb 115).

10. Plutarch, *Life of Alcibiades*, 17.4–5 (Loeb 4:43), and *Minor Attic Orators*, 2 vols. (Loeb Classical Library, 1941–1957): Andocides, *Against Alcibiades*, 22 (1:561).

11. Thucydides, 3.37.

12. Ibid., 3.33.5ff (Loeb 2:63).

13. Ibid., 3.48 (Loeb 2:85).

14. Ibid., 3.49 (Loeb 2:87).

15. Plato, *Apology*, 32E (Loeb 1:119).

16. Plutarch, *Life of Nicias* (Loeb 3:257).

17. Plutarch, *Nicias and Alcibiades*, translated by Bernadotte Perrin (New York, 1912), 221.

18. Diodorus Siculus, 14.5, quoted from Ferguson's *Source Book*, 187.

19. Aristophanes, *Birds*, 1.1282.

20. See Douglas M. MacDowell's *The Law in Classical Athens* (London: Thames and Hudson, 1978), 180–181, 188–189. The fullest and most judicious account of this painful affair is still that of George Grote in his *History of Greece* (London: J. Murray, 1888), 6:392ff.

21. Plato, *Apology*, 32B (Loeb 1:117). Substantially the same account is given in Xenophon's *Hellenica* (1.7.1–35) and briefly in Aristotle's *Athenian Constitution* (100.34), but there, curiously, without mention of Socrates.

22. Ibid., 32C–D (Loeb 117).

23. Juvenal, *Tenth Satire*, 1.356.

24. Plato, *Apology*, 30B (Loeb 1:109). The Loeb translates this passage as "the perfection of your persons," but "persons" fuzzes the antithesis with souls. The Greek word the Loeb translates as "persons" is *somaton*, the genitive plural of the word *soma*, or body. For the ancient Greeks generally perfection of the person involved both body and soul.

25. John Burnet, *Euthyphro, Apology of Socrates and Crito* (Oxford: Clarendon Press, 1924), 123.

26. Aristotle, *de Anima*, 413a3 (Loeb 73).

Chapter 9: The Prejudices of Socrates

1. *Memorabilia*, 3.7.2–7 (Loeb 4:215–217).

2. Of course the worst example of snobbery in the Platonic canon is Plato's supercilious description of rival upstart philosophers in the *Republic* — "that multitude of pretenders unfit by nature, whose souls are bowed and mutilated by their vulgar occupations even as their bodies are marred by their arts and crafts," whose picture is "precisely that of a little bald-headed tinker who has made money and has just been freed from bonds [i.e., the bonds of servitude, having just purchased his freedom] and has a bath and is wearing a new garment and has got himself up like a bridgegroom and is about to marry his master's daughter who has fallen into poverty." (*Republic*, 4:295E [Loeb 2:47–49]). But Plato put this into the mouth of Socrates many years after the latter's death. There is no evidence that the historical Socrates ever spoke so unkindly and pretentiously. Otherwise Socrates could not have kept the lifelong affection of his oldest disciple, the "low-born" Antisthenes; his mother was a Thracian, hence he was twitted for not being of pure Attic blood (Diogenes Laertius, 6.1). Several scholars believe this was Plato's slur against his fourth-century rival — and Socrates' old friend — Isocrates. See the comment on this passage in Adam's edition of Plato's *Republic* as revised by D. A. Rees (Cambridge: Cambridge University Press, 1963), 2.29. The "little tinker" passage in the *Republic* was a curious way for Plato to demonstrate his own superiority as a philosopher and a gentleman.

It is easy to understand why Antisthenes hated Plato, and — according to Diogenes Laertius (3.35 [Loeb 1:309]) — wrote a dialogue attacking him under the name of Sathon, an obscene pun on the name Platon.

The Liddell-Scott-Jones Greek lexicon blushingly takes refuge in Latin in helping us to understand the pun. It does not mention Antisthenes' satire on Plato but says that *sathe* (from which Sathon presumably originated) was the Greek word for *membrum virile*. Such was the less-celestial underside of ancient philosophical controversy.

3. Xenophon, *Oeconomicus*, 2.3 (Loeb 4:375).

4. Plutarch, *Life of Aristides*, 1.9 (Loeb 2:215).

5. Libanius, *Apology of Socrates*, cited in a footnote by Eduard Zeller in *Socrates and the Socratic Schools* (1885; New York: Russell & Russell, 1962, reprint), 3.7 (56n).

6. Demosthenes, 7 vols. (Loeb Classical Library, 1984), *Against Eubylides* 1.30 (6:253).

7. Xenophon, *Apology*, 29 (Loeb 4:659–661).

8. *Meno*, 95A (Loeb 4:351).

9. *Theaetetus*, 173C–E (Loeb 2:119–221).

10. The most complete account of this minority view of Athens is François Ollier's *Le Mirage Spartiate* (Paris, 1933; New York: Arno Press, 1973, reprint).

11. Aristophanes, 3 vols. (Loeb Classical Library, 1931–1938), *Birds*, 1.1281–1282 (2:251).

12. Plutarch, *Life of Alcibiades*, 23.3ff (Loeb 6:63).

13. *Gorgias*, 515E (Loeb 5:495).

14. *Gorgias*, translated by Eric R. Dodds (Oxford: Clarendon Press, 1959), 357.

15. Plato, *Crito*, 45A (Loeb 1:157).

16. See, for example, the brilliant effort to resolve them made by the great American classicist Gregory Vlastos in "Socrates on Political Obedience and Disobedience," *Yale Review* 63 (Summer 1974), 4:517–534.

17. *Crito*, 52E (Loeb 1:185).

18. Burnet, *Euthyphro*, 207.

19. *Memorabilia*, 3.5.13–15, 4.4.15 (Loeb 4:197, 317).

20. *Republic*, 8.544C (Loeb 2:239).

21. *Crito*, 45Bff (Loeb 1:159).

22. *OCD*, on Thyrtaeus.

23. *Protagoras*, 342Aff (Loeb 4:195).

24. In this passage we are using W. K. C. Guthrie's version of *Gorgias* (London: Penguin Press, 1960), 77.

25. Alfred E. Taylor, *Plato: The Man and His Work* (New York: Dial Press, 1936), 255.

26. *Birds*, 1.1013.

27. Thucydides, 2.39 (Loeb 1:325).

28. Xenophon, *Scripta Minora*, 14.4 (Loeb 7:185).

29. See C. D. Hamilton, *Sparta's Bitter Victories* (Ithaca: Cornell University Press, 1979).

30. *Protagoras*, 342D (Loeb 4:195–197).

31. Plato, *Laws*, 2 vols. (Loeb Classical Library, 1934), 950 (2:505).

32. The best discussion of this is still in George Grote's monumental *Plato and the Other Companions of Socrates*, 3 vols., 2nd ed. (London: J. Murray, 1867), 3:578ff. In James Adam's indispensable two-volume commentary on the *Republic*, the index lists no less than fourteen different references under "Spartan features of Plato's city." Plato had some reservations about Sparta and Crete, especially their educational focus on the martial virtues only. But in the main he admired them, especially because they were closed societies.

Chapter 10: Why Did They Wait Until He Was Seventy?

1. On espionage in Sparta see Thucydides, 4.80; Xenophon, *Lacedaemonian Constitution*, 4.4; and Plutarch's *Life of Lycurgus*, 28.

2. *Politics*, 5.9.3 (Loeb 461).

3. These fragments are conveniently collected in Ferguson's *Source Book*, 172–173.

4. Plutarch, *Moralia*, 16 vols. (Loeb Classical Library, 1956, reprint), *On Education* 10C (1:49).

5. Plato, *Apology*, 18B–D (Loeb 1:71–73).

6. Ferguson, *Source Book*, 173.

7. Plato, *Apology*, 18B–19C (Loeb 1:73–75).

8. *Republic*, 379A.

9. Freeman, *Ancilla*, 22, Frag. 116, 117, and 12.

Chapter 11: The Three Earthquakes

1. Aristophanes, *Clouds*, 1397–1400.

2. His only recorded word of disapproval is a brief and passing reference to the dictatorship of the Thirty in his *Seventh Letter* (Loeb Classical Library, 1966), 324D (479). There Plato writes that the Thirty "within a short time caused me to look back on the former government" — meaning the democracy — "as a golden age." But scholars are still undecided whether the *Seventh Letter* is genuine.

3. Plato, *Apology*, 36B (Loeb 29); B. Jowett, *The Dialogues of Plato*, 5 vols. (Oxford: Clarendon Press, 1892).

4. Burnet, op. cit., 153.

5. Aristophanes, *Knights*, 1.479–480 (Loeb 1:169).

6. *Republic*, 365D (Loeb 1:137). To the argument that "neither secrecy nor force can avail" against the gods and their punishment for deceit, Adeimantus has a cynical response. "Well," Adeimantus continues, "if there are no gods, or they do not concern themselves with the doings of men, neither need we concern ourselves with eluding their observation." But what if they do exist? Adeimantus says the poets, who are the source of knowledge about the gods, say their forgiveness can be assured by "sacrifices and soothing vows." So, he concludes, "the thing to do is to commit injustice and offer sacrifice from the fruits of our wrong-doing." Socrates combats that view. His thesis is that "justice is better than injustice" (368B [Loeb 1:147]).

7. *Laws*, 856B (Loeb 1:209).

8. A. W. Gomme, A. Andrewes, and K. L. Dover, *A Historical Commentary on Thucydides* (Oxford: Clarendon Press, 1981), 5:129.

9. Thucydides, 6.60 (Loeb 3:287).

10. Ibid., 8.65–66 (Loeb 4:301–305, slightly amended).

11. *Athenian Constitution*, 34.3 (Loeb 101).

12. Ibid., 35.1.

13. Plato, *Apology*, 39D (Loeb 1:139).

14. *Athenian Constitution*, 60.2–3 (Loeb 113–115).

15. Plato, *Euthyphro*, 15D (Loeb 1:59; italics added).

16. The Liddell-Scott-Jones *Greek-English Lexicon* defines the Homeric use of the word *thes* as serf or bondsman. But both Cunliffe's Homeric lexicon and Georg Autenrieth's older German dictionary of Homer agree that it

meant hired laborer, as opposed — Autenrieth adds — to *demos*, "vanquished serfs or slaves." The corresponding verb *theteuo* meant to work for a fixed wage. Stanford in his commentary on the *Odyssey*, where the words also appear (18.3.12), agrees with Cunliffe and Autenrieth.

17. *Iliad*, 1.444–445.
18. *Euthyphro*, 4C (Loeb 1:15).
19. Ibid., 4B (Loeb 1:13–15).
20. Plato, *Apology*, 21Aff (Loeb 1:81).
21. Ibid., 23C (Loeb 1:89). It is worth looking at the Greek phrase that the Loeb translates as "of your democratic party." The Greek is *"humon to plethei,"* which is literally "of you the masses or common people." *Plethos* is defined in the Liddell-Scott *Greek Lexicon* as "a great number, mass, crowd . . . hence the people, the commons . . . also the government of the people, democracy." There is an element of disdain in the very word. Plato's Socrates does not use the term *demokratia*, or democracy, which had the same favorable sound to Athenian ears as to ours.
22. Burnet, op. cit., 90.
23. Lysias, *Orations* (Loeb Classical Library, 1930), 10.4 (199–201).
24. Ibid., 16.4 (Loeb 375–377).
25. Ibid., 12.52 (Loeb 253).
26. Xenophon, *Hellenica*, 2.4.8 (Loeb 1:147).
27. Ibid., 2.4.43 (Loeb 1:171).

Chapter 12: Xenophon, Plato, and the Three Earthquakes

1. *Memorabilia*, 1.2.32 (Loeb 4:27).
2. *Hellenica*, 2.4.21 (Loeb 1:157).
3. *Athenian Constitution*, 35.4 (Loeb 103).
4. *Memorabilia*, 1.2.33–38 (Loeb 4:29–31).
5. Ibid., 1.2.29–31 (Loeb 4:25–27).
6. Plato, *Seventh Letter*, 342C (Loeb 479).
7. Ibid., 176D (Loeb 91).
8. The *Eryxias* may be found in Jowett's *Plato*, 2:559; or in the Bohn edition, 4:59.
9. Plutarch, *Life of Theseus*, 24.2 (Loeb 1:53).
10. *Iliad*, 2.547 (Loeb 1:91). Here, however, *demos* is translated as "land," and this rendering is supported by Cunliffe's Homeric lexicon, though in line 198 of the same book of the *Iliad* both the Loeb and Cunliffe translate *demou andra* as "man of the [common] people." Ancient detractors of Athens claimed that this reference in Homer was a later Athenian interpolation in the text. The still unsettled controversy is ably summarized in Alan J. Wace and Frank H. Stubbings, *Companion to Homer* (London: Macmillan, 1962), 239.
11. Plato, *Timaeus*, 19E–20B (Loeb 7:25–27).
12. Ibid., 21C (Loeb 7:31).
13. *Hellenica*, 2.3.25 (Loeb 1:125).
14. *Republic*, 414C–415A (Loeb 1:301–305).

15. *Statesman,* 293A–C (Loeb 3:131). The italics, of course, are added.

16. *Republic,* 4.424A, 5.449C, 457Cff (Loeb 1:331, 427, 453ff).

17. Ibid., 5.459C–E (Loeb 1:461).

18. Ibid., 540Dff (Loeb 2:231–233ff).

19. Ibid., 6.500C (Loeb 2:69).

20. The Greek word in the text is *sophrosyne,* usually translated as "moderation." Shorey's rendering of it here as "sobriety" sounds ironic in this context — the idea is hardly a sober one. *Republic,* 500D (Loeb 2:71).

21. Ibid., 501A–C (Loeb 2:73).

Chapter 13: The Principal Accuser

1. Plato, *Apology,* 23E (Loeb 1:91).

2. Ferguson, *Source Book,* 177n.

3. *Athenian Constitution,* 34.3 (Loeb 101). Aristotle explains that when Athens finally lost the long war with Sparta, two disaffected elements sought an end to democracy. One group was made up of aristocrats who had been exiled under the democracy and were brought back by the Spartans or had been members of the *hetaireiai* or "comradeships," the antidemocratic clubs. The other group were "those notables who were not members of any Comradeship but who otherwise were inferior in reputation to none of the citizens." The latter "were aiming at the ancestral constitution." This was a euphemism for a limited democracy. "Members of this party were Archinus, Anytus, Cleitophon, and Phormisius, while its chief leader was Theramenes." So the rule of the Thirty was imposed on Athens.

4. Isocrates, 3 vols. (Loeb Classical Library, 1928–1945, reprint), *Against Callimachus* 23–24 (3.269). Thrasybulus was an Athenian statesman and general, an aristocrat who gravitated in both 411 and 404 to the democracy and became the military leader of the opposition that overthrew the Thirty. His biography is eloquently told in *Lives of the Great Generals* by the Roman writer Cornelius Nepos.

5. *Athenian Constitution,* 27.3 (Loeb 82–83).

6. Diogenes Laertius, 2.43 (Loeb 1:173).

7. Ibid., 6.10 (Loeb 2:11).

8. *Themistius,* 20.239C.

9. That relationship seems to have inspired another charming but spurious anecdote about Socrates in Diogenes Laertius. He reports that Lysias, the most famous speechwriter of his time, wrote a speech for Socrates to deliver at the trial but Socrates rejected it. Socrates said, "A fine speech, Lysias; it is not suitable, however, to me." Diogenes Laertius explains that "it was plainly more forensic than philosophical." Lysias argued, "If it is a fine speech, how can it fail to suit you?" "Well," Socrates replied, "would not fine raiment and fine shoes be just as unsuitable to me?" (Diogenes Laertius, 2.41 [Loeb 1:171]). This delightful anecdote could have happened but didn't, or we would have heard about it elsewhere. The text of an undelivered defense of Socrates by Lysias would have been a prize addition to his orations, so many of which have been preserved as models of Attic style. In any case, even Lysias could not possibly have woven finer raiment for the defense of Socrates than Plato's own *Apology.*

10. Lysias, 22.8ff. But an engaging story dies hard. The venerable German "Pauly-Wissowa" encyclopedia of classical antiquity, though it mentioned the Lysias speech about the corn dealers, still swallowed the story whole about Anytus' exile from Athens and "alleged" eventual death by stoning in Heraclea. The *OCD* only concludes circumspectly that "accounts of his [Anytus] banishment and murder may be later inventions." But the newer *Der Kleine Pauly* (1:col. 417) finally concludes that Anytus' later service as an *archon* "refutes the legend" of Anytus' tragic end.

11. Diogenes Laertius, 2.44 (Loeb 1:173).

12. The fourth-century orators Lysias and Isocrates were both younger friends of Socrates. Lysias, who suffered so much under the Thirty, never defends Socrates. Isocrates, who lived to be ninety-eight and did not die until sixty-one years after the trial, makes only one brief and defensive reference to Socrates in his voluminous surviving works, which fill three volumes in the Loeb. In his *Busiris,* nine years after the trial, in reply to the lost pamphlet of Polycrates attacking Socrates, Isocrates said, "One would have thought you were writing a panegyric of him when you gave him Alcibiades as a disciple. No one ever thought him a pupil of Socrates, though everyone would accept his [Alcibiades] outstanding qualities." (Ferguson, *Source Book,* 177.) Isocrates discreetly omits any mention of Critias, whom Polycrates linked with Alcibiades as the two worst examples among the pupils of Socrates.

13. Aeschines (Loeb Classical Library, 1919), 1.173 (139).

14. Xenophon, *Apology,* 29 (Loeb 4:661).

15. *Meno,* 92E–93A (Loeb 4:345).

16. Ibid., 94A (Loeb 4:351).

17. Xenophon, *Apology,* 30–31 (Loeb 4:661).

Chapter 14: How Socrates Did His Best to Antagonize the Jury

1. Plato, *Apology,* 36A (Loeb 1:127).

2. Xenophon, *Apology,* translated by Sarah Fielding (1762; London: Everyman, 1910).

3. Xenophon, *Apology,* 4–8 (Loeb 4:643–647).

4. Ibid., 32 (Loeb 4:661).

5. The main sources for this later usage of *megalegoria* are three ancient treatises on Greek literary style: Longinus, *On the Sublime* (8.4), the critical essays of the historian Dionysius of Halicarnassus, *On Thucydides* (27), and Demetrius, *On Style* (29). Longinus is generally believed to have written in the first century A.D.; Dionysius of Halicarnassus began to teach rhetoric in Rome about 30 B.C.; Demetrius' *On Style* is usually regarded as no earlier than the first century B.C., though the LSJ strangely attributes it to Demetrius of Phalerum who lived at the end of the fourth century B.C.

6. One of these schoolbook editions, W. S. Tyler, *Apology and Crito* (New York and London: Appleton, 1871), in a note on this passage, linked it directly to Xenophon's *Apology* and said, "*Mega legein* properly denotes boasting . . . it has the seeming *pride* and *arrogance* of what he [Socrates] said, which, he feared, would give offence, and which did actually give offence to the judges." Tyler added that Xenophon "speaks of the *megalegoria* which all the *Apologies* ascribe to Socrates in his defense." Thus

the Platonic account lends support to the Xenophontic. One of the best editions of Plato's *Apology and Crito,* by John Dyer and revised by Thomas Day Seymour (1885; Boston: Ginn and Co., 1908), explains that *mega legein* is to be read "in the sense of *megalegorein*" (*Apology,* 20E note). The best of this century's commentators on the *Apology* of Plato, John Burnet, in his *Euthyphro, Apology and Crito* (Oxford: Oxford University Press, 1924), writes: "No one who reads the 'Platonic Apology' of Socrates will ever wish that he had made any other defense." He argues against the Xenophontic view that Socrates deliberately provoked his judges but admits that "It is the speech of one who deliberately forgoes the immediate purpose of a defense — persuasion of his judges" (p. 65). Burnet goes on to agree "that *megalegoria* is generally used in a bad sense, and that the Socrates of Hermogenes and Xenophon really is insufferably arrogant." But is Plato's Socrates really less so?

7. LSJ.

8. Xenophon, *Apology,* 13 (Loeb 649). I have slightly amended the Loeb translation to fit the Greek original. It says *ho theos,* "the god," not "God." Too many translators convert Socrates to monotheism. Anyway, he is referring to his personal familiar spirit, not to "God."

9. Ibid., 13–15 (Loeb 4:649–651).

10. Ibid., 25 (Loeb 4:657).

11. Diogenes Laertius, 2.42 (Loeb 1:171).

12. Burnet, op. cit., 161.

13. Xenophon, *Apology,* 23 (Loeb 4:655).

14. Plato, *Apology,* 38Bff (Loeb 1:135).

15. Even so reverential a scholar as Burnet was appalled at the way Socrates handled the counterpenalty. He commented that in the Prytaneum proposal, "Socrates is making what the court would consider a monstrous claim" and adds sadly, "that is the *megalegoria* which puzzled Xenophon." Burnet, op. cit., 156.

16. *Crito,* 45A–E (Loeb 1:157–161).

17. *OCD.*

18. The Dyer-Seymour edition of the *Apology* and *Crito* (Boston, 1908), for example, says, "At Athens, as at Rome, the law allowed a man to go into voluntary exile" (122). Burnet, in his note to the same passage of the *Crito,* suggests, "No doubt Anytus would have been quite satisfied if Socrates had left Athens" (45E4 [186]).

19. Plato, *Apology,* 37Aff (Loeb 1:131).

20. *Crito,* 46A (Loeb 1:161).

21. Plato, *Phaedo,* 59Eff (Loeb 1:209).

22. Ibid., 60A (Loeb 1:209).

23. Ibid., 116Aff (Loeb 1:395–397).

24. Ibid., 61A–62AC (Loeb 1:213–217).

25. Ibid., 64A–B (Loeb 1:223).

26. Ibid., 65C–D (Loeb 1:227).

Chapter 15: How Socrates Easily Might Have Won Acquittal

1. Plato, *Apology*, 24B (Loeb 1:91).

2. *Memorabilia*, 1.1.1 (Loeb 4:4), and Diogenes Laertius, 2.40 (Loeb 1:171).

3. *Rhetoric*, 1.8.13 (Loeb 145).

4. Plato, *Apology*, 26Cff (Loeb 1:97–99).

5. The earliest surviving use of the word *atheos* is given in the Liddell-Scott-Jones *Greek-English Lexicon* as line 162 of Pindar's Fourth Pythian Ode, sung in honor of an Olympic victory in 462 B.C. There it refers to a hero saved from "*atheon* weapons." The *o* in this transliteration is the *omega*, not the *omicron:* the word is the genitive plural of the adjective *atheos*. It would be ludicrous to translate this as "atheistic weapons." Both the Loeb and the Bude French bilingual edition (Paris: Société édition) translate it as "impious" weapons. Another rendering would be "ungodly weapons" in the colloquial sense that we might call the H-bomb an "ungodly" or "devilish" weapon.

6. *Clouds*, 1.367.

7. In B. B. Rogers' rollicking verse translation (Loeb 1:401).

8. *Memorabilia*, 1.3.1 and 4.3.16.

9. Theseus himself, the legendary founder of Athens, was regarded as the lawgiver who gave political equality to the poor. A British nineteenth-century classical handbook reports touchingly that at the Theseia, the annual Athenian festival in his honor, "in consequence of this belief donations of bread and meat were given to the poor people at Theseia, which thus was for them a feast at which they felt no want and might fancy themselves equal to the wealthiest citizens." Article on Theseia, *Smith's Dictionary of Greek and Roman Antiquities* (London, 1878).

10. It is alluded to at four points in the story of the wanderings of Odysseus: 1.298–300; 3.304–312; 4.546–547; and 9.458ff.

11. Peitho makes her appearance in Hesiod (Op. 73) but there she is a daughter of Ocean, a sea nymph, linked to the Graces and Aphrodite. Sappho too called her the daughter of Aphrodite in Henry T. Wharton's *Sappho* (London: J. Lane, 1908), still the most useful and delightful edition (160: Frag. 135); the most scholarly is the new Loeb *Greek Lyric: Sappho and Alcaeus,* edited by D. A. Campbell (Cambridge: Harvard University Press, 1982). In another fragment Sappho calls her Aphrodite's "handmaiden bright as gold" (Wharton 107). In these earlier references Peitho seems to be Temptation or Seduction rather than Persuasion. This is so when Peitho is first mentioned in the *Oresteia*, at line 385 of its first "act," the *Agamemnon*. H. W. Smyth of Harvard in the Loeb edition and A. Sidgwick of Oxford in the Clarendon edition (1898) of *Agamemnon* translated Peitho there as Temptation. In this passage, the Chorus is speaking of the ruin brought about by the infatuation of Paris for Helen and Peitho is the child not of Aphrodite but of Ate, blind and destructive Fate. Political changes are reflected in the evolution of the word and the myth. Peitho took on new meaning and status with the rise of Greek democracy. On Peitho the latest study is K. G. A. Buxton's *Persuasion in Greek Tragedy: A Study of Peitho* (Cambridge: Cambridge University Press, 1982), which did not come to my attention until this book was completed.

12. *Oxford Book of Greek Verse* (Oxford: Clarendon Press, 1930), xxiv.

13. Pausanias, edited by Paul Levi (New York: Penguin Press, 1971), 1.22.3 (2:61).

14. Demosthenes, *Pro.* 54; Isocrates, 5.249A.

15. See footnote to line 970 Eumenides citing Pausanias, 1.22.3, in George Thomson's edition of *Oresteia*, 2 vols. (Prague, 1966, revised) 2:229.

16. *Corpus Scriptorum Atticarum*, 3.351.

17. Sculpture by Praxiteles: Pausanias, 1.43.5; by Phidias: Pausanias, 5.11.8.

18. I rely for this statement on the admirable analytical indices in the one-volume complete *Plato* edition by Edith Hamilton and Huntington Cairns (Princeton: Princeton University Press, 1971), and in the third edition of Jowett's *Plato*, vol. 5. I also consulted des Places *Lexique* to the Bude edition of Plato (Paris, 1970) and Leonard Brandwood's *Word Index to Plato* (Leeds, 1976).

19. *Phaedrus*, 260A (Loeb 1:513–515).

20. *The Complete Plays of Aeschylus*, translated by Gilbert Murray (London: G. Allen and Unwin Ltd., 1928).

21. Lewis R. Farnell, *The Cults of the Greek States*, 5 vols. (Oxford: Clarendon Press, 1896–1909), 1:58–59.

22. See Cunliffe's *Lexicon*.

23. Georges Chantraine, *Dictionnaire etymologique de la langue grecque* (Paris, 1984).

24. Pausanias, 1.3.5 (Penguin 1:18).

25. Ibid., 1.1.3, 1.3.3. (Penguin 1:11, 17).

26. Sir James G. Frazer, *The Golden Bough*, 9 vols. (1915; London: St. Martin Press, 1966, reprint); Wilhelm H. Roescher, *Ausfuhrliches Lexikon der griechischen und romischen Mythologies* (Hildesheim: Gp. Olms, 1965). I cannot resist mentioning one other tidbit in the *KP* article. It reports that on the gravestone of the dictator Critias there was carved a relief showing Oligarchy putting the torch to Democracy.

Chapter 16: What Socrates Should Have Said

1. Ferguson, *Source Book,* 269.

Chapter 17: The Four Words

1. See under *isos,* Chantraine's *Dictionnaire.* Contrast this with Cunliffe's *Lexicon* which lists only five *isos* compounds, none of political significance.

2. Herodotus, 5.78 (Loeb 3:87).

3. The exception, as we know from Thucydides, was the highly unusual count taken when the Peloponnesian war was declared.

4. J. A. O. Larsen, "The Origin and Significance of the Counting of Votes," *Classical Philology* (July 1949), 44:178.

5. In the most important Roman assembly, the *centuriata,* each "century" had a fixed number of votes and the majority in each century cast that fixed number. The century of the proletariat or poor, the overwhelming majority of the population, had only one vote out of a total of 193. The wealthiest class had 80 votes and the next richest 20, so between them they

had a majority. When they agreed, as they usually did, the decision was announced and the presiding officer did not even bother to poll the other classes.

6. Chaim Wiszubski, *Libertas as a Political Idea in Rome* (Cambridge: The University Press, 1950), 18.

7. *Protagoras*, 319D (Loeb 4:127).

8. Euripides, *Orestes*, 885, and Demosthenes, *On the Crown*, 18:170.

9. The compound appears in three forms: the noun *eleutherostomia*, meaning freedom of speech; the verb *eleutherostomein* (to speak freely); and the adjective *eleutherostomos*, meaning free-speaking. This turns up in the *Suppliant Maidens* (1.948). Aeschylus uses the verbal form in *Prometheus Bound* (1.182) where an anguished chorus of sea nymphs begs the shackled but still defiant rebel god not to speak so boldly against Zeus. The noun form, *eleutherstomia*, does not appear until much later, in the historian Dionysius of Halicarnassus.

10. Aeschylus, *Suppliant Maidens*, 523.

11. Sophocles, *Antigone*, 732–739.

12. *The Theologisches Woerterbuch zum Neuen Testament* (The Theological Dictionary of the New Testament) (Stuttgart, 1933) is a rich storehouse for classical as well as New Testament Greek — plus the Hebrew and Aramaic equivalents of key Greek terms in the Gospels. It calls *parrhesia* a word of *Athenisches meldung* — Athenian coinage — and says it first appears in the latter half of the fifth century with the achievement of full democracy. It is a compound of two words — *pas* (all) and *resis* (speaking).

13. Euripides, *Ion*, 672. Ion turns out to be the offspring of an Athenian queen and Apollo. He proceeds to exercise his own free speech in a bastard's bitter comment on his divine father. Ion speaks scornfully of the lustful habits of the Olympian gods, who so often came down to earth in order to ravish mortal maidens, as Apollo had done to his mother. Ion estimates sardonically that if three gods, Zeus, Poseidon, and Apollo, were sentenced to pay the current Athenian fine for deflowering a virgin, the sum total would empty the treasuries of all the temples in Greece!

14. Euripides, *Phoenician Maidens*, 1.391.

15. Euripides, *Hippolytus*, 1.422.

16. Euripides, *Bacchae*, 2.668ff.

17. Euripides, 4 vols. (Loeb Classical Library, 1925–1935), *Children of Hercules*, 1.178ff (3:269).

18. Euripides, *Andromache*, 2.957–958.

19. Euripides, *Orestes*, 1.551 (Loeb 2:530).

20. Fragment 275 quoted here from James Loeb's translation of Paul Decharme's *Euripides and the Spirit of His Dream* (New York: Macmillan, 1906), 121–122. This is the same James Loeb who founded and financed the Loeb Classical Library.

21. Euripides, *Phoenician Maidens*, 3.504–506.

22. Quoted here from the literal translation of E. P. Coleridge in the Bohn edition of *Euripides* (London: G. Bell, 1891), 2:234–235.

23. *Republic*, 3.568A (Loeb 2:329).

24. Ibid. (Loeb 2:328).

25. Adam, 2:260.

26. *Republic,* 1169.

27. The translation is Milton's. Milton, *Complete Poetry and Selected Prose* (London: Nonesuch Press, 1964), 683.

28. Such an appeal would have been all the more effective because in Athens the theater was as participatory as its democracy. The Athenians were more than a passive audience. A substantial portion of the citizenry actually took part in preparing and producing the plays, just as it took part in the assembly and the law courts. The theater itself was a venerated component of annual religious festivals. The magnitude of popular participation in them was described by William Scott Ferguson, who estimated in his *Greek Imperialism* (Boston: Houghton Mifflin, 1913), "upwards of 2,000 Athenians had to memorize the words and practice the music and dance figures of a lyric or dramatic chorus." A normal Athenian audience, he concluded, "must have been composed in large part of ex-performers" (59–60). Fully to appreciate this one must compare the theater in Athens with that of Rome, a kindred civilization but with a contrasting social and political structure. The theater occupied a place of honor in Athens; it was looked on with suspicion in Rome. The Greek theater grew out of the popular and democratic religion of Dionysus, a poor man's god. In preaching democracy and free speech, the tragic poets reflected its popular audience. In Athens, the comic theater was the equivalent of a crusading newspaper. There was neither a libel law nor a censor, as in Rome, to curb the tongues of the comic poets. Their art flourished with democracy and died with it. In Rome, the oligarchy feared the theater for its democratic potential, and its threat to senatorial dignity. Rome never permitted Aristophanic social or political satire. A Roman comic poet would never have dared write, as Aristophanes did, during the Peloponnesian war, some of the greatest antiwar plays of all time. The attitude of the Roman ruling class to the theater is expressed in Cicero's treatise on the Republic, written in its last unhappy days. His discussion of the theater is preceded by an outburst against democracy itself. "When the applause and approval of the people, as of some great and wise master," Cicero wrote, "have been granted to them, what darkness they produce!" *de Re Publica* (Loeb Classical Library, 1961, reprint), 4.9 (239). The Roman aristocracy, he says, considered the dramatic art "disgraceful" and "desired that all persons connected with such things — writers, actors or producers — should be disfranchised. But in Athens, as Cicero notes with disapproval, actors not only enjoyed rights of citizenship but held high political office. When he came to discuss Athenian comedy, Cicero was venomous. Political comedy had been stifled early in Rome by a stringent libel law, designed originally to protect aristocrats from vulgar lower-class derision in the rustic lampoons from which Roman comedy originated. Cicero recalls approvingly that though the original Roman lawgivers established the death penalty "for only a few crimes," they did "provide it for anyone who sang or composed a song which contained a slander or insult to anyone else." There was another, less well known, reason for Roman hostility to the theater. Almost down to the last days of the Republic, the aristocracy prevented the erection of a permanent theater building lest it be used for popular assemblies. See Lily Ross Taylor's seminal study, *Roman*

Voting Assemblies (Ann Arbor: University of Michigan Press, 1966), 107–108.

Chapter 18: The Final Question

1. *Crito,* 51C (Loeb 1:179).
2. Ibid., 50E (Loeb 1:177).
3. Xenophon, *Cyropaedia,* 1.3.10–11 (5:37).
4. *Laws,* 694A–B.
5. *Protagoras,* 319D (Loeb 127).
6. *Republic,* 8.557B (Loeb 2:285).
7. Ibid., 493D (Loeb 2:41).
8. Ibid., 557C–D (Loeb 2:287).
9. Ibid., 563Bff (Loeb 2:309–311).
10. *Gorgias,* 461D (Loeb 5:309). The LSJ also gives instances where *exousia* means "abuse of authority, license, arrogance." Dr. Bernard Knox disagrees with my interpretation and believes the choice of the word *exousia* may merely have been an echo of the related impersonal verb *exesti* used by Polus when he asked whether he was not to be "at liberty to say" (the Loeb translation for *exesti moi legein*) as much as he pleased.

Epilogue: Was There a Witch-hunt in Ancient Athens?

1. Eric R. Dodds, *The Greeks and the Irrational* (Berkeley: University of California Press, 1951), 189.
2. *Dictionary of the History of Ideas,* edited by Philip Weiner, 6 vols. (New York: Charles Scribner's Sons, 1973), 2:252–263; 565–566.
3. Artistophanes, *Knights,* 1085; *Wasps,* 380; *Birds,* 988.
4. Plutarch, *Life of Pericles,* 32 (Loeb 3:95).
5. Thucydides, 2.59–65.
6. Plutarch, *Life of Pericles,* 33 (Loeb 3:93).
7. Aristophanes, *Acharnians,* 1.527.
8. *Cambridge Ancient History,* edited by J. B. Bury, S. A. Cook, and F. E. Adcock, 11 vols. (New York: Macmillan, 1923–1953), 5:478.
9. Mary R. Lefkowitz, *The Lives of the Greek Poets* (Baltimore: Johns Hopkins, 1981), 110.
10. Plutarch, *Life of Nicias,* 23 (Loeb 3:289–291). Plutarch himself was not wholly enlightened. As a priest of Delphi and a Platonist, he was also uneasy with rational theories about the movements of the heavenly bodies. This is indicated by his final comment, "It was not until later times that the radiant repute of Plato, because of the life the man led, and because he subjected the compulsions of the physical world to divine and more sovereign principles, took away the obloquy of such doctrines, and gave their science free course among all men." In fact, Plato regarded the heavenly bodies as gods. To treat them as material objects was punishable as atheism in his *Laws.*
11. A less elaborate version of the same story had appeared earlier in Cicero's treatise on the gods, *de Natura Deorum,* 1.23.6 (Loeb 19:61).

12. Euripides, *Ion*, 445–447.

13. Euripides, *Trojan Women*, 886.

14. *Meno*, 91D–E (Loeb 4:341).

15. John Burnet, *Greek Philosophy: Thales to Plato* (London: Macmillian, 1928), 111–112.

16. Ibid.; *Theaetetus*, 152A; *Helen*, 10.2.

17. *Meno*, 91E–92B (Loeb 4:341–343).

18. Diodorus Siculus, 12 vols. (Loeb Classical Library, 1976), 12.39.2ff (4:453ff).

19. For references to Anaxagoras in Cicero's philosophical works see the *Academica*, the *Tusculan Disputations*, and the *de Natura Deorum*. For references in his essays see *de Oratore*, 3.138, and *Brutus*, 44.

20. Diogenes Laertius, 2.13–14 (Loeb 1:143–145).

21. Daniel E. Gershenson and Daniel A. Greenberg, *Anaxagoras and the Birth of Physics* (New York: Blaisdell, 1962), 348.

22. A. W. Gomme in his article on Pericles in the *OCD* takes the stories about the attack on the statesman through his friends, Aspasia, Anaxagoras, and Pheidias — and the decree of Diopeithes — as historical fact. One looks to him for some explanation of why Thucydides makes no reference to them. In Gomme's great *Historical Commentary on Thucydides* one finds a six-page essay on "The Prosecutions of Pericles and His Friends" (2:184–189). But, disappointingly, he offers no explanation other than one sweeping phrase — "about all of which Thucydides was *deliberately silent*" (184, italics added). In discussing Plutarch's story that the comic poet Hermippus prosecuted Aspasia, Gomme did recognize that while there was "nothing to prevent" a comic poet from prosecuting Aspasia, "there is a natural suspicion that this is a misunderstanding of a statement that Hemippus attacked her in a comedy" (187).

23. *Memorabilia*, 6.7.6 (Loeb 4:351).

24. *Phaedrus*, 270A.

25. *Gorgias*, 516A.

26. Burnet, *Greek Philosophy*, 112.

27. Plato, *Apology*, 26C–D (Loeb 1:99).

28. W. D. Ross's still indispensable *Aristotle* (London, 1923), 7, traces the story to Ps. Ammonius' *Life of Aristotle*.

29. Anton-Hermann Chroust, *Aristotle*, 2 vols. (Notre Dame, Ind.: University of Notre Dame Press, 1973), 1:153.

30. William S. Ferguson, *Hellenistic Athens* (London: Macmillan, 1911), 104–105. Ferguson was a professor of history at Harvard before World War I.

31. Acts 17:16–32.

32. Edward Gibbon, *Decline and Fall of the Roman Empire*, 6 vols. (London: J. Murray, 1938–1939), 2:522.

ACKNOWLEDGMENTS

THIS WORK might never have been written down if Roger Donald of Little, Brown had not taken a geriatric gamble when I had just turned seventy-seven and made an offer for the book. Until then I was satisfied to have developed its theses in a series of extemporaneous lectures at various places: the 92nd Street Y.M.H.A. in New York; Georgetown University in Washington under the auspices of the Institute for Policy Studies; the University of California in Berkeley; Harvard; and McGill in Montreal, where my lectures won an annual Beatty award. I developed my idea of the four words in Athens for free speech in an annual William Kelly Prentice classics lecture for 1979–80 at Princeton.

Early in my Greek studies, American University in Washington gave me facilities and many friendships as scholar-in-residence, and the use of interlibrary loan for many out-of-print works on the classics.

I treasure encouraging words at the beginnings of my autodidactic labors from Professor Gregory Vlastos, retired, of Princeton and from the late Huntington Cairns, who never lost his joy in the classics.

My studies were aided by the access generously accorded me to the library of the Hellenic Studies Center in Washington by its director, Dr. Bernard Knox, and later by his successor, Dr. Zeph Stewart, and by its librarian, Mrs. Inge Hynes. I was also helped by access to the Library of Congress and to the rich collections at Georgetown and Catholic Universities.

I am grateful to my friend Bernard Knox for agreeing when Little, Brown asked him to read the manuscript as technical adviser and earlier for many a helpful hand during desperate wrestles with that protean monster, the ancient Greek verb.

I also wish to express my gratitude to Michael Mattil of Little, Brown for his devoted copy editing; to my friend and literary agent, Andrew Wiley, who sold the idea to Little, Brown; and to my friend and film biographer, Jerry Bruck, Jr., who made the film about *I. F. Stone's Weekly* and arranged the lectures at Harvard and then at McGill. Finally I pour a libation to my Macintosh word processor. Its large fat black 24-point Chicago Bold type enabled me to overcome a cataract and write the book.

— I. F. Stone

INDEX

❧❦❧❦❧